The dissolution of communist power

The dissolution of communist power
The case of Hungary

Ágnes Horváth and Árpád Szakolczai

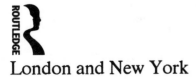

London and New York

First Hungarian edition published
by Akadémiai Kiadó, 1989

English edition published 1992
by Routledge
11 New Fetter Lane, London EC4P 4EE

Simultaneously published in the USA and Canada
by Routledge
a division of Routledge, Chapman and Hall Inc.
29 West 35th Street, New York, NY 10001

© 1992 Ágnes Horváth and Árpád Szakolczai
Typeset in Times by
NWL Editorial Services, Langport, Somerset TA10 9DG

Printed and bound in Great Britain by
Mackays of Chatham PLC, Chatham, Kent

British Library Cataloguing in Publication Data
Horváth, Ágnes, *1957–*
    The dissolution of communist power The case of Hungary
    I. Title   II. Szakolczai, Árpád, *1958–*
    943.9053

    ISBN 0–415–06709–X

Library of Congress Cataloguing in Publication Data
Horváth, Ágnes, *1957–*
    The dissolution of communist power: the case of Hungary/
    Ágnes Horváth and Árpád Szakolczai
    Includes bibliographical references and index.
    ISBN 0–415–06709–X
    1. Europe, Eastern – Politics and government – 1945–1989
    – Case studies.   2. Hungary – Politics and government –
    1945–1989 – Case studies.   3. Communism – Hungary –
    Case studies.   I. Szakolczai, Árpád.   II. Title.
    DJK50.H67   1992
    320.9439–dc20   91–41752
                                                          CIP

To Dániel, Péter and János

How could anything originate out of its opposite? ... This way of judging constitutes the typical prejudgement and prejudice which give away the metaphysicians of all ages; this kind of valuation looms large in the background of all their logical procedures; it is on account of this 'faith' that they trouble themselves about 'knowledge,' about something that is finally baptised solemnly as 'the truth.' The fundamental faith of the metaphysicians is the faith in opposite values. It has not even occurred to the most cautious among them that one might have a doubt right here at the threshold where it is surely most necessary – even if they vowed to themselves, 'de omnibus dubitandum'.

(Nietzsche, *Beyond Good and Evil*, 2)

Contents

Preface

The series of revolutionary changes that destroyed the so-called communist systems in Eastern Europe took everyone by surprise in the West. They were almost completely unforeseen and unpredicted. The very fact of collapse and especially the way it happened overthrew all existing theoretical frameworks used in the past for the analysis of the internal structure of these states.

In some Eastern European countries, the changes were less abrupt, and to some extent foreseen.[1] In the case of Hungary, at least since the middle of the 1980s, there had been an increasing awareness that the existing situation could not continue for much longer and that some changes were hanging in the air. Some of the most influential writings of the period expressed both the pervasive uneasiness and the feeling that the end was near.[2] But even here, the acceleration of events, the extent of the changes and especially the successive fall of all systems took everyone by surprise. Even in January 1989 in Hungary, when the aura of irreversible changes was present everywhere, it was still possible for leading intellectuals to argue seriously that the single most important factor distinguishing right-wing authoritarian regimes and bolshevik-type party-states was that, while the former eventually disintegrate and thus open up the possibility of a more democratic system, the latter – as history shows – never change.

There are, of course, many views proposed to explain these changes. There is the obvious influence of the reforms of Gorbachev. The problem is that this leaves open the question as to what made such reforms both possible and necessary. The existence of these regimes depended upon the presence of the Red Army. But this does not explain in detail what exactly was happening inside, what made the establishment and survival of these systems possible, under fairly stable circumstances, and finally what made them collapse so quickly. Others rather emphasise economic variables, the deepening and unsolvable crisis. But economic problems had been facts of life in these systems since the beginning. An explanation centring on economics fails to account for the timing, and also for the fact that the events of 1989 centred so much on the political sphere. Still others are talking about the impact of the so-called new social movements, the 'long march' of the opposition. But that strategy was based on the assumption that the system was fairly stable and could be altered, in the long run, only through piecemeal evolutionary changes. Nothing comparable to the present collapse was anticipated. And, referring to the burgeoning of alternative movements in Hungary at the end of the 1980s, that explanation does not specify how and why these movements and the emerging opposition parties suddenly became relatively tolerated in the first place.

Neither the quantitative force, nor even the indirect mobilising and enlightening impact of the opposition, could have resulted in the changes that have happened. The space in which the opposition suddenly found room to breathe was not made by their open struggles or efforts. Rather the opposite is true – a space opened up somehow, nobody really knew why; a vacant field that only had to be occupied, and which, by the way, was taken up only slowly and hesitantly.

The end of communism in Eastern Europe was a truly peculiar phenomenon. In a sense, the events were running against the main currents of modern sociology. They proceeded without agents. It is a commonplace that in sociological theory, after the rule of structuralism in the 1960s and the early 1970s, there came a resurrection of agent-based approaches. The simplest objection was put to the structuralist theories: no matter how important structures are, nothing happens without conscious or at least active agents. The events of the last years clearly flew in the face of such views, as not only was there no consciousness on the part of the actors themselves, but very often there were hardly any actors at all; or, at least, the stage itself was prepared well before the actors could have entered the scene.

The difficulties of explaining the sudden fall of a system that was thought by most experts to be unshakeable, even a little while ago, raise fundamental problems concerning the understanding of the nature of the system itself. They point out that there must have been serious gaps, omissions, failures in the former theoretical and empirical analyses. Things that had been taken for granted and had become fossilised as the very grounds of thinking and analysis now had to be questioned. Otherwise, the events ought to have been foreseen. And, indeed, there was a hidden area in research, a topic that was formerly almost completely closed to serious sociological or political research. That was the activity of the communist-party apparatus itself.[3]

In the past, even a factual description of the activities of communist party workers was not possible; and for a number of reasons. Not only because the topic was taboo, and that consequently we had no idea even about what was really going on inside the party, but also because we did not have the distance necessary for any analysis. What we saw of the party from the outside was repugnant and alien, yet its power seemed to be unassailable. It was deemed repulsive even to deal with the whole topic; there was no question of curiosity at all. However, the question of distance had a different aspect as well. While, from one perspective, the alien and unknown character of the party's activity presented an insurmountable wall, from another our sight was blinded by the closeness of the party, by the fact that the consequences of its existence and activity were taken for granted. Imperceptibly the style, the methods, the mentalities, the ways of thinking that were characteristic of bolshevik-type state-parties became part and parcel of our daily life.

In order to be able to describe the daily mechanism of communism, two impossible things had to happen at the same time. First, one had to obtain a permit to do research. This was an impossibility, as the party, by definition, did not allow external analysts, let alone sociologists, to come close to it. Second, one had to be at once inside and outside the system. One had to be inside, had to live in Eastern Europe in order to understand what was going on; to be acquainted with this peculiar system where – at the discursive level – every sentence, every word, every emphasis and intonation had a special sense;[4] where, in daily reality, every instance of behaviour was – or could have been – relevant; where everyone, in each segment of life, lived under the feeling that 'anything you do or say can be used against you'. But it was also necessary to step outside, to be detached in some way from the system. This had to be different from a final internal or external exile. Such a complete break led not only to a separation, but to an existential change, stemming from irrevocable acts or decisions which precluded the possibility, even the desirability, of such an analysis. By coincidence and accident we both found ourselves in a situation of separation and existential change. In order to understand every possibility of how this book could have happened, it is necessary to give some accounts of these accidents, without going into unnecessary and non-public personal details.

When finishing university in 1981, both of us, independently, faced the same situation as most of our generation. We had to get ourselves accommodated within a system that we could not accept, especially because at that time, in the university, the atmosphere was open enough for the deformities, the conformism, the seemingly pointless compromises of 'real life' to seem even more difficult to accept. But, on the other hand, we did not see any prospect in joining the opposition either. We considered that a pointless act of suicide, when, after all, we hardly even had the opportunity of committing such acts, as these activities were the business of a different generation, people a dozen years older than we, having quite different backgrounds and experiences, who in most cases were themselves victims of certain official recriminations rather than self-made dissidents. Thus, our situation was basically the same as that of anybody else of our age, perhaps with a difference in shading: we had a strong feeling of disgust with the whole system. For us, the most important characteristic was not repression. It was rather a deformed, muddy, distasteful situation without solid values and respect for true achievement, and an all-pervasive cynicism not restricted to the official sphere. We found ourselves personally unable to relate to the reality into which we were supposed to 'socialise' ourselves. Neither could we fight it. We felt that one could fight against repression and oppression, but not against mud, except by becoming muddy oneself. We considered these characteristics of ours not an asset, but a liability. We were as unable to become fully part of this world, of which we had been a part since our birth anyway, as we would have been unable to assist in a dissection. Our inability to come to terms with the daily reality of a 'soft' communist system was rooted not in an ethical quality inside us, but in a physical handicap.

Perhaps many people had the same feelings at that time. But we were fortunate enough that we were not forced to accommodate. Both of us succeeded in escaping. One of us married and had two children, living almost in seclusion in an outer, working-class district of Pest. The other finally succeeded, three years after the original application, in getting permission to accept a personal scholarship and went to study in the United States.

Each of us felt that we needed a complete break, a total escape from the system we were living in. And yet, none of us had left everything behind; nothing 'irreversible' had happened in our existence. We simply preserved ourselves, physically and intellectually. We did not make an existential or ethical commitment, only satisfied our most basic physical needs. This break was so complete that for years we did not even want to hear the news. We did not read Hungarian newspapers or periodicals for years. One of us even finished a Ph.D. that had nothing to do with contemporary Eastern Europe – though the question of what was and is going on there was a motivating force in the background.

It was in 1987 that we 'returned' to Hungary, one in a real, the other in a metaphorical sense. We found many things changing. The silent waters were stirred up, the air was strange and exciting. There was a possibility of free and open talk about politics. Yet all this happened in a small circle of people who knew each other all too well, repeating the day after what somebody had said the day before. To our greatest surprise, we discovered the truth of an old commonplace: the more things change, the more they remain the same. We became curious about the deep changes that might have happened beneath these surface movements. We wanted to analyse it, to check on it, to question it.

It was at this point that an accident happened to us, an accident that brought us together and transformed our hesitations and doubts into a concrete strategy of research. This story started very far from us. Some sincere reform communists in the mid-1980s wanted to analyse the party sociologically, as a precondition for serious internal reform. In 1985 it was even agreed that the Institute of Sociology at the Academy of Sciences should host this undertaking. Everything was ready, including the researchers that were allocated to this task, when at the last minute the whole project was undermined. 'Let no one study the party, except the party itself.' But with that, the case was not completely closed. A new attempt was made, this time through the research institute of the party itself – a hideaway for reform communists anyway. This time, on the basis of a more modest proposal, one researcher was employed for the study of decision-making and interest-representation inside the party apparatus. It was this job that one of the authors received. Not being a party member, she became based in the Political Science Department at the Faculty of Law, but was employed on the research money of the Social Science Institute of the central committee of the HSWP (Hungarian Socialist Workers' Party). Though her employment started in June 1987, she only received permission to start actual research in February 1988.

A pilot study was conducted in February and March 1988 in one of the largest districts of Budapest.[5] The paper summarising the results of this study was distributed at a conference in May 1988.[6] After this, and now together, we constructed a questionnaire on the basis of the pilot study, and included questions from international surveys on élites and the communist party, and previous surveys done in Hungary at the Centre for Value Sociology at the Hungarian Academy of Sciences. We got permission to go ahead with the questionnaire in August 1988, and collected the data between 1 September and 4 October 1988, in all the other twenty-one districts of Budapest.

Acknowledgements

First of all, we would like to express our thanks to our project leaders, Péter Schmidt and Milhály Bihari, and to Elemér Hankiss and Iván Szelényi, who gave important advice on both method and content. We would like to mention our colleagues who read and helpfully commented upon the first draft of the Hungarian book version: Lászlo Bruszt, Csaba Gombár, Tamás Gyekiczky, István Herédi, György Lengyel, Róbert Manchin, Zsolt Papp, András Sajó, István Schlett, Julia Szalai, and István Vida. Special thanks are due to Eva Juhász for her computer assistance.

We also got important advice and encouragement in England concerning one or more segments of the book. First of all from John Keane, who helped our work in many ways when we were on a British Council scholarship in England. Concerning the works of Foucault, we profited especially from discussions with Colin Gordon, and also with Graham Burchell, Peter Miller, and Nikolas Rose. With respect to the analysis in our study, we should mention the names of Zygmunt Bauman, Archie Brown, and especially Richard Sakwa. Concerning the historical part, discussions with David Starkey were most helpful and reassuring.

Finally, in Florence, during the last stages of the work, we were helped by discussions with Jean Blondel, Alessandro Pizzorno, and especially Steven Lukes, and the graduate students of the seminar on the East European transition. Special thanks to Maurice Glasman, who took the trouble of reading the whole manuscript, and besides correcting syntax errors, also made fruitful suggestions.

Our research was also furthered by several libraries and librarians. In Hungary, especial thanks are due to the inter-library loan facilities of the libraries of the Faculty of Law and the Institute of Sociology. In England, we are especially grateful for the possibility of using the facilities of the British Library, the London School of Economics library and the library of the Polytechnic of Central London. At this point, we should also express our gratitude to the British Council for a scholarship which helped our work a lot, and to the Polytechnic of Central London which proved to be a generous host institution.

Versions or parts of some chapters appeared in the following periodicals: *Social Research* (1990), vol. 57, no. 2, pp. 275–301 (Chapter 7, section 1); *The British Journal of Political Science* (1991), vol. 21, no. 4, pp. 469–88 (Chapters 5 and 7); *East European Politics and Societies* (1991), vol. 5, no. 2, pp. 268–305 (Chapter 6). The extract from Friedrich Nietzsche, *Beyond Good and Evil* is reproduced by kind permission of Random House, Inc, New York. We are also thankful for the assistance of Márta Gelléri, at the *Akadémiai Kiadó*, for the proper care of the Hungarian version of the book.

Finally, needless to add, all the – doubtless many – remaining errors are solely our own.

Ágnes Horváth and Árpád Szakolczai

1 Introduction

My aim is, firstly, to indicate the reasons why it was in France rather than elsewhere that the Great Revolution, stirrings of which were perceptible in almost all European countries, came to a head; why it presented itself as an almost natural outcome of the very social order it made such a haste to destroy; and, lastly, why the monarchy which had weathered so many storms in the past collapsed so suddenly and catastrophically.

Tocqueville, *The Old Régime and the French Revolution*, 1856

If the dissolution of the system should, however, begin to take place from below, even so great a master of the art of wielding power as Stalin would be unable to hold his throne.

Avtorkhanov, *The Communist Party Apparatus*, 1966

The single most important characteristic, the *differentia specifica* of communism, of communist political systems, is the existence and role of bolshevik-type communist parties. And the most distinctive feature of these parties is their apparatus. No matter how we characterise or baptise the system – Stalinism, communism, bolshevism, 'formerly' existing socialism, totalitarianism, or post-totalitarianism – its identity is given by the decisive influence of this apparatus. Such statements are truisms. Nevertheless, as often happens with commonplaces, their highly specific character in this way goes unnoticed. The place of the communist party apparatus in Soviet and Eastern European studies provides a remarkable example both for the omission of crucial agents and concepts and for the power of the language to conceal, confuse and blur.

'Apparatus' is a word most often used in the context of communist political systems. It is much less clear what exactly is meant by this term. In journalism and in the public opinion, its meaning has become ever more overblown, through an identification of the apparatus with unspecified, general totalitarian power or with the bureaucracy. Another aspect of the same phenomenon is the practical identification of the apparatus with the *nomenclatura*.[1] This is characteristic not only in popular assessments, but in most academic writings not specifically concerned with the internal organisation of the communist parties as well. In the media, apparatus and nomenclatura are considered as synonyms, as epitomes of the old power structure that only appropriates resources and represses the population. In scholarly literature, they are also often lumped together, or are considered to be different aspects of the same coin.[2] According to this view, these concepts cover those people who actually occupy important positions in the party-states, who make the decisions, who wield power and who are the beneficiaries of the policies. The nomenclatura in this sense covers the leaders of central and local bureaucracies, the managers of firms and local councils, and all members of the party apparatus. They are the ones who go hunting, who build their houses from public funds, who place their friends and relatives in well-paid positions. The problem with this model is not just that it generalises from the abuses, and therefore fails to present the 'complete picture', but that the place and function of the apparatus are completely misplaced here.

Studies devoted exclusively to the party apparatus are rare. We could locate only one book devoted exclusively to the study of the communist-party apparatus.[3] General studies of the communist party do discuss the apparatus, but in a way that presents a distortion of the common usage. Here the meaning becomes not all inclusive, but rather restricted. Often, especially in straightforward Kremlinology, the word 'apparatus' stands only for the apparatus of the central committee.[4] When an overview is given of the whole party network, it is more often than not reduced to giving the bare bones of the hierarchical structure, and to a discussion of the 'apparatchiki', characterised as faceless bureaucrats, the main obstacles to reform. It is acknowledged that the apparatus represents a vast layer of party organisations and function- aries providing a connection between the top levels of the party and its membership. But the activity of the actual agents and the modalities of the connection are left hanging in the air.

There are several reasons that may account for this strange neglect. One could argue that literature in the field merely reflected the fact that the activity of the apparatus was hidden from the eyes of the population at large, from the outside world. A more plausible, seemingly obvious explanation would be that access to the apparatus and an exhaustive study of its activity were not possible in the past; it was not even possible this last year in the Soviet Union.[5] The apparatus was not studied as there were no data available and none could have been gathered.

However, exclusive reliance upon such a 'supply-side' explanation would be unwarranted. There were considerable problems here with the lack of interest, of curiosity, thus with the 'demand side'. Even the data that were available on the detailed activity of the communist-party apparatus were hardly used at all.[6] The literature took seriously and followed closely the model of democratic centralism. The principle of democratic centralism defined a hierarchical structure with the complete subordination of the lower levels to decisions made at the top. From this perspective, the party apparatus played its role either as the obedient transmission-belt of top party resolutions, or as a brake, an obstacle to decisions or reforms. The specificity of the apparatus was grasped only in negative terms. In its positive activity, it was seen merely to fulfil a subservient role.

Moreover, it was not just the apparatus that was little dwelt on in the literature on communist politics. No matter how paradoxical it may seem, the party itself seemed to have gone out of fashion in discussions of the Soviet Union or Eastern Europe in the last decades. There were exceptions that put the party in the centre of the analyses of these systems, the two most notable examples being Bauman's concept of 'partynomial power' and Avtorkhanov's idea of the partocracy.[7] But there was a proliferation of approaches where the role of the party was either subordinated to other concepts or general trends – like the idea of the party-state, or the 'iron laws' of bureaucracy or oligarchy – or was left out altogether (authoritarianism, corporatism, interest-group theories, clientelism, etc.). By reducing the specificity of communist systems to such general categories, the question that was the most important concerning this (or any particular) system was forgotten: what difference did it make?

One can again list a number of reasons for this development. It was definitely linked to the requirements of the discipline of comparative political science, the attempt to develop and use categories that are applicable for the description of all modern political societies. International developments also have played their role. Among other things, the downplay of the role of the party may well have been indirectly related to the increasing contacts between Eastern and Western scholars. And in the Eastern European countries, the discussion of the party had very specific overtones. In the media, only the current party line could be represented concerning this question, which was dominated by slogans like the party's being the leading force of society. For anybody else and for any other purposes, even the mention of the party was taboo. Thus, in scientific or semi-official publications, a double talk developed, where words like 'state' and 'bureaucracy' stood as substitutes for the party. These were phenomena that – occasionally – could have been subjected to criticism. Did not Lenin himself say some nasty things about the state and the bureaucracy? But, as time went on, these euphemisms came to be accepted and taken seriously by specialists and the (educated) public in both East and West. Interestingly enough, these reasons are all external to the study of the characteristics of communist political systems. But the most important cause is related to the fate of a concept with which the study of the communist party was intimately linked from the beginning: totalitarianism.

TOTALITARIANISM: THE FATE OF A CONCEPT IN WEST AND EAST

This concept, so crucial in the political thought of the twentieth century, ran a peculiar course in the last decades. Just when it was discarded by Western theorists as analytically useless and empty, it was taken up by dissident writers in the East. This is not the place to analyse these developments in detail – it has already been accomplished by recent studies.[8] Yet, without giving a comprehensive account of the different meanings of 'totalitarianism', we must review some of the crucial assumptions and parts of the career of this theoretical framework that cast such a lasting, looming shadow over our understanding of the specific reality of communism.

It is often said that the theory of totalitarianism became just a slogan of the cold war.[9] But the concept itself, together with all its problems, was rooted not in an ideology, but in a quite tragic perception of reality: shocking, personal experiences of Nazism and Stalinism. The classic works on totalitarianism were attempts not so much to explain as to 'write out' this feeling: the horror caused by the existence of a twentieth-century European political system using terror, repression and fear; a system that pervades and rules practically everything, that is everywhere; that is, in one word, 'total'.[10] The standard books of the 1950s on totalitarianism were attempts to systemise these experiences.[11]

This literature connected the full specificity of the nature of communism to these experiences. It made assumptions about the nature of the system which proved to have been valid only for certain periods. These assumptions served as positive or negative reference points for most later studies. First, the theory of totalitarianism claimed that terror and repression were necessary parts of the daily life of totalitarian regimes. Second, due to this identification of the system with repressive measures, it found no theoretical grounds to distinguish between the party and the secret police. We do not mean that the two institutions were actually identified, only that in the theoretical framework of totalitarianism they both performed the same function. Third, it attributed an overwhelming role to ideology in maintaining social cohesion. Fourth, according to it, power was strictly hierarchical and coming only from above; in the final instance, from the single hand of the ruler. In sum, to present a somewhat overdrawn picture, the party was a power machine, controlled completely by the leader, which repressed the whole population on the basis of an ideology.

In the late 1960s and 1970s, these views were increasingly impossible to hold on to as both the international situation and the internal affairs of the Soviet Union were changing considerably. In international relations, *détente* replaced cold war, making the language of totalitarianism something of a nuisance. As to the internal developments of communist systems, all basic assumptions of the theory seemed to have become obsolete. Terror and repression ceased to be regular parts of daily existence. The role of ideology also receded into the background. The central tenets were not discredited officially and remained binding in both the media and in academic literature, but daily existence was no longer permeated by ideological mobilisation. Ideology became a ritual which could not be questioned, but which was hardly taken seriously by anyone. In economic policy, there was more concern with efficiency and pragmatic goals than with conformity to ideological purity. And the control of the centre also seemed to have been relaxed. The personality cult of Stalin was replaced by a less violent and more collective leadership.

Soviet and Eastern European studies reflected these changes, and also the opportunities that opened up to research. Denunciation of the impact of the regimes by voices from the outside was replaced by analytical studies of how decisions were actually made from the inside. As the new approach itself acknowledged, it was concerned more with the input side than the output side.

However, while the new orientation defined itself as opposed to the theory of totalitarianism, it was still conditioned, negatively, by the fact of this denial. Starting from an arguably crude version of totalitarianism, it was surprised to find that reality, both in the past and the present, was different from the pervasive, total control it expected. Instead, it found a relatively high degree of arbitrariness in the decision-making process. The centre was far from being able to impose its desire at will. There was a considerable amount of local struggle and bargaining going on between different segments of the élite. Instead of landing on the moon, they found a landscape that seemed to be all too familiar. This led them to propose the new paradigm of pluralism of interest groups.[12]

The similarity obviously did not mean a complete identity, and most writers within the paradigm used caveats to distinguish interest-group struggles in the Soviet Union from those within the United States, but the whole perspective was definitely shifted. Instead of talking about certain similarities in basically different systems, they were rather pointing out differences in societies that were basically using identical mechanisms. The literature tended toward interpreting these differences as left-overs of an ideology that were difficult to discard, but that were losing all their importance and were practically defunct.

In this framework, moral indignation and outright rejection were replaced by understanding. It was acknowledged that industrialisation and modernisation had to be accomplished, and that these were processes not without costs. And it was accepted that the drive toward industrialisation had had important successes, that it had lifted a backward country to a place among the first powers of the world. Even the bureaucracy was interpreted as a rational solution to the problem of development administration. A curious parallel development occurred between standard academic and leftist writings in the West: the former started to acknowledge some successes, while the latter became disillusioned and put more and more emphasis on failure and moral abnormalities.

Academic writings from the 1960s started to compensate for the simplistic views of the earlier theories of totalitarianism. But they certainly overshot their target. In an attempt to establish similarities and to understand, they downplayed what was specific and still outrageous. Apart from Kremlinology, studying top-level policy-making, the very terms 'apparatus' and 'party' went out of use – as if gentlemen were not supposed to mention such words.[13]

However, at the point when Western academic literature started to question the desire and the ability of communist systems to exercise an all-powerful control over the population and therefore to drop the idea of totalitarianism, it was taken up by Eastern dissidents, and with a vengeance.[14] One may say that the attitude of these writers to standard totalitarianism theory is analogous to Khruschev's attitude to Stalinism. According to Khruschev, Stalin's methods represented a deformation of the true mission of the party. They did not invalidate the importance of and the need for the party; quite the contrary, it was only after Stalin that it was possible to return to the true mission. The importance of the party in a consolidated, developed socialist society should increase, and not decrease. And some key dissident writers agree with this statement, only to change its strategic sense. Thus, according to Havel, the true nature of the communist, or post-totalitarian, system was shown only once the crude, terroristic methods were abandoned (Havel 1985: 24–7).

This was based on a dual perception. First, it was asserted that in spite of all the attempts at reform, the basic structure had not been altered. The crude, overt aspects of repression had no doubt disappeared, but the system still aspired for a total control of all aspects of public life in the same way as before. Dissident writings in the last decades took upon themselves the task of informing the world that, despite all the promises and discussions, the changes were only cosmetic.

Disillusionment with the possibility of reforms, together with the general softening of the system, led to changes in both perspective and strategy within the different segments of dissident or opposition circles.[15] If the system could not be changed at the top or through the top, then an alternative power base would have to be constructed from below. It implied that a new importance was to be attributed to daily existence and society at large; a single perspective with two distinct emphases in different writings. In some, there was a total disillusionment with politics, and the ideal of a quiet, Epicurean life without any involvement in public life was voiced. In others, the desire for political activity was preserved, but with a different orientation. They still wanted to push for a change, but they were turning toward a different audience. They now addressed the whole population, instead of segments of the power élite. The new catchwords 'civil society', 'antipolitics' or 'power of the powerless' were all connected to the duality of this orientation. Instead of advising enlightened despots, the new programme of the long march of the civil society was proposed.[16]

This strategy, which today can not only be seen more clearly but also written about, had a number of defects. First, there are many signs that the new emphasis on daily life was only tactical. The struggle against the system was reoriented toward the micro level only because of lack of a better opportunity. Second, the very concept of daily life as a strategic field was dangerously close to the bolshevik strategy of transforming daily life, even if the means and the aims were obviously different. It preserved an instrumental view of daily existence, where every concrete deed immediately became the sign of something else; where everything was important only to the extent that it represented something else. The system – as we'll later see in detail – defined all social and public questions as political ones, and brought them within its own competence. Being excluded from open politics, the opposition began to be involved in social questions. There was a danger that the re-politicisation of existence by the opposition, starting from the micro level and daily life, might prove successful, but only to reproduce some of the ideals and realities of bolshevism. Moreover, the catch-word 'power of the powerless' contained the idea that power was already possessed by society. It was only our failure to perceive or cowardice to realise it that kept the system in its place. No matter what concrete intentions were, all this was dangerously close to the 'blaming the victim' syndrome.[17] Third, despite all talk about power coming from below, it did not lead to a reconceptualisation of the 'nature' of power, involved no interest in theoretical, historical or conceptual problems related to the emergence and working of mechanisms of power in modern societies. All the more so as, in the view of the opposition, bolshevism was generally considered as a specifically Eastern, Russian phenomenon that had nothing to do with the mainstream of Western development.[18] And even if there was talk about the power of society, it often turned out that, according to them, 'real power' was vested in the system, at the top levels.[19] And, finally, it is obvious that the strategy was not successful. Apart from Poland, where it contributed to the creation of Solidarity, the opposition was not able to gather massive support and make large-scale impact, although this was a crucial element of the new strategy. The system fell down, but all this was only vaguely connected to the efforts of the opposition, no matter how laudable they were.

The first perception concerning the unchanged basic nature of the system after the death of Stalin was joined by a second perception which stated that, on the contrary, the relation between the system and society did change in the last decades. The politically active opposition, for both tactical and existential reasons, tried to operate with clear-cut dividing lines, with the same language separating 'us' and 'them', the society and the party-state, that was used and was, for a large segment of the population, valid in the 1950s. However, many analytical writings within the opposition in the last decades questioned exactly the existence of such straightforward divisions. While formerly the dominant colours were black and white – or red and white – they were now replaced by pink and grey.[20] The most influential Hungarian writer of the 1980s, Péter Esterházy wrote the following sentence at the moment when the opposition in Hungary tried to take up the discourse[21] of 1956: 'Even if it were true – which still must be proved – that the country shook off communism in 1956 as a dog shakes off water, today it is not at all clear where the dog ends and where the water begins' (Esterházy 1988). In a way, the purpose of our book is nothing but to analyse how this could have come about, and what it means in the present.

Moreover, an influential minority within the dissident circles moved even further. From this observation about the blurring of division lines and from their own personal experiences, which included not only persecution by police, but bitter experiences in the workplace and even in everyday life, they drew the conclusion that the system had succeeded in its efforts to penetrate society. The concepts of 'homo sovieticus' or the idea of a 'velvet prison' where external repression disappears because everybody polices himself belong in this category.[22] The serious consideration of the lasting impact on society was thus immediately connected to the success of the system on its own terms. Today, the error of this view is so obvious that it hides both the important and the dangerous aspects of these and similar views. Their authors were the ones who correctly observed some important changes in the reality of these societies, who had an eye to the deep and lasting internal effects of the system, the impossibility of maintaining a discourse according to which the system remained solely external, even if they obviously connected this observation to a false world-view and conceptual framework. But, on the other hand, the dangers inherent in this perception can be all the more pertinent today, when the opposition has gained an important influence on public policy.

Dissidents always resented the lack of involvement on the part of the general population. However, beyond this denunciation, perhaps today it is high time at least to pay more attention to popular concerns and to opinions concerning popular attitudes towards the different élite strategies. This other side of the issue is becoming even more important today, and may be behind some of the most puzzling aspects of the present changes in Eastern Europe. It is no doubt true that the population was conformist in the past, that it was thoroughly permeated by elements of bolshevik attitudes and reality. But most people also preserved a high degree of independence and had both a moral sense and an awareness of their own interests. Most of all, they became extremely weary of other people's speaking in their names, assuming they knew what their interests and opinions were, and of any attempts to mobilise them. After all, the history of bolshevism was nothing but successive waves of calls to action and involvement.[23] They had become fed up with it all; therefore the language of the current changes, attempting to raise enthusiasm and involvement, was not very popular, nor effective. Most individuals resented being pawns in or targets of someone else's games.

Dissident writings, as opposed to academic sovietology, did lay an emphasis on daily-life experiences in communist systems. But their perspective was highly specific and ambivalent. They proposed that the opposition between state and civil society should be the major conceptual framework into which their struggles could be formulated. But daily life for them was a source of constant anxiety, caused not simply by the repressive organisations, but also, and perhaps more disturbingly, directly or indirectly by the population at large. Society, or civil society, thus became not only a source of resistance, but a sphere that itself had to be created. If society policed itself, if it were inhabited by species of the *Homo sovieticus*, it would have to be dissected and re-educated, civilised again. Paradoxically, civil society became at once the source of power and a target. Finally, although the opposition considered that the way power was present in the daily life of communist systems was of crucial importance, it was not interested in the exact daily workings of the power apparatus itself. Not that they would have had a chance to do a concrete study, but the curiosity to do so was also missing.[24] It was asserted that everything was known to the point of suffocation about the mechanism of the communist party-state.

No matter how different academic and dissident writings were in the past, they both shared a common perception, and behind it a common assumption concerning the way power was exercised in the system. The common perception was of the stability of the system, the idea that this system would be with us for a long time to come. The common assumption was that power is simply the ability to make and enforce decisions, that it can be localised in the centre, is related to the taking up of certain positions, was flowing downwards from above, and was closely associated with privileges. The lower organs of the power mechanism were considered to be solely the executants of decisions made at the top; thus the specific activity of the apparatus was neglected.

The basic perception has clearly proved to be incorrect. Systems of power that were thought to be unshakeable and eternal have been falling at an unbelievable speed and ease. It is necessary to give up some of the certainties held for decades about the 'nature' of the system. The framework of thought in which we lived and viewed the communist systems cannot explain, let alone accommodate, what is happening.

In a way, the fact that the changes were so unpredictable only highlights a statement made by several people that there was a definite lack of theoretical innovation and imagination in this field.[25] But, to be fair, the assumptions mentioned are commonly accepted for most studies of power. There may be problems with the very concept of power in the political and social sciences. The field is underconceptualised and there is a general paucity of tools for analysis. Not that there is a lack of theories concerning the 'nature' of power. But there is a definite lack of studies designed to describe the actual mechanisms and impacts of power with an eye to conceptual problems. In most accepted theoretical frameworks, the study of politics and aspects of daily existence have not been connected at all.

'REVISIONISM' IN THE HISTORY OF ABSOLUTISM

However, in the last few decades, in a field completely unconnected with Soviet and Eastern European studies, a novel conceptualisation has been developed about the relationship between power, daily life and individuality. This came from a reinterpretation of the experience of modernity.[26]

The study of the origins of the modern world, the emergence of the modern state, economy and society were for a long time considered to be almost exclusively macro-level concerns – in the same way as the study of the Soviet political system was. This holds true as much for the classical theories describing the successive stages of this process – one only has to mention the names of Saint-Simon, Comte, Hegel, Marx, Spencer, Durkheim and Parsons – as for most of the more recent literature (from the 1970s, see the writings of Skocpol, Anderson or Wallerstein; from the 1980s, those of Giddens and Michael Mann). As a counterpart to the global character of these analyses, they were often supplemented by a concern with the similarly abstract character of 'man' or 'human nature', as a reality or potentiality.

Nevertheless, in the last decades, there has emerged a definite, widespread reinforcement of the feeling that all this is not enough to explain the specificity of daily existence in modern societies; that something crucial has been left out of the macro-level accounts. Assumptions were made, connections were taken for granted that are nevertheless highly problematic. The workings of automatic mechanisms or organic developments were assumed in areas where one should rather have talked about explicit strategies. It was realised that there were certain aspects of daily existence in modern societies that were connected to the experience of modernity or the modern world, but that could not be explained away in terms of historical or anthropological necessities. Among these, certain activities and forms of behaviour became intolerable or extremely difficult for an increasing number of people, and there was a need for analyses that would be able to account for these novel experiences.

The study of the connection between daily existence and the impact or requirements of the modern state, society or the economy is not novel in itself. But in the accepted frameworks, the perspective on problems of daily life was limited, and the causation was unidirectional. On the one hand, questions of daily existence were raised with respect to the failures of modernity. The problems of exploitation, poverty, alienation were all connected to abuses, vested interests, the betrayal of the true path, where the reaffirmation of the potentials always lay at hand. In this respect, there was no difference between, say, the neo-classical and Marxist versions of the modern economy. On the other hand, the links between daily existence and the requirements of the different aspects of modernity were posited as external ones. Accounts that were critical of the modern state, economy, society or modernity 'as such' saw it as an external threat to daily existence, as an alien, irresistible force, a repressive factor destroying the life-world, interpersonal relations, the human personality itself. While this perspective represented a complete rejection of the whole of modernity on the one hand, it left no escape on the other. Modernity represented here a rationalisation and bureaucratisation of all spheres of life, with the – independent or combined – impact of the modern state and the capitalist market economy and was rooted in the realisation of an anthropological constant. This view, already present in the works of Tönnies and Weber, reached an almost apocalyptic vision in the writings of some members of the Frankfurt school, due to a specific connection made between two perspectives, the 'hard' Marxist analysis of exploitation and domination, and the 'soft', cultural-aesthetical criticism of modernity.[27]

The increasing popularity of this novel perspective is undoubtedly due to the fact that 1968 represented a break for thinking. On the one hand, it became obvious that the critical theories of the 1960s that attempted to break away from the simplistic world-view of the macro-level development and modernisation theories of the 1950s led to a dead end. On the other, the events in the West proved that the theory according to which the 'enemy' is only external – the state, capitalism, the world market – could not be maintained any longer.[28] The macro structures were undoubtedly present as all-encompassing global frameworks. But they did not determine what was happening at the level of daily existence. If structuralism presented itself in the 1960s as *the* outcome of centuries of work trying to establish a real and true social science, then the failure of structuralism proved that the very project[29] was a mistake. It is not possible to account for the actual link between structure and behaviour in a universalistic, scientific way.

The new perspective offered a conceptualisation of the relationship between modernity, and daily existence and forms of individuality in a different way. The connection between the macro and the micro became internal. Forms of individual behaviour and aspects of daily existence became central concerns and not just external, secondary effects of the emergence of modernity. The very project became, in its heart, linked to and contingent upon transformations at the minute levels of daily life; transformations that were conditioned by macro-level changes, like the birth of the modern state and capitalism, but that were also the foundations, the grounds of those changes: the 'preconditions' and not just the consequences.

The new approaches obviously represented an attack on classical, macro-level theories, but in a special sense. They criticised not what was said, but the very things that were taken for granted. Macro-level theories were not denounced as false or ideological, but as irrelevant for an approach that was concerned with the formation of the very players and the rules of the game which had been assumed by the macro-level theories to be fixed.

This post-1968 sensibility was not completely novel. It had to rely upon previous works in order to be able to express itself. And there were some classical, empirical-historical studies that attempted to explain not just the impact of civilisation or modernity on the individual and daily life, but that played with the idea of an opposite causation. Particularly important in this respect were the writings of Nietzsche, Weber and Freud. Interestingly enough, they were all Germans, and, not surprisingly, they were all critical of the major figures of the macro-level, abstract perspectives, especially Kant, Hegel and Marx. Though each of them said many things that are strange or unacceptable to us today, they provided crucial insights into the problematic relationship between the macro and micro level, modernity and daily existence. And there were also writers who, not independently of the above three, were working on similar topics before or after the Second World War, but who gained real popularity, or were even discovered, only after 1968.[30]

While these developments were related to works that studied history from specific, theoretical, philosophical or contemporary political or social perspectives, similar approaches emerged in the field of history as well. Social histories of the Reformation, debates about the meaning of bureaucratisation in mid-Tudor England, or studies concerned with the daily impact of the political centre all attempted to revise our common knowledge about the reality and impact of absolutism.[31]

This is not the place to give a comprehensive analysis of the similarities and differences of these writers, and to compare their works to other historians' – something that is, however, strongly overdue. Just a few remarks. One common concern is that, while the actual connection, or the nature of this connection between the macro and micro spheres, was always taken for granted in the classical accounts of modernity, now exactly this became problematical. They all asked the 'very empirical' question of 'how?'. How were individuals actually connected to the concerns of the state or the economy? How did this influence interpersonal, 'social' links? What happened when power was exercised? Second, they did not stop here, and posed the question concerning modern man itself: what was the type of individual created correlatively with the modern state and the economy? Opposed to all liberal accounts, they refused to endorse the concept of free individuality as a universal fact or potentiality, and refused to accept the concept of progress along these lines. But they also refused the idea that the individual was a mere product of society or of socio-political or economic changes, and that questions of individuality were only second-ary to the broad macro issues. Rather they asserted that a specific type of individuality was at once the precondition and product of modernity. Truly modern societies could only develop correlatively with the development of certain types of character and forms of behaviour.

In this way, a type of analysis that was specifically concerned with and connected to the present necessarily entailed a historical investigation. From diagnosing certain elements of daily existence in advanced modern societies it went back to the past to search for the 'effective' origins of these forms of behaviour.[32] It studied history not in order to discover general laws or to see the face of the future, but in order to locate the causes of present problems. And it discovered a moment in history that was previously either neglected or considered as a practically or theoretically irrelevant episode: the age of absolutism.

According to the Whig interpretation of history, absolutism was an aberration, a detour from the normal path, a useless and meaningless episode that disappeared without a trace. According to the Marxist perspective, absolutism was a step necessary for the establishment of capitalism. The new approach also considered the experience of absolutism crucial, but in a different way. Divesting the interpretation of all teleology, and considering absolutism and Protestantism not as opposites but as aspects of the same general problematic, it saw the lasting legacy of absolutism in the decisive transformation of the conditions and stakes of daily existence, and the shaping of human personality. Where others saw the failure and complete demise of absolutism, it pointed out its latent, lasting success.

THE EMPIRICAL STUDY OF THE COMMUNIST-PARTY APPARATUS

Given our specific questions detailed in the Preface, and armed with the perspective provided by the 'revisionist' analyses of absolutism, we thus turned to the empirical study of the communist-party apparatus. We chose an approach that was different from what others expected and suggested to us. We were interested in the routine daily activity: how the system was governed in daily life, how it was possible at all and what its lasting and hidden impacts were. We were motivated and increasingly reinforced by a feeling that the party was in no way simply a repressive institution, that the dangers it represented were more extensive than those of a simple dictatorship, and that the power of the party could be located neither in other repressive state organisations, nor in the top leadership. We had to realise that the very concept of the 'party-state' was misleading, and therefore we substituted for it the idea of the 'state-party'.

We were not the first attempting to shed light on the daily reality of the party and its apparatus, who emphasised that though decision-making was centralised in the party, the 'Party' itself was not simply built from the above, but also based on the bottom. Thus twenty years ago, on the basis of quite different material and background, Avtorkhanov stated the following:

> The usual study of the organs of party power is limited to an analysis of the functions and functioning of the higher levels of the party and government pyramid. Although the entire party structure is created from the top and these higher levels are the summit, they top a gigantic base composed of elementary power cells.... The strength of the communist régime resides not in the party and government summits, but in its brilliant hierarchical system of power and the use made of that power, resting on the mass base of the party itself and a great network of organisations subordinate to the party. It is this mass base that chiefly distinguishes Soviet partocracy from autocracy or oligarchy.
>
> (Avtorkhanov 1966: vii)

The same idea was reiterated more than ten years later by Alexander Zinoviev. He states that, in spite of the fact that in the critical literature the basic characteristics of the role of the communist party in the society seem evident, there is an almost total misunderstanding concerning the nature of this power. He claims that these misapprehensions were either because the claims of the party about itself were taken seriously, or because it was considered to be merely a political phenomenon, applying the modern Western concept of a political party to the state-party. However, according to Zinoviev, 'it must be understood what exactly the party is at the micro-level of the base communities, thus, at the basis of society itself. The modifications effected by the party on the macro-level of society can only be understood after' (Zinoviev 1981: 185).

Finally, in a book published a couple of years ago, Yuri Glazov went even further in emphasising the micro-level aspects and grounds of the power of the party. Related to the problems of party membership, of the question of whether or not to join the party, he discusses crucial aspects of relations and attitudes toward oneself under a communist system. And he hoped that 'by interpreting the phenomenon of party membership we may be able to penetrate some depths of this peculiar and quite unprecedented society' (Glazov 1988: 14).

These writers all voiced concerns that the exact connections between the party and the society, or even basic aspects of the self, are issues that were not discussed in the past, but that are nevertheless crucial in order to come to terms with the nature of the system. Although all writers quoted here came from the Soviet Union, such considerations are now increasingly becoming important in all post-communist countries, from the perspective of the legacy of the past. We want to support and supplement their views from this perspective, on the basis of a detailed empirical analysis of a communist-party apparatus, that of Hungary, carried out at the last minute before the final dissolution, but at a moment when it was still working, and in a certain way was fighting for its life. A curious fight it was, no doubt, as at that period it was led solely inside the party, with hardly any attention being paid to the emerging alternative movements. As the time and the topic of our study were both unique, some details of our research must be given here.

The particular line of investigation we chose – to map out the regular, daily workings of the lower organs of the party apparatus in all the twenty-two districts of Budapest – was a choice that was not without risks. At the time of our research – the pilot study was done in the spring of 1988, the major survey between 1 September and 4 October – none of the former monopolies of the communist party was yet relinquished. Though the signs of the deepening economic crisis were clearly visible, and the voice of alternative movements was growing, the party itself at that time was still in full command. It was just in February 1988 that four well-known members of the reformist wing of the party, including Mihály Bihari, the supervisor of our research, were expelled. People who commemorated the thirtieth anniversary of the execution of Imre Nagy on 15 June were beaten up by the police. And at the infamous meeting in the Sporting Hall in November 1988, Károly Grósz, then first secretary, made the threatening comments about the gathering of counter-revolutionary forces, aiming to re-introduce a 'white terror'.[33]

When doing our survey at the district party committees, we had the feeling that we were entering the lion's den. We knew that, though formally our papers were in order, we really did not have the 'proper licence' to conduct such an investigation. In our interviews, we strayed far from the original topic for which the permit was valid. None of us were party members. Arpád Szakolczai was from the Institute of Sociology, belonged to the research team led by Elemér Hankiss that was considered to be a 'fifth column' of the opposition and had spent four years studying in the United States. His only 'official certificate' was a paper signed by the project leader – a paper that could have provided some formal defence, but whose presentation would not have helped in completing the study.

We thought and still think that it was a series of accidents that helped us to complete the research in a situation where, due to the turbulent times, the very logic of the inner mechanisms of the communist party happened to work in our favour. An original permit was obtained through the project manager, and after that our research somehow became officially acknowledged, and the subsequent steps slipped through at a period when, perhaps, the internal control mechanisms were already lax. Thus, we could go ahead with our survey, but still felt that we were on a very uncertain footing, and should proceed as quickly as possible. We wanted to complete our study before information spread about what we were doing. Here, again, bolshevik organisation helped us a lot. District party committees had no horizontal ties; therefore there was no flow of information between them. But still we collected our data in a hurry. We did all the work alone, with minimal external help (typing and some computer assistance). We prepared the questionnaire, personally administered it, held the interviews, put the data into the computer and made the analyses. As soon as we were ready with the first draft, we sent both our study and the background data to forty people in Budapest – well-known sociologists, political scientists, philosophers, historians – in order to prevent its being simply put in a drawer somewhere.

In the 'field', in order to prevent unnecessary and dangerous questions, we attempted to create an atmosphere that everything was official around us and in proper order. Curiously, no doubt due to our good luck which never once left us in this study, our strategy worked better than we expected, sometimes even all too well. We came to realise that, in a system that is based so much on pure power, on personal hierarchical relations of subordination and control, if one implies a certain degree of power, one has to accept that others will behave accordingly. In quite a number of cases we got into a very curious, uncomfortable situation, in a way that no doubt will never happen to us again. We were confronted with people who had a substantial influence over matters in their district, who controlled, among other things, the nomination of important economic or local political positions, and it was they who were wary of us. We, who were uncomfortable enough with the reverential attitude shown by students toward us, had to put up with a situation in which people showed obvious signs of fear in our presence – due to our presence. And in this situation there was nothing we could have done to alleviate this tension, as we simply could not afford it. Thus, in the very process of going ahead with our research, we became thoroughly acquainted with the basic life experience of communist power: always be feared and be afraid.

Thus, even though we couldn't diminish the tension when administering our questionnaires or the interviews, and had to acquire our information under such strange and stressful circumstances due to the nature of the mechanisms investigated, we at least wanted to be fair. As our interviewees told us many things that at that time could have been very disadvantageous to them from the point of view of the party, we not only left out all names from the final study, but cut them out from all copies of the interviews as well. We were also faithful to the texts in the preparation and interpretation of the material. Though we considered the 'stealing' of this information permissible, we did not think that it gave us a licence to do anything with it. We did not want to use the material for propaganda reasons, to help any of the new political parties in formation, and later we did not want to give handy food to the emerging wave of anti-communist rhetoric. We wanted to lay bare and reconstruct the mechanisms of communist power, but in a form that was without unnecessary rhetoric and defensible even in front of our former interviewees. We thought that the material we presented spoke for itself – there was no need for magnifying comments. It would have been indecent, both ethically and stylistically.

When collecting the data, in September 1988, there was a moment when we looked at each other saying 'Good heavens! Could it be that we are documenting the dissolution of the party?' This perplexing feeling is available only to those who lived in – or were born into, like us, after 1956 – a world that was thought to be unalterable. But it took a long time even for us to realise the full extent and validity of this presentiment.

Today, one may say, any study of the communist party is obsolete, is of mere historical interest. Who still talks about communism? Nevertheless, we think that such an approach destroys the dividing line between serious work and explanation, and mere journalism – a line that, due to the modern forms of media politics, is becoming blurred anyway. We feel that perhaps our study might be more helpful in the new situation than in the old.

The present situation, rather than presenting ready-made answers to the past, or giving solutions for the present and the future, raises a number of questions for consideration. The changes that were happening in 1991 overthrew most of the accepted truisms. On the basis of the available theoretical frameworks, they were unpredictable, even inexplicable. At the level of thought, new theories are proposed and rejected each day, stretching the limits of the former frameworks until they break. In politics, the hard-won concessions gained by the opposition one day become burdens to be carried, unwillingly, into the future. The changes take place not only at the level of thought and politics, but also at that of perception, of sensitivity. The very framework through which we saw things had to be changed, as our existence changed. The existential feeling of living under communism is now almost lost.

In this period, nevertheless, we were able to maintain a consistent approach to our project. This, we hope, was not due to our stubbornness or insensitivity, but to the fact that – perhaps because in the first half of the 1980s we were distanced from current debates – we were able to notice both deep changes and an even more perplexing continuity in the atmosphere, and could direct our attention toward the level of power mechanisms invested at the level of daily existence. We were interested not just in current political changes, nor simply in the history of the system. Rather, we happened to accomplish an on-the-spot study of the order of the history of the present.

This was all the more possible as our whole approach was strongly influenced from the start by the works of the French philosopher and historian, Michel Foucault.

2 Michel Foucault and the study of power

> Power is less a confrontation between two adversaries or the linking of one to the other than a question of government. . . . To govern . . . is to structure the possible field of action of others. The relationship proper to power would not therefore be sought on the side of violence or of struggle, nor on that of voluntary linking (all of which can, at best, only be the instruments of power), but rather in the area of the singular mode of action, neither warlike nor juridical, which is government.
>
> (Foucault 1983a: 221)

Foucault is a writer who is much referred to but is little used. Today, there is an enormous number of references to his work in almost all fields of study related to human and social activities (Megill 1989). But there is very little actual work done in applying his methods and analyses. It is often stated that it is not possible to use them as a starting point for empirical research. Most of the references about his work are in the nature of a commentary – something he no doubt would have found quite perplexing. It was his explicit goal that his works should be used as tools for analysis while they have any utility, and not as subject matters for exegetic comments and academic debates.

Moreover, and not independently of the first concern, much of the secondary literature on Foucault is marked by grave misunderstandings and mistaken interpretations of his work (Gordon 1990). The point is not to supervise the correct functioning of a discourse, especially not in the case of a thinker like Foucault. But openness and pluralism should not be a licence to say that anything goes. Concerning Foucault's work, the literature abounds in basic errors of fact and wrong assessments of his objectives. Many of the remarks are due simply to insufficient knowledge of basic original texts, or are criticisms made concerning the omission of subjects he considered irrelevant to his problem, and criticism is often simply based on the interpretations and behaviour of some of his propagators.

Past studies analysing the system of power in Eastern Europe did not pay attention to the theoretico-philosophical aspects of the problematic. They probably deemed such considerations unimportant, irrelevant or academic – either because they thought that the type of power exercised did not require very sophisticated methods and did not represent a problem of thought, or because it was thought that such an analysis would help only to hide away the truly oppressive and intolerable aspects of this system. Such an analysis was not made because it was perhaps thought that it would involve only the same types of discussion that had been held concerning human rights: the official ideologists of the system were engaged in discussions at – supposedly – philosophical levels concerning the 'true meaning' of human rights and whether it was possible to talk about individuals outside society, where the real issue was the neglect and suppression of the real concerns of concrete human beings at the level of daily existence.

We have different goals in a different situation. The perception that the actual exercise of power in communist societies did present a problem of the order of the 'theory' of power does not present inherent ethical difficulties now. And it was this perception that motivated our whole research: could the frameworks generally employed for the study of power accommodate, explain what was going on in daily reality within communist societies? Could it be accepted that this exercise of power did not present problems worthy of serious consideration or thought?

This book presents an empirical sociological investigation motivated by Foucaldian concerns and methods. It tries to show that such an analysis is not an impossibility. And by introducing the work of Foucault into the field of Eastern European studies, it intends to make the point that the way power was exercised in these countries would still have serious implications for the future, and it does present a problem that is far from being obvious and that is worthy of some serious consideration in relation to the central characteristics of the exercise of power in modern societies.

PARADOXES OF FOUCAULT

All the works of Michel Foucault have dealt with the past. And more than that: they were related not to recent events, but to the distant past, to certain aspects of the sixteenth to eighteenth centuries, never going beyond the 1840s. In his last works, he even went back to antiquity (Foucault 1986a, 1987). Nevertheless, he always emphasised that his work is connected to and starting from the present; present concerns and sensitivities led him to study the past. It was in order to get a clearer sight, a firmer grasp on contemporary problems that he went back to the earlier periods.

Many of his works were closely related to the question of power, especially concerning the deployment of extensive apparatuses and technologies of power correlative with the emergence of the modern state. It is fair to say that the problematic of power was one of the leading threads throughout his oeuvre.[1] The functioning of power was a central element in all his investigations; we could say that he was deeply interested in the 'nature' of power if it were not that he aimed to move the question away from the whole idea of 'nature'. He refuted the idea that power had an 'inner essence' or 'nature', but he was motivated in a certain way by the same difficulty as those writers who were trying to find the 'nature' of power (Foucault 1983a). But the way he was looking for the central questions concerning the application of power was itself highly peculiar, even idiosyncratic. Instead of trying to get ever closer to the centres of decision-making, the top levels of the political and economic spheres, 'real power', he restricted his attention to problems that were always considered to be minuscule, not to say marginal – the problems of madness, criminality, sickness, sexuality. He was careful to keep clear of the study of the state, the large corporations, capitalism, or other macro-level concerns.

We have thus two paradoxes. We have a philosopher deeply interested in the present – and doing nothing but historical investigations; and an analyst of power relations, a philosopher trying to come to terms with the functioning of 'power' – and doing nothing but detailed, empirical investigations of micro-level aspects and applications of power.

In this chapter, we do not want to pursue a comprehensive study of the basic ideas of Foucault. There are many studies at hand that fill this purpose.[2] We only want to present the methods followed in our research, to explain the particular choices taken, and for that purpose a discussion of these two paradoxes seems to be particularly helpful.

APPROACHES TO THE STUDY OF POWER

The discussion of power is conducted in a field spanned by the tension between two opposite views. One concentrates on the actual, observable aspects of power. According to this view, power is the ability to direct, subject, constrain others, to use the visible, concrete, material aspects of domination, whether legal or non-legal, legitimate or non-legitimate, and the enjoyment of benefits that accrue to those who hold important positions or who have control over the instruments of force. This view focuses on the monopolisation of decision-making and its enforcement: who are the people who have the initiative to rule, to govern, to dominate, to decide;[3] and what are the means that are available to enforce these decisions? Therefore, it centres around the study of the élite, the ruling strata, and the question of legal means of and constraints on power.

If this first approach is concerned with the empirical, visible, obvious, immediate, manifest aspects of power, the second perceives here a philosophical problem. It tries to go deeply, to look beyond mere phenomena, to uncover the nature, the hidden essence of power. By a shift in perspective, it attempts to lead us behind the scenes. It shows the apparent potentates as mere pawns in a game whose stakes are really defined at a deeper level. The most characteristic views belonging to this category are not the ones that represent a simple extension or duplication of the first, plain empirical approach – for example, conspiracy theories, or questions about the control of the political agenda[4] – but those theories that posit an explanation of a different order, irreducible to empirical categories: an inherent nature or a hidden force lying behind actual actors, and not just 'other' actors. The manifest decision-makers are directed by internal, abstract forces, like a will to power, desire, interests or by structural constraints like the existence of social classes, relations of production, or mentalities. While this approach was made necessary, among other things, by the obvious failures of the first approach to describe the complex relations of power existing in a modern society, due to its separation from empirical reality it had serious problems in returning to the real world. Here we are not just concerned with the question of testability. But, after all, concepts like 'classes' and 'interests', on the one hand, claim to represent not just abstract theoretical constructs, but a reality of a higher order than mere classes and interests that can be observed through the study of social stratification and behaviour. On the other, they cannot be identified with real phenomena. In a different way, they represent the same unsolvable dilemma as the search for 'true meaning', always enclosed in the hermeneutical circle: an undying echo reverberates forever between reality and 'true' reality.

The works of Michel Foucault represent an important contribution to the study of power, as he was able to move the whole problematics to new ground, to displace it, by opening up new dimensions that helped to undermine the dichotomies between individual and structure or between empirical reality and hidden essence. He did so by pursuing a dual strategy, at once empirical and philosophical. First, he opted for an empirical approach to the study of power; but in a special way (Foucault 1983a: 217). One may say that he was more empirical than the 'empiricists' themselves. The usual perspective of the latter is limited to two instances of the application of power. They are interested only in the way a decision is arrived at in the top level of the political system, and in the eventual resistance to this decision at the bottom level. With some exaggeration, one may say that most scholars and historians of politics are interested only in the mind of the prime minister and the actions of policemen; the discussions in the cabinet and the fights in the street. The whole vast zone of power exercised in the social body was either left out of the framework, or was assigned to – often boring – studies of organisations.

Second, Foucault displaced the tension between reality and essence to chronological sequences between the application and effects of power. And again in a special way: not simply replacing the synchronic concept of a hidden nature with a diachronic idea of the 'origin'; something that has been done already, without overcoming the dilemma, but by a dual innovation in methods: first, by reintroducing, in a novel way, the concept of 'thought' in the empirical study of power; and second, by positing an inherently pluralistic view of power that is present in the whole social body.

FOUCAULT ON THOUGHT AND PROBLEMATISATION

There is nothing new in the statement that the exercise of power involves thinking. It is well known that power is not equivalent to the use of force, but refers to the making of decisions, the formulation of objectives, the influencing of behaviour. Power is related to the possibility of solving problems about influencing and directing human beings which does present a problem for thinking. But Foucault here shifts the locus of thinking from the subject – the agent who is making or is resisting decisions – to the level of discourse and thought – the way a certain framework was set up that conditions both positively and negatively the thinking of an individual. Thinking is not merely the mental reproduction of external necessities, nor does it happen in a vacuum where the mind of the subject reigns sovereign. Foucault attempts to reconstruct the process of thinking that lies behind the exercise of power outside the traditional framework given by objectivity and subjectivity (Foucault 1967, 1973, 1984c). Even here, he is not much interested in general universal laws. He rather tries to map out the fragility of the whole process, and this is what he calls 'problematisation'.[5]

For Foucault the philosopher, what is at stake in his work is the study of the specific connections between thought and reality. This is the central concern of his investigations and not the topic studied in itself. The abstract pursuit of such a general question would no doubt seem pointless to him. Instead, he tries to pin down, to excavate in a number of specific investigations what difference thought makes in reality. For Foucault as a person with a passionate interest in reality and having strong ethical concerns, the starting points of these analyses are not given accidentally, by mental exercises, but by problems posed in the contemporary reality of human and social existence. The epistemological question about the impact of thinking on reality is linked to the ethical problem on the implications. From this perspective, the whole activity of thinking is reconceptualised.

We have a very special and restricted perception of thinking, especially concerned with activities like philosophy and theory, but even in the daily use of the word. According to this, thinking represents an activity of reflexion. It is a mental process that starts from and aims at the representation of the real and eventually at the formation of general explanatory theories. After the original, positive – and in modern neo-Kantian theories optional – contact with reality that means the acquisition of the 'ideas', it is a self-referential process that turns back to reality only with the end-product, the theory to be confronted again with reality; to be tested (if it ever is). This basic model of thinking originated with classical Greek philosophy, Socrates and Plato. For Foucault – and here he closely follows Heidegger – the whole conceptualisation of the process of thinking must be returned more closely to existence (Foucault 1986a: Introduction; 1988d). But Foucault is interested neither in digging out the forgotten truths of pre-Socratic philosophers, nor in restoring the purity of existence, in retrieving the original difference between thought and unthought, in grasping the depths of the unthinkable – another undertaking that he again no doubt would have considered as futile. He is not implying that somehow we forgot how to think after the pre-Socratics. Quite the contrary, thinking – and not just at the obvious level of individuals – has been constantly done since, but often quite outside theoretico-philosophical interests. This thinking is closely interwoven with reality, is rooted in reality. However – and here is Foucault's philosophical originality – its starting point is not a positive, but a negative instance.

Foucault returns to thought its volatility, its activity, its deep involvement with and interest in reality. He poses the same major question to thought that Nietzsche posed to truth: 'why truth', after all; why the 'will to truth' (Nietzsche 1966)? Foucault's question goes even deeper. Why think? Why does it happen that we think and how? Certainly not only due to abstract, theoretical interests. Thinking starts not with the positive aim of formulating 'true' representations – and eventually a theory – of the real, but with a difficulty, a gap. Foucault returns to the primary level of thinking from the secondary one – that of representations and theories – to the original confrontation of the gap. This whole process is described as 'problematisation'.

Thinking starts with a gap, a distance, a loss of familiarity with respect to reality, whether this reality is given as certain practices or experiences – the first being closer to the social and the second to the individual subject (Foucault 1986a: Introduction). At this level, the interest is not 'idle', theoretical; it rather involves a deep, existential dilemma. The loss of certainty creates a stimulus, generates 'irritation' – or, the other way round, it may be a feeling of pain with respect to certain elements of reality, leading to the loss of what was formerly taken for granted, toward problematisation.

Problematisation, the work of thought, is thus rooted firmly in the real. But reality – or rather the part of reality that has become a problem – plays only the role of the instigator. Thinking begins when the original difficulty, the feeling of pain is formed into conceptual terms and is thus localised; when an answer is found as a question.[6] The former hazy feelings that could only be described in negative terms give place to a clearly formulated problem. Thus starts the search for answers.

This concept of problematisation enables us to solve a paradox often mentioned with respect to the work of Foucault – one between the accidentality or even whimsical nature of thinking and the iron logic of a system from which no individual can escape. Foucault reverses here the usual places assigned to freedom and constraint in the process of thinking. According to the taken-for-granted view, the transition from the perception of a problem to the formulation of the question follows an unproblematic, almost necessary, course outside thought. The freedom of thinking comes with the proposition of alternatives. For Foucault, it is the other way round. Where formerly necessity ruled, he sees freedom, the real work of thought; and where free alternatives were pictured, he sees them fundamentally constrained by the former work of thought. The commonality of these answers is derived not just from the 'objectivity' of the difficulty, but also from the specific way the problem itself was formulated.

The simultaneity and systematicity of different eventual answers are rooted in the common problematisation. But it is not the only source of constraints on answers. Even if the original perception of a difficulty resulted in a dislocation from existing practices and reality, in the creation of a gap, the answer is not posed in a complete void. Problematisation lifted the concrete, real difficulty into the realm of thought, but this realm has its specific reality.[7] The answers to a problem are limited by the existing discursive resources; their conditions of possibility are constrained by the available stock. Even if the novel problematisation uproots the truths of the whole discursive system, the new solution must still be based on the at least partial reorganisation of the existing elements, 'primary units' of thought. For Foucault, these elements are not ideas or concepts, but 'techniques'.

A 'technique' is a procedure, a 'know-how', close to the common meaning of the term. It gives steps that are to be performed in order to attain certain goals. In the case of techniques of power, the targets are human beings. These procedures can range from simple commands to complex scenarios. They contain both discursive and non-discursive elements. The development of techniques of power is a contingent answer to a given problematisation.

But as the existence of a problem does not explain or justify the application of a particular technique of power, neither does the use of a given technique depend on the concrete problem which led to its emergence. Techniques are open. They can be applied under circumstances different from their original application. Techniques of power are not rigid, localised answers to concrete problems, but imply the work of thought embedded in the creation and the bridging of a distance, that make possible the application of these techniques for the solution of a quite different problem, the bridging of another gap.

The openness of techniques is a three-sided phenomenon. They are open not only towards the possible fields of application and targets of intervention, but also the possible users. The problem of resistance against a given system of power thus cannot be reduced to the take-over of the power apparatus or the refusal of such a take-over, but means questioning and resisting the techniques themselves. This is a more subtle question as techniques of power are often hidden.

The hiddenness of techniques of power lies in their similarity to routine or customary behaviour. No matter how much they are embodiments of thoughts, the results of rational considerations, in time techniques also become part of everyday activities, routine behaviour. This characteristic is especially important from the perspective of their mobilisation. The fact that they become accepted as part of routine behaviour does not mean that they become static forever. The element of thought contained in them can be accessed at any time, for different purposes. But their availability and familiarity help their smoother application in a novel situation.

This use of the word 'technique' has an important corollary, concerning the return of thought to reality. If the process of thinking started with a gap in reality, it must end with bridging this gap. The deployment of a technique is a solution to the problem, a link between the two sides of the perceived gap. But it is a link in another sense as well – it provides a link between thought and reality. The end-product of thinking is to effectuate a change in reality. It is the technique that makes this change possible. Technique as a bridge presents a circular relationship between thought and reality. It gives a procedure to effectuate change; but thereby it becomes a part of reality itself, something that can be re-mobilised and re-deployed again, to solve a different problem; something that becomes an instance of reality and thus a condition of possibility for the solution of novel problems.

If reality is produced partly by thought, then the question of truth must also be posed in a novel way. Problematisation started with a distance from reality, the existing state of affairs. This also means an overthrow of the established order of truths. If search for the solution involves more than a simple return to the previous order, then it must involve a reinterpretation of truth. Foucault calls this the 'games of truth' (Foucault 1984c, 1986a, 1988c). This concept is not concerned with the validity of the representation of reality; it has nothing to do with lies and falsity. It rather poses the problem of truth at the level of the production of reality in terms of the positive truths of human existence and social behaviour. The reorganisation of truth may lead to a new paradigm concerning the status and acquisition of knowledge – this is what Foucault calls discourses or discursive formations (Foucault 1976a). But such a change is not restricted to the level of knowledge. Knowledge concerning the truth of human behaviour is intimately linked with behaviour itself. A particularly good example for the relationship between thought, knowledge and the production of reality is the concept of the 'norm' (Foucault 1979a: 177–84, 304; see also Canguilhem 1978, and Gordon 1980: 248–9).

'Norms' and 'normality' are descriptive, statistical categories applied to the study of mass phenomena. But in the case of individual behaviour, they have an inherent prescriptive sense. The deviation from the norm, for all human and social sciences, involves a value judgement, a statement that something is unhealthy, even dangerous. It implies that such a behaviour, such an individual has to be corrected, returned to the normal, 'normalised'. A series of almost imperceptible connections lead from 'objective' statistical analysis to the project aiming at the transformation of individuals, where the reality and impact of such an intervention are hidden in the language of scientificity.[8]

This explains Foucault's attitude concerning theory, his refusal to engage in 'theoretisation' (Foucault 1983a: 209). Theory is secondary to a reality on which it is superimposed. The theoretician uses mental constructs to categorise and explain reality. The only question is the explanatory power. Foucault displaced this whole problematics toward the question of reality itself, here closely following Kant.[9]

For Kant, there is an eternal ontological gap between reality and knowledge. The nature of reality is different from that of experience. This gap can be bridged only by the attributes of transcendental reason, *a priori* categories shaping and interpreting experience. But this also means that experience – and thus knowledge – can never break out of the trap imposed by these categories. For Foucault, this ontological gap is partially broken down by the proposal that reality is already invested with thought: thought that is not related to processes of understanding, but to the solving of problems. Foucault's solution to a complex epistemological problem is so simple that it makes one wonder how it comes that nobody noticed it before. Students in the social and human sciences were puzzled by the problem of how to explain a reality that exists outside us, and were lately also troubled by the Heisenberg effect – the impact of the observer on the thing that is being observed. They took over the epistemological problem of Kant, voiced basically from the perspective of the natural sciences, where external reality – at the level where these questions are posed – exists outside human activity; transposed it to the study of men and societies, and realised that the problem there presents insurmountable difficulties, on both epistemological and ethical grounds. First, the interference between observer and observed as a problem is much more serious. Second, the whole project is ethically ambivalent as it places human beings in the position of objects. If these problems appear, though not with a uniform severity, in all areas of human and social 'sciences', they are especially acute in the case of political science, where, on the one hand, there are serious limits to empirical analysis (can a scholar observe the 'real' process of how decisions are made?), on the other, ethical considerations are *a fortiori* present.

Foucault's methodological considerations, needless to say, do not solve all the problems discussed above but, by displacing the dividing line between the ontological and epistemological questions, open up vast new areas for study and thought. Perhaps Foucault turned the eternal disadvantage of the social and human 'sciences', their irreducibility to objectivity, to their advantage. He liberated thinking at the same time when he made the 'objective' study of 'man' and 'society' almost meaningless. Thought and thinking are no longer restricted to an external and *a posteriori* application to a reality already lying there, waiting to be discovered, and are no longer connected to the 'realisation' of the unity of theory and practice by the conscious putting of the 'correct' theory into practice – a project that, by abolishing the distinction between scholarship and politics, turns scholars into social engineers, and even prescribes this as a duty. Quite the contrary, research is connected to the excavations of elements of thought that are present in real forms of behaviour and social relations; that were invested in them.

In this way, thinking does not want to grasp an elusive objective reality that always evades it by being inaccessible and by changing itself whenever the observer thought that it succeeded in pinning it down. It does not want to objectify human beings partially or in their 'wholeness'. It does not want to uncover and restore hidden meanings that are either inaccessible from the outside or long forgotten and buried deep in the past. It simply addresses itself to elements of thought that were invested and are therefore present in concrete activities.

Finally, this restatement of the relationship between thought and reality has several implications concerning actual work to be done. First, on the epistemological level, it gives a different task for the thinker from the formulation and testing of theories concerning the 'true' representation of the 'real'. It is the reconstruction of thinking as a historical process. And as this concept of problematisation is linked to very concrete problems, the line of analysis to be followed should also be empirical – on the order of the history of thought. Specific problems have to be reconstructed in their uniqueness and accidentality. The singular process of thought cannot be 'explained', as there is no fixed external reference point to which this process could be attached – the reference point in reality being stable, but only in the negativity of the difficulty. However, even if explanation is impossible here, thinking can be used to reconstruct the original process of thought, as it would represent the application of thought upon thought – present thinking upon the process and results of past thinking. This empirical work can start from the reconstruction of the original concerns – thus a 'history of problematisations' – or can take its starting point as the end-product, the answers that were given and became parts of existence, the 'truth' conditioned by the problematisation; it is in this sense that he is talking about the 'history of truth' (Foucault 1977b).

Second, if thought does not simply follow reality from a distance both in space (exteriority) and time (*a posteriori*), then the retrieval of the original problematisations may have consequences beyond reconstructing past games. Reality, social and human existence, is not outside thought, but is already thoroughly invested with thought, as a result of the former problematisations. We live in a world that is permeated by the results of past thinking. The reconstruction of past problematisations has a crucial relevance for the status of the present. In this way, declared universals may retrieve their fragility.

Third, this implies that if the present was made, it can then be unmade (Foucault 1979a, 1984c, 1986a, 1988c). This is not a licence for deconstruction and destruction. Foucault is talking about limited, concrete investigations rooted in present concerns and difficulties. For the pointless mental exercise of the deconstruction of 'reason', he substitutes the questioning of certain concrete techniques and rationalities; questionings where he does not play the role of the universal intellectual, only one who takes up issues that have been raised by others (Foucault 1983b).

Foucault's investigations concerning 'power' can be situated in this general framework of thinking as problematisation.

FOUCAULT ON POWER AS GOVERNMENT

Foucault was constantly trying to step back from his own studies, to re-think the specificity of his interest in relations of power, and to reassess the importance of questions of power for his own undertaking. Throughout his career, he rejected the view that limited power to negative instances. For him, power – like thought – always involved an activity, and was also intimately related to knowledge. The specific way positive power was conceptualised, however, shifted several times. In his first writings, power was connected to the link between certain techniques of exclusion and the collection of knowledge, and the power involved in the application of language and discourses, under these circumstances (see Foucault 1961, 1975, 1976b, 1979a). Even if power was classified here in negative terms – exclusion, coercion, objectification through knowledge – it was always connected to the production of individuals and rituals of truth. Later he got closer to viewing war as the best metaphor for power (1979a, 1980a). In his last writings concerning power, he implicitly reclassified this view as only one of the possible meanings of strategy,[10] the one that seeks confrontation and victory over the adversary (1983a: 224–5) and proposed to conceptualise power rather in terms of a generalised concept of 'government' (Foucault 1978, 1979b, 1979c, 1981, 1983a).

The definition of power as government pins down the specificity of Foucault's meaning of power both in a negative and a positive way. First, negatively, it separates his concept of power from related concerns.

Positive power does not equate with capacity, the ability to do something, a view that is in certain ways close to both the perspectives of Nietzsche and Bacon. Power does not equate with the opposite of the above concept, the preventing, the taking away of capacities or the possibility of their exercise – whether this negative concept of power is couched in the highly specific and problematic discourse of repression (about which Foucault has very strong and basic epistemological–ontological reservations), or simply in the terms of force, violence and domination which Foucault does not think to be the sole bearers of power. Exclusion, oppression, exploitation and domination do have a real existence, but they do not exhaust the problem of power, especially concerning the type of power exercised in modern societies. Foucault calls this peculiar form of exercising power 'governmentality' (Foucault 1979b).

In a positive sense, identifying power with the broad sense of government, Foucault plays with the triple sense of the French word '*conduite*', meaning conduct, the government of others, 'behaving oneself'. In this sense, '[t]he exercise of power consists in guiding the possibility of conduct and putting in order the possible outcome. . . . [It is] a mode of action upon the actions of others' (Foucault 1983a: 221). Power as government is a specific relation between human beings that can never fully be explained by external constraints. It is not restricted to external confrontations and conditioning, but may involve the internal formation of actions themselves.

Power as government immediately involves a problem and also the possibility of freedom. The problem is how to exercise power, how to lead others. This question has a technical aspect – how to perform the very activity of government, what are the preconditions of effective government; a question of mobilisation, related to rationality, persuasion and faith – how to convince the object-subject to follow the course prescribed; and an inherent ethical dilemma. The possibility of freedom is given by the fact that power in the positive sense as government is exercised over the acts of others, therefore the possibility of non-acting is always given. Force breaks individuals; government makes them act. At this point, the problem of subjectivity enters the scene in the discussions of power.

Before pursuing these two issues, let's notice that Foucault's concept of power as government permits an interesting play between power in general and political power. The tension between the current use of the word and Foucault's definition already indicates this ambiguity. Political science employs the term 'government' as almost a synonym of the state. But Foucault, through a play with the French meaning, goes back to the more general sixteenth–seventeenth-century meaning.[11] The point is partly analytical, and is oriented, for example, against current slogans claiming that 'everything personal is political'. But Foucault's aim is not restricted to analytical concerns. Rather, the purpose of separating political power from other aspects of power is to make the analysis of their interconnection – something that he thinks is especially crucial for the emergence of modern societies – possible.

Power relations as instances of government, thus, cannot be localised, are not only restricted to the political centre. They may occur at any point in the social body. Any relationship between individuals may be transformed into a power relationship. Society is not outside power; it contains a vast network of actual and possible power relations. But the idea that power and social relations are coextensive must be qualified in three ways. First, this statement refers to a possibility and not to an actuality. Foucault is not saying that power is everywhere. All he says is that power cannot be excluded *a priori* from any social relationship. He is not asserting the unavoidability of power and the impossibility of freedom; rather, he states that freedom is an activity that must be exercised. Freedom cannot be 'warranted' for ever by the once-and-for-all exclusion or taming of power. The exercise of power should be opposed by the exercise of freedom.[12] Second, the unavoidable possibility of power does not represent for him a 'potentiality', something of the Hegelian–Marxian–Freudian concept turned inside out. According to that concept of 'potential', there is something beyond the actual things as a hidden – if immature or repressed – possibility, an internal force that has an ontological existence and that will eventually be realised. Foucault's whole philosophy is directed against the very idea of the existence of such 'possibilities', an inherent human nature or authentic existence that should only be 'found' and 'realised'. It would be more than unfair to reproach him with the cynical concept of an inherent potential of power. Third, especially in his last writings, he states that power does not necessarily have a negative value (Foucault 1983a, 1984f). It is unavoidable that sometimes human beings be governed for one reason or another. The task of social thought is not to denounce power in general, but to be alert to its actual exercise, to map out its rationality. The dream of a society without power would only help existing relations and exercises of power to go unnoticed and become reinforced.

Power relations as possibilities are thus coextensive with the social body. The turning of a possibility into a reality, however, depends on a number of factors; especially if we are talking about the possibility of the centre's vesting itself in the local networks, and turning them to its own uses. It depends on the top level, on the existence of a will for such an intervention; a will that was missing in the feudal period in Western Europe and that was missing in Eastern Europe even up to the end of the Second World War.[13] On the bottom level, it depends on the level of civilisation, the availability of certain techniques of behaviour. But the crucial question lies in between these two extremes. It involves the co-harmonisation, the bringing together of these two ends, the filling of the vast space between them. It involves more than a simple will to rule or govern. It means, on the level of thought, the formulation of strategies which attempt to invest, mobilise and include local techniques of power; on the level of reality, the actual ways in which such attempts were confronted with daily existence and the result of the interaction and confrontation of these two factors. The first part is described by Foucault under the categories of programmes, technologies and governmental rationality (or, in an earlier terminology, programme of power); the second is the contingent systems of practices and apparatuses.

GOVERNMENTAL RATIONALITIES AND TECHNOLOGIES OF POWER

Governmental rationalities represent a collection, assessment and valorisation of sets of procedures that can help to mobilise and apply particular techniques for the attainment of the strategic ends (Foucault 1979b, 1980c, also Gordon 1980, 1991). A strategic aim cannot be open-ended; it must have a specific objective in mind. A strategy is a purpose that always has a target; it is intentional in the Husserlian sense. Governmental rationalities or programmes, however, are results of a thought-process. They are answers to specific problemat- isations, but can be deployed for different uses. Programmes of power are complex scenarios. They define a set of objectives, prescriptions, desired states concerning the objects of government, the targets of intervention, and delimit specific positions for those who govern. They have explicit objectives, but a programme as a consistent project with an intrinsic rationality may well have a validity and applicability beyond the concrete strategic aim (Foucault 1983a: 224–6).

Such programmes are made possible by the availability of techniques of power, spread inside the social body. These techniques are themselves collected, classified, rationalised into complex systems, technologies, where the relationship between techniques and technologies is somewhat analogous to that between ideas and ideologies. While it is easy to make a distinction between an end and a means, or between a strategic aim and a technical tool, the distinction between a programme and a technology is more difficult to make in concrete cases. Even Foucault is confusing in his terminology. Sometimes he calls pastoral power or police a programme, at other points a technology. Still, this separation is crucial for assessing the implications of Foucault's methods for socio-political analysis. Programmes have a higher degree of rationality than technologies. They do possess an inherent logicality and not just a technical consistency. They are not just passive tools, ready to be deployed for different uses, but mobile and dynamic in their openness. They have a certain degree of automatism in their activity, they can 'work themselves'.

Programmes thus have the explicit aim of transforming reality. They also have instruments to effectuate this transformation, complex technologies using techniques of behaviour available in the social body, and investing other techniques to make its exercise possible. But these programmes must be deployed in a vast and complex field of reality, penetrated by numerous social networks and individual strategies. It is in this context that the question of the impact, the effect of a governmental rationality and the often voiced concern about resistance can be located.

The conceptual framework outlined above – the omnipresence of (possible) power relations within the social body, and thought as problematisation transforming reality and leaving its marks in techniques and rationalities embedded in the real through games of truth – make the analysis of the concrete interconnections between governmental rationalities and actual practices possible. These tools were worked out for the analysis of the conditions of possibilities for the emergence of modern state power. The concept of governmental rationality – as opposed to ideas like the 'colonisation of the life-world' and the incessant growth of state power – reflects that central strategies had to take account of and mobilise for their own purposes existing social networks and had to increase and organise the forces of individuals. The final effect of these programmes in reality – what Foucault calls 'practical systems', or 'systems of contingencies' – is the result of these multiple interactions between central initiative and micro-level relations and techniques (Foucault 1979b, 1980c, 1984a).

Finally, four comments related to this conceptualisation of the intermeshing of central and local concerns and the establishment of solid networks of practical systems and apparatuses. First, programmes are explicit, and are deployed as part of a conscious strategy. The results of their deployment, however, cannot be predicted in advance. Central initiatives from the top levels of political power confront micro-level power relations rooted in the nexus of social networks in daily life. Even if the relative strength of the different sides, especially concerning the possibility of the use of force, is not equal between the different sides, the results of the encounter cannot be predicted precisely at the outset. The impact of a programme on the real is not limited to its success. Foucault's problem is not to show that we are all trapped in a diabolic programme, but to point out the difference such governmental rationalities make in the real.

Second, it is in this sense that resistance is correlative with power from the outset. We have here a delicate interaction of forces where power and resistance are correlative elements of these struggles, each irreducible by the other, but nevertheless conditioned by it. There is thus a category of resistance in Foucault's work, though his perspective is different from standard accounts. The dividing line is not between social classes, not even between the state and (civil) society. The question rather is the extent to which governmental rationalities were successful in vesting themselves in and mobilising social networks and individual behaviour. The point of attack should be not the state, but the specific connections, the historically established and consolidated links between governmental rationality, social networks of power, and the construction of forms of behaviour and subjectivity.

Third, even if the establishment of these connections meant a long process of bargaining, struggle and coercion, using numerous instances of micro-level social networks rather than the simple imposition of a repressive apparatus from above, the possibility of the whole project was rooted in a major breakdown of the practical systems that formerly represented the horizon and the integrative force at the level of daily existence. Had this practical system remained intact, the central programmes would not have been able to penetrate social networks. The possibility of the establishment and utilisation of positive power at the micro-level by the political centre was established by such destructive struggles as the Italian wars around 1500, the religious and civil wars in the sixteenth century and the Thirty Years War, among others. The same holds true for the twentieth century as well, where all major efforts for the government and transformation of social reality were closely connected to the two world wars.

Fourth, a central paradox of power is that its most overwhelming, rigid and ossified aspects, the ones that seem to be unassailable, are also the most unstable, or, at least, the most ephemeral. Governmental rationalities result in the crystallisation of practical systems, supervised and controlled by the material reality of an apparatus. It is these solid networks of power, with the positions and privileges they offer, that represent 'real power' for most political analysts, on the basis of which they reject as futile all attempts to study power as a problem for thought. Still, it is these material aspects that are always subject to breakdowns – as both the history of absolutism and the current events in Eastern Europe, and also in Latin America and Asia demonstrate. Paradoxically, while the reality of practical systems may be quite different from the original programmes, it is exactly the element of thought contained in technologies and rationalities embedded in daily reality that may best survive the disappearance of the whole systems.

These methodological considerations suggest to us two different lines of analysis for the study of relations of power: two initial points of attack on a long and complex process. Power can be empirically studied, starting from the two ends. These are not the same as the well-known distinction between the ruler and the ruled. Rather, it suggests, on the one hand, a study of the nature of a history of thought, the reconstruction of forms of problematisations and the formations and investment of governmental rationalities (programmes of power); on the other, it demands empirical analyses of the actual exercise of power at the level of daily existence.

These two lines of analysis make each other intelligible and possible. An analysis of programmes of power, in itself, could easily remain an exercise in the history of ideas. An empirical analysis of the actual, contemporary exercise of power would limit itself to the study of effects and appearances, would not be able to escape the trap set up by the internal rationality and external insupportability of this exercise. Foucault is interested in and developed tools for the linking of these two investigations, for the analysis of the interconnections between the original programme and its actual application at the level of daily life, as it is at that level that thought, through problematisations, has become part of reality in the past, and may have a life-span well beyond the former system of programmatic and practical rationality, constraining and conditioning the present and the future. In this way, the two paradoxes mentioned at the beginning of this discussion can be resolved together: a serious critical work on the present is possible only through an investigation that is at once historical and empirical at the level of the history of thought and practices.

METHODS AND DATA

The specific circumstances and topic of our research required some modifications in methods. First of all, concerning the actual vesting and exercise of power, we did not have to rely upon the archives – something not only Foucault, but also Tocqueville and Fainsod had to put up with. We could talk with the actual agents of power, could conduct interviews. We could ask our own questions, and could get the 'feeling', the atmosphere of the whole place. This atmosphere in a situation where the whole apparatus was obediently present, including the first secretary, was really something extraordinary – among consenting adults, it is probably impossible today to observe anywhere else this particular atmosphere. It was a peculiar mixture of business meeting, classroom and military protocol. Moreover, we were fortunate enough to be able to do our research exactly in the moment of the major transformation, the coming dissolution of the whole system. Our interviewees felt that the end was near and therefore did not hide anything. On the contrary, they were trying to reveal everything, to emphasise their own importance. This only reinforced the general view that a system can be best understood at the moment of its dissolution. Also, in our study of the exercise of power by the party apparatus, we could already direct our attention toward aspects of these activities that we considered to be interesting from our perspective of the present. Because of this, we were fortunate enough to carry out a contemporary and not just a retrospective analysis in the way of a history of the present.

Second, we had to develop our own methods concerning the conduct of the interviews and the questionnaire. We followed an elaborate strategy to open up our respondents and reduce their suspicion. First we asked everybody present to fill out the questionnaire. With this we had a dual purpose: the gathering of concrete information and background facts; but, more importantly, the preparation of the interview. The questionnaire included many personal items concerning childhood experiences, personal aspirations and relations with their own children. In this way, we tried to get apparatus members involved. Also, both of us were present when respondents filled out the questionnaires, and could select individuals who seemed to be the most suitable for our purposes. We needed interviewees who were willing to participate in our investigations, and who also were intelligent enough to have some ideas about the activities and the working of a party committee. We wanted to reconstruct a rationality, and we needed partners for that exercise.

In the actual interviews, we started with a very mundane and empirical question, asking our respondents to describe in detail the content of their daily activities, without reference to ideologies or empty generalities. Once an in-depth description had been made, we tried to reconstruct – with the help of the respondent – the internal rationality of these activities. In this process, we made our respondents face the nature and the impact of their activities in an often novel way, helping them to give explanations or make connections that they perhaps would not have done otherwise. With the help of this mutual effort of reconstruction, we also gained access to topics that were deemed the most sensitive by the respondents themselves. By trying to make our interviewees come to terms with their own activity, we often aroused their interest in our research, and at the same time succeeded in overcoming their internal resistance and suspicion. We consider this ethical as these activities were political ones, concerned the whole country and therefore had to be made public.

Third, in a Foucaldian analysis, the study of the actual exercise of power must be complemented with the study, at the level of thought, of the original programme embedded in these activities. In our case, it was a highly problematic question. Which programme to study, after all? The distinction made by Foucault between programme and ideology is relevant here. A programme, as was discussed above, is a discursive scenario with the explicit aim of transforming reality. An ideology, however, starts with the claim of giving a correct account of reality. It is a science of ideas that also aims at the transformation of reality according to this 'truth'. This whole idea is pre-Kantian (thus the immediate importance of all neo-Kantian philosophies in Eastern Europe), and is by definition dogmatic. Our problem is not the question whether an ideology provides a correct representation of reality or not. It is rather that an ideology contains not just representations of the 'real' as a reality existing outside thought, but embedded and often distorted discursive programmes. In an ideology, elements of thought vested in reality are mixed together with explicit attempts to change the real, all formed into a complete system at the level of consciousness. It is an amalgam that does not lend itself to analysis without some external reference point in the way of a history of thought.

The apparent solution of extracting the programme embedded in the activities of the party apparatus, an analysis of bolshevik ideology, seemed to us of dubious value for another reason as well. Such an exercise would have been dangerously close to an exercise in ideology criticism, a comparison of actual practices to the original ideology. It has already been done by many works, and also it would not be very promising concerning the enormous gap between the pronouncements of ideology (working-class power, genuine participatory democracy, economic progress, the end of alienation, etc.) and the actual – past – reality of these countries.

These methodological considerations only reinforced our belief that the original works of bolshevik ideology are not particularly useful for understanding the programme embedded in the daily reality of communism. Instead, we chose to extract and reconstruct this programme from the actual practices, and to search for the original governmental rationality and technology that may have given the bolshevik strategy its positive orientation and content in a literature apparently unconnected to the field of communist studies.

The subjects of our study were the district-level 'political workers' of Budapest. The number of political workers in a given district depended on the number of party members (an unwritten rule was that one such worker was to be employed for every 1,000 party members). Apart from the first secretary and the two or three district secretaries, there were six or seven political workers in the smallest districts, while in the largest areas this number could rise to twenty. We attempted to include all members of the political apparatus of the twenty-two districts in our study. The completion of the questionnaire was optional, but with one exception all the political workers present filled out the questionnaire; only those absent for various reasons were missing. Although our permit was not extended to the district secretaries, in a number of cases they were glad to express their opinions and even agreed to an interview. Altogether, we held twenty-five interviews and collected 202 questionnaires, which, in our estimate, represents about two-thirds of the district-level political apparatus of Budapest.[14]

3 The activity of district party committees

'Well, and about the business of the agora, and the ordinary dealings between man and man, or again about agreements with artisans; about insult and injury, or the commencement of actions, and the appointment of juries, what would you say? There may also arise questions about any impositions and extractions about market and harbour dues which may be required, and in general about the regulations of the markets, police, harbours, and the like. But, oh heavens! shall we condescend to legislate on any of these particulars?'

'I think', he said, 'that there is no need to impose laws about them on good men; what regulations are necessary they will find out soon enough for themselves.'

(Plato, *The Republic*, 425. c–e.)

The objects of our study were the regular, day-to-day activities of the district party committees, their relations with the population, firms and the public institutions of the area, and the reasons and methods of these interventions. Our object was thus not 'politics', in the sense of the highest decision-making level, but regular, everyday 'political' activity. For us, this approach was suggested by the fact that public perception of these activities was not only distorted, but in most cases simply missing. The population met the party at two different levels: one was that of the documents and resolutions issuing from the centre, as reflected in the media, and the other was at the concrete level in the firms or the residential area. The wide and influential area of intermediate party organs fell outside our horizon in Eastern Europe; we were unacquainted with their existence. In the words of one of our interviewees:

The public perhaps only perceives the party as this building. It is the local council that maintains contact with the population. It is [a question] whether the population is aware of the fact that the council, on the other hand, is told what to do by us; I feel they are not aware of this.

(G.D.)

Our goal was thus to assess the exact impact of the district party committees through a detailed analysis of their concrete day-to-day activities and the reasons for this type of activity.

THE CONCRETE ACTIONS OF DISTRICT PARTY COMMITTEES

How large then was the actual extent of the sphere of daily influence of a district party committee (PC)? At a first approximation, the answers can be given on two different levels, in principle and practice. On the level of principles, the answer is quite obvious: the area of responsibility of the district PC includes all political questions, or all phenomena that may have a political aspect, that may be qualified as political. The only problem here concerns the relation between the two sides of the equation 'all political questions = the competence of the party': does it mean that the party should deal only with political questions; or that it is only the party that is supposed to deal with political questions? The first interpretation means a restriction: the party should deal with only political questions; the second is an exclusion: everybody else is excluded from the political arena. It was only in 1988 that one could witness a shift in the interpretation; and later we'll discuss how and why up till now the two interpretations were meshed together in the everyday activity of the party. Let's first discuss the practical level: what type of questions are defined as political, i.e. what does the party deal with?

A part of this activity corresponds to what, without any objection, can be termed as political. These issues include such conflicts as massive lay-offs, the possibility of a strike, the attention paid to the political rivals, the alternative organisations, the direction of the activities of local party units, or the education of party members.

There is nothing surprising in the fact that the apparatus of a political party is engaged in such activities. The only questions that arise are whether there is an attempt to exclude others, and whether this work is done efficiently. The latter doesn't fall within our brief, and we'll return to the former later on in our study at several places. But it seemed extremely interesting that, besides the areas listed above, a district PC dealt with a number of others as well. It was engaged in a much broader scope of activities. Let's review, then, a few such examples, not from the distant past, but from the concrete 1988 practice of the district PCs.

We'll give only examples that were related to the work done at the given PCs at the time of our interviews or the immediate past.

THE SUPERVISION OF ECONOMIC ORGANISATIONS

A group of the examples belongs to the economic field, related to the businesses in the district. Until the very end, the district PCs still paid minute attention to the performance of businesses, their results and the fulfilment of their targets:

> Firm X modified its yearly plan when it failed to meet the targets in the first half. I remarked that this was the easy way to show a successful completion at the end of the year. Well, a big battle broke out about this, there were no two subsequent EC[1] meetings when this fact was not brought up against me. How shall I put it: history proved me right as they even fulfilled the original plan.
>
> (G.E., secretary)

Besides evaluating the activity of the firms, it was often the party committee that established links between businesses, or provided them with the conditions to carry out their regular work. Thus, it may have been the task of a district secretary to obtain raw materials, if they were not available in any other way.

But it was not only the linking of businesses for economic reasons that belonged to the profile of the work of a district PC. A similar example was the 'one business, one child-welfare institution' initiative, which was created to serve a dual purpose. First, to establish links between the population and the different institutions of the district; second, to provide hidden financial support for child-welfare institutions (schools, day-care centres, hospitals) through district enterprises. Let's look at an example related to the closing of a restaurant where workers of a nearby factory had their organised daily meals:

> Well, where should they go for lunch? And then the linked school immediately made them an offer. They were really very grateful as, in the process, we reshuffled a few of the brigades, we tried to figure out what were the possibilities, who can talk with whom, both in material and other respects, and it turned out that we hit it right on target. And they are still grateful. What a nice group we found for them, say the workers of firm Z. And the Y-street girls' school says the same thing as they can get some work at firm Z and so earn some extra money.
>
> (G.E., secretary)

The same goal of connecting people and institutions appeared in the activity done by local PCs during the snowstorm of the winter of 1987–8:

> Well, now the question is the following: somebody must make a decision. Who is in the centre? The council and the party. They oversee the whole area, and somebody must pick up the phone, and must organise the links or at least try to do so. Who has cars, who can go to the bread factory, and who can't? This is the situation. So in case of emergency, one must and can help effectively. . . . Here at that time there really was a hot line between the district council and the party. We discussed what to do, as here was the factory, there were the cars. I know it sounds funny, but really, the regular cars couldn't get there. Now, we solved this problem, we solved it in a day.
>
> (G.E., secretary)

HELPING THE WORK OF THE COUNCILS

The other major targets of the activities of district PCs were the district councils. Formally these consisted of an elected body and a paid apparatus directed by the elected officials. In practice, the lists of candidates were provided by the communist party, and the apparatus was often directly governed by the communist-party apparatus. The personnel of the district PC was also heavily represented at the top levels of the district council.

The impact of the party on the different branches of the council was not identical. In the case of some, the supervision was occasional and distant; in others, even yesterday, it meant actual direction. One such area concerned the development plans of the council. So in one district, during the preparation period, that is, before the plans were even shown to the elected bodies of the council, the district PC had twice discussed the seventh five-year district plan. One of the participants gave the following opinion on this:

> Here the situation is different from that of the plans for individual firms, as things related to the population of the area belong to us at least as much as to the council. . . . The seventh five-year plan which is now with the district council is the result of a joint activity. The district PC took an active part in this. . . . The elected bodies of the council did not take part in the preparation stage at all. . . . But it would be an abnormal thing if this body had to sit down every other week because a new version had emerged.
>
> Q: May I say that the seventh five-year plan, in the process of preparation, and before it made its way to the elected bodies,

was a joint effort of the two [party and council] apparatuses?

A: Yes, you may say so.

(J.L.)

Another example of direct control was the department of education, health and sport:

The department of education, health and sport was completely taken over by the instructor [for a definition of 'instructor', an inadequate translation of the Hungarian *instruktor*, see Chapter 6, page 93] from the PC who directly governed them. Or in the case of public health, things went in the same way.

(G.D.)

The other side of the interweaving between the local council and the party committee was given by joint initiatives when the party was directly helping the councils, mobilising the population to carry out the policies of the latter or to improve its financial resources. One such example concerned the organisation of 'communist shifts' (shifts worked for no pay), whose returns went to the budget of the district council. The concrete questions of organisation were not at all clear. Sometimes even the agents of the process were uncertain about the meaning:

Q: Who initiates this with the firms? In fact, who does initiate this?

A: The local council would like it if this money came in. And the PC takes care of the matter. To put it mildly. It is rather the PC that is the initiator. Or, if the leadership of the council fails in some respect, then it is the leadership of the PC that carries the case further. We're talking about the [district] secretaries here, there is no need for fetishisation.[2]

(J.L.)

Even today – though a lot of people tried to convince me – I still don't understand why the organisation of communist shifts is a task of the district PC, when it increases the budget of the council.

(G.C.)

The third major area of guidance given to the local council by the party concerns public institutions, like the schools or medical establishments of the area. The PC decides whether there is a need for a new school in the district, or whether it is necessary to close or change the nature of an existing school; whether the boundaries of the local medical centres' areas need to be re-drawn; how to allocate the funds made available locally for grants to deserving local organisations and for teachers' merit awards; what the situation is concerning the training of skilled workers; how the new school year started, etc., etc. The examples seem to be haphazard and could be continued without an end, as almost anything happening in the district may have become the object of the attention of the district PC.

Before further analysis, let's point out two factors, two aspects of these activities that play a crucial role both from the perspective of the accomplishment of the tasks and of our whole discussion. The first is the question of information, the second is that of personnel, or 'cadre policy'. The former is important because it is through information that the PC can get close to the events and activities. Through the latter, the attention of the PC is extended to all sorts of persons who may be considered in any way to have leadership potential. 'Cadre policy' was not restricted to the cadres of the party, not even to the infamous practice of the nomenclatura. The party raised its voice whenever it felt that the work done by any of the managers was not satisfactory, or if it wanted their removal for some reason. If the district PC had no licence in terms of its competence list, it tried to contact the level where the appropriate decisions could be made.

THE DIRECT REASONS FOR INTERVENTION

Let's take up one after another the reasons given by the members of the apparatus for the activity of the district PC, for the constant, regular, positive, helping intervention into the ordinary business of day-to-day life. Why was there a need for minute attention to be given by a political party to the everyday working of economic organisations, public institutions or the local council? Part of the reason was already alluded to above, as it is not possible to separate completely the activities from the justifications. Here we'll complement and summarise the arguments that have already been discussed in part.

A realistic understanding of the situation

According to some, the PCs should not really be pursuing any of these concrete activities. They should not even have to guide or steer businesses or the council in any particular direction. They only have to ensure that these organisations really do work and achieve their aims properly:

> With respect to the schools, I think our concrete task is not to provide particular schools with computers. . . . Rather we should be ensuring that, where they really need a computer, there is one. They shouldn't give a computer to a school simply because the district PC demanded it – that would not be proper.
>
> (D.F., secretary)

This instance also gives some indication about the actions a district PC must take in order to reach its goal, a situation where everybody dutifully accomplishes his/her own work. Some other arguments also point in the same direction:

So we were not really interested in the practical details of their work – what they do in this school, how many directors are there, etc. – but how successfully they are able to accomplish their work.

(V.K.)

Another detail of this same interview emphasises directly that political workers, in their current job, were not concerned with the activity itself – even in cases where it happened to be their former profession: thus, where teachers were supervised by a former teacher:

Not one [school] party secretary has invited me to sit in on his/her classes. I would really like to do so. But I don't have time for that, and it is really not my job. I am there for meetings, on training days; I see how they try to 'fortify' the teachers.

(V.K.)

The next instance illustrates the fact that, even if the direct influence of the district PC was restricted to the local party cells, the government of the latter in practice coalesced with that of the whole economic or public organisation:

The question is whether the party organisation over there is really able to accomplish its tasks properly or is doing something else. It may have some problems concerning leadership or something else, and because of this, it couldn't –
Q: And in what direction should he influence a process?
A: Who? The instructor?
Q: Yes. In the firm.
A: Well, in the direction of making them aware, as soon as possible, of their own capabilities, weak points, troubles, the means to overcome these; so that they may work and make decisions independently. Besides that, as I mentioned earlier, the question of profitability also belongs there. In sum, they must cope with the problems where they work.

(B.C., secretary)

Thus, according to this chain of reasoning, the task of the party was not to give a concrete direction for the firms or the institutions to follow, and to enforce the pursuit of this goal, but to help them realise and follow the direction that they are supposed to follow and accomplish the task that is their job. The tasks of supervision are combined with the raising of self-awareness and self-knowledge:

> They should not alter [the work of elected bodies].
> Q: Then to influence?
> A: No, not even that, but to bring them to a realistic understanding of the situation.'
>
> (D.F., secretary)

The evaluation of economic activity must be linked to the question of 'efficiency'. District PCs were not only supposed to ensure that the workers did work, and that businesses did produce, but had to pay attention to its being done efficiently. The measure of efficiency, using standard economic methods of evaluation, is profitability, in terms of revenues exceeding costs. But reliance on this method made the work of the district PCs much more difficult, if not impossible:

> The economic activity of businesses is so complicated today that for a layman the data are a jungle. You can hardly find your way through all this. Our committee on economic policy does so only because the majority are economic experts who are only incidentally party workers. Finally, they figure out something, which then the EC – well, all this makes five or six rounds of internal discussion.
>
> (B.C., secretary)

The situation was even more complicated by the fact that, given the system of wage and price regulations, it was difficult to know whether an activity that was profitable on paper really brought in more than it cost. In any event, in the case of firms operating at a loss, the only possible way for a PC was to work on decreasing this loss:

> It may happen that a manager is acting against the common interest precisely when he is stimulating his own workers to more or better work. When the firm produces a loss, he shouldn't stimulate. He should work on how to diminish this loss.
>
> (B.C., secretary)

This leads to two possible conclusions. First, there is a need for economic experts who can decide about profitability. Here, a district PC was obviously not competent; and why should it have been, as in this case the interest of each and every firm is to find out the profitable paths for itself. Second, if we start from the premise of economic efficiency, then, in the given situation, the activity or even the very existence of the party was questioned. The whole orientation of the party was tuned toward mobilisation and stimulation, on the premise that this is the way to promote the common interest. This whole system was simply not prepared for a case where the growth of production went against the common interest. There follows only one logical conclusion from all this, one that can be found almost literally in the quotation above: the party should mobilise its members to commit sabotage.

This absurd consequence in its extreme form illustrates the conclusion that the purpose that gave the motivation for the activity of the party earlier loses any conceivable meaning at the moment when enterprises begin to be assessed in monetary and not quantitative terms. We think the statement that 'socialism' and a market economy are incompatible is quite correct, if we assume that a party apparatus is a necessary condition of 'socialism'.

This whole chain of reasoning is based on the background assumption that without the helping and at the same time evaluating supervision of the party things would not be done properly. In one of our interviews, related to a concrete example (the reorganisation of local schools and medical facilities), this assumption came almost directly to the fore:

> Now, let's take the doctors – where does their interest lie? Good working conditions, only a few patients, as a doctor's interest lies in having more time for leisure, time which is not spent in the examination of sick people; so it is in their interest to hold on to a somewhat easier situation.
> (B.C., secretary)

We could have presented a similar statement about the teachers who, in order to maintain the existing state of affairs, due to the same 'love of comfort', wanted to prevent the transformation of a local elementary school into a high school specialising in computer education. In other words, to state explicitly the mental attitude underlying all this: people would not work of their own volition. They needed somebody with a stick standing behind them to prevent this 'laxity'. This attitude is surprisingly similar to that of the conservative British economists of the early nineteenth century, writing in defence of the Poor Laws.[3] According to the latter, the poor were provided with regular subsidies, thus keeping wages at an artificially low level, below market prices. Paley and his contemporaries justified this practice by saying that if workers received more money they would work less, as they only worked in order to maintain their subsistence level. A pay rise would lead to the decrease of gross output, and would be detrimental to the commonwealth.[4]

The same argument was made concerning the supervision of the activities of the local council. On the one hand, supplying the population with essentials must be ensured by the party:

With the Department of Education, Health and Sport, the PC definitely must maintain contact on a daily basis. Here, we are talking about 20,000 kids, so things that must be taken notice of happen there much more often than in other departments.

(D.F., secretary)

On the other hand, the party should not carry out work instead of the responsible council organs, but should ensure that they work efficiently: 'The district PC has an impact on the efficiency of the work done at the council. That's the basic goal' (G.E., secretary).

But there is more here. As we mentioned earlier, a key aspect of the party supervision of work done at the council concerned development plans. There, our interviewee emphasised the difference between the assessment of the five-year plans of the council and the businesses, and considered the former to be much more important. From another interview, we can see the exact reasons:

There must be a body that is always one step ahead of the practical work of the councils. There must be a vision of the future, and it must be provided by the district PC – measured by the elected bodies of the council. We shouldn't create a myth of infallibility, but we must perform a leadership role from this aspect as well, that would be the ideal. I consider the existence of a district PC to be a great force.... We should show the way by being one step ahead. And not just show it to the council, but help them find their own way.

(T.C.)

A new objective appears here, that of 'showing the way'; and in a very special way, not just giving direction from the outside, but making people aware, as if from the inside, of the correct direction. Thus, if we are looking for the model of this intervention, it will not be found just among those of the ancient lawgivers, a Solon or a Lycurgus; not even among the great Hebrew prophets who discovered the truth and thus showed the way. We should rather evoke the famous analogy of the midwife by Socrates,[5] according to which it is not the wise man who creates true knowledge; he simply brings it out of his subject, contributing to the birth of a thought. The really wise man tries to have an impact from the inside.

It would be only too easy to say that, concerning the past and present activity of the district PCs, the analogy with Socrates is much too exaggerated. No doubt, in the majority of cases the party was only giving advice, directions, or commands, and was not following the model of Socrates' sage. That's quite true. Still, we think that we must take the above argument, if not at its face value, still in its positivity, as something that is much more than a mere ideology.

Thus, people must be forced into facing themselves, realising their tasks and potentials. Party members must be in the vanguard of this process:

> Our task is to prepare the party members in our business enterprises, and to provide them with the appropriate political information so that they themselves know what they should do. . . . Our real task is to prepare our party members so that they automatically become the opinion-makers in any associations or mass organisations, within the council or the firms. They shouldn't be listened to because they are the representatives of the district PC, or because they represent the party on the elected bodies, but because they say clever things. We have to choose the right men, and to prepare them so that they may convince the members of the given bodies of the rightness of their views simply by the facts, and not because, say, they speak in the name of the party.
>
> (D.F., secretary)

The direct task of the district PC is the training of party members only. But indirectly, this internal work, this impact on the way of thinking about and approaching problems, should be extended to all the leading persons of the district:

> Those who sit there, who decide these questions, they must have all this in their heads; the only thing that may prevent realisation is the lack of funds. If we can't organise things so that the people at the Department of Education or the finance department of the council understand it, know that there is a need for this or that, then –
>
> (D.F., secretary)

The major target of the party should not be the material conditions or the concrete results of production, the mere figures. The party should mostly be concerned with people. It must pay attention to the needs of the population, going into minute details, and it must have an impact on individual thinking and behaviour. It must ensure that the key positions are filled by men who are able to perform their job, to realise and meet the demands. The practice of the 'sphere of competence list'[6] serves exactly this purpose:

> After all, we still have our competence list – those who belong to our sphere of competence [i.e., to the nomenclatura]. We pay special attention to them, we are curious whether they can think in a way that meets the demands of our time. And if we are careful about the few

key positions, if, together with the continuous retreat [the party strategy of relinquishing control of less important posts] we keep these positions firmly in our grasp, then it will have an impact on the rest as well. Thus, if the head of the council understands the demands of our time, the demands of the population and young people, if he grasps their interests, then he will be able to spread this perception through his apparatus so that the others understand it as well. And those who don't will be removed.

(D.F., secretary)

In the present circumstances, it is necessary ...

Another often repeated statement, that it is only in the present given situation that the party should deal with these issues, provides a summary of the previous arguments and a connection with the rest of this chapter. According to this, the problem is that those who should accomplish these tasks fail to do so properly: 'And there is an enormous number of similar things that – well, it should not be a task of the PC, but in the present circumstances, it is necessary that the district PC helps' (V.K.). Here the idea that was only lurking behind the statements of the previous sections emerges to the surface: the party performs this regular supervisory activity because of the lack of a better solution. This motive was stated several times in our interviews, in relation to the control of both the enterprises and the councils. Let's give a few examples:

Q: And is it sure that it is the task of the party to mediate the economic activities of businesses?

A: Not at all. It is not the task of the party. Just that it is not working properly. ... Look, at the moment I am the link who can bring them together. There is nobody else. Should I not do it just because it is not the task of the party? I say, I bring them together even if it is not the task of the party. I won't do any harm to the party with it.

(A.T.)

Here the activity of the party embodies the good uncle. As he is single and available, he has the time and energy to accomplish, without apparent charge, things that others should have done. From the next quotation this folk-tale-like modality is missing, but the idea is the same: 'Today, there is no institution that would deal with economic units in such detail as the local PC' (G.C.). The next statement sets forth the most detailed and explicit summary of the arguments given above and at the same time projects the question of the next chapter:

It is certain that this supervision could have been accomplished by somebody else. But as political questions may arise related to the activity of the businesses, I think it important that the supervision and the exchange of experiences [with new methods and techniques] be done by the district PC as well. . . . It is really the district PC that can quickly and efficiently talk with all the businesses and other economic organisations, that can ask help or coordinate work. We have the capability through the party organisations. It is quite obvious that we have it. Nobody else has this capability.

(J.L.)

How does all this look in relation to the councils?

Under normal circumstances, the [elected] members of the council should decide about these matters. I hope that slowly they will be able to take over these tasks. So the party may play a mediating role or whatever, it may create opinions, the mood, may organise the meetings or the negotiations, the discussions, but it should not make the decisions.

(G.E., secretary)

The following lines come to this conclusion: 'We shouldn't be one step ahead of "the" council, but of the existing council, which is not identical with "the" council' (H.O., secretary). And the party organisations should be 'ahead' of the councils because the latter have not yet found themselves, the system of popular representation is not working properly:

I don't think this council is suited to take on the role of the owner. According to my own experience, I would say that in a number of things that could have been done, they did not take the initiative. Of course, there are material and other constraints, but I think that the intentions are perfectly clear concerning the role of ownership at the district council as well. There are positive counter-examples. But they can't do without the guidance of the district PC in matters of principle. Even if this guidance includes concrete questions of development. The responsibility of the party is at least as great as that of the council concerning the life of the district. In a number of cases, it should even be greater. So, until the system of popular representation will work as I think it ought to, where the council would have much more independence and much greater capability to manage the affairs of the area, then there is a need for [the direction of the district PC].

(T.C.)

The party has a double purpose in helping concrete economic and administrative work. On the one hand, it must accomplish tasks that, for some reason, are not completed by those who should be responsible. On the other hand, it must prepare the people for the time when they may accomplish all this independently. This is done in two steps. First, it must prepare its own members for independent activity in the area. In the final count, they should help the others, the governed (the workers, the members of the council, the population) as well, to find themselves and to be able to accomplish their tasks independently, without any further help from outside.[7]

They are not independent enough

On the one hand, the goal of the activity of the party is to make party members and non-members capable of accomplishing their tasks independently, without any external constraint and control. People should be autonomous when they are just a 'cog in the machine'. As a compensation, on the other hand, the party takes care of them throughout their lives, provides for their subsistence, frees them from the troubles of making a living. It is the task of the party to solve everything.[8] The result is a trap, a dual, interconnected failure, as if the long strive to teach independence led to the loss of even the need for independence on the part of the governed. Again and again we encountered the claim that the area or the members do not want to be independent; do not want to use the new possibilities:

> I feel that slowly the schools and the teaching bodies could start this work if they were mature enough. So now they do have the chances. But a lot of teachers say 'this is how things are, and that's all.'
> Q: What do you mean by maturity?
> A: Perhaps they are not used to the idea that they may have something to say about their own lives, about the direction of their school.
>
> (V.K.)

> Today I have 19 party cells, but at that period I had 15. Now you should not imagine that they all march along independently, with the flag high up in the air. Some must lead the others by the hand. Now do this, now do that, now this must be said. The secretaries' meeting is not enough, because they misunderstand something, do not find the information sufficient, forget to put down what has been said. So, some of them require a lot of support.
>
> (A.T.)

Sometimes one must intervene actively, because they are not independent enough, these party organisations. Apart from a few exceptions.

(P.G.)

Perhaps it is needless to state that the statements about the dependency of the 'people' should not be taken at face value. If we had wanted to study popular attitudes and behaviour, we would not have gone to district PCs. But one thing is certain. The activities accomplished by the district PC in the place of other people failed to meet their goal. They didn't teach independence, only discouraged it. And, on the other side, the district PC itself became caught in the web created by its own all-embracing activity.

The project of self-direction failed. This is all the more surprising as, concerning both the goals and the methods employed, it was not that different from what was applied in the process of 'organic', Western development in promoting a certain work ethic in order to raise efficiency, productivity and intensity. The constraint was not internalised; it remained external. At least in the 'first economy', the official economic sector, centrally controlled, that worked under the guidance of the party, the slow work style remained dominant. 'People don't work here', said Western experts. But it was exactly this distance that made it possible for a long time, up to the 1970s, for people to preserve in their everyday life, in what remained relatively free from the official world, their personal connections, the trust toward each other, the immediacy, the inner harmony and autonomy, the ability to live and feel. The 'fight of all against all' mentality which today characterises all strata of society was earlier restricted to only those groups that were close to the internal power struggles.

The emergence of the second unofficial economy and the commercialisation that found a momentum in the 1970s has effectively realised the goal that the party was not able to reach directly. While the party destroyed existing communities, human relations and self-esteem from the outside, the new method of self-exploitation has eliminated the remains of surviving humanity, composure and personal relations from the inside.

While the first part of the project (at least directly) had failed, in the other aspect, the party had more 'success'. It successfully discouraged a large number of people from being able to lead their own lives, express their opinions, and discuss public issues and their interests in a civilised form. And thus the trap is closed – there is again and again a need for the intervention of the party to act, to decide, to work instead of the immature, infantilised people. This circle could only be broken as a whole.

The district PC is engaged in substitute activities

It is not surprising that a large part of the activity of the district PCs is 'substitute activity'. Doing other people's work made them unable to perform their job in the future as well, and ready to need further help:

> According to my experience, in a number of questions the district PC is engaged in substitute activities. It gets bogged down in things or carries out activities that should not require the intervention of a political apparatus, that have no political content.
>
> (G.C.)

Why, then, does all this happen? Do we not encounter here, in this attitude which tried to supervise and control everything, only the remains of an obsolete, outdated practice? In our interviews, we have often been told that there are big differences between the current and past practices of the district PCs. This meant, first of all, that the belief in the earlier, hand-operated system was shaken everywhere:

> There are a number of issues that I can influence only to a limited extent. Earlier one could ensure by an order that the proper decision be made, or that which was expected by the higher organs.
>
> (M.B.)

Moreover, the emphasis on difference was part of a conscious strategy employed by some members who have only recently joined the apparatus:

> I tried to make it plain, especially in the first period, why I will behave in that way. And I also called their attention to the fact that I am not the same person as their previous instructor.
>
> Q: Where did you put the emphasis, on what differences?
> A: I basically told everybody that I will not turn to them with any special central demand or call. I won't prescribe anything to them, nor do any similar things.
>
> (L.G.)

> I tried to show them – in almost all areas – that I really want to help.
>
> (M.B.)

There were changes, then, at least concerning the methods employed; though we also found that not everybody interpreted the new style in the same way:

Q: And you meet the managers of the firms here, at the PC, or is there some other –?

A: Both. Well, earlier, it happened that from time to time we asked them to come in to give a report, but it is no longer the practice. Rather, we observe the trends, and then we sit down with those who seem to be in trouble, or when we experience some problems –

Q: So it is they who turn to the PC?

A: No, rather it is we who look after them, but it may happen that they ask us.

(B.C., secretary)

The following details are even more revealing:

Earlier the system was that the resolution was declared, and then nobody said a word, they accepted it. . . .

Q: But [the new system] delayed the carrying out of the resolutions?

A: Not at all. It only required some extra work on the part of those people who had to face the public in certain forums: the parents, the teachers, the party members. Now we sometimes handled the party members here inside the PC or at the teacher organisation's committee, because we have such an organisation, and started to work them together – well not like that – we just explained that see, this is the interest of society, this is your personal interest, this is the common interest, and these are the possibilities.

(B.C., secretary)

The above examples present at the same time the pronounced desire for changes, some real changes, and the lack of movement throughout. Compared to the earlier period, the scope of the activities of district PCs has not changed. Is it possible, then, that this all-encompassing activity is just a left-over, a vestige of times past? If this is the case, then the district PCs are engaged in a number of activities which, according to the opinion of the majority of apparatus members, they should not be. This leads to the question: what should then be the task of such intermediate party organisations? In one part of our questionnaire, we tried to get an answer to exactly this question. We listed sixteen areas where, according to our pilot study, district party committees were engaged in some sort of activity. Some of these were stated in general terms, and were related to different social groups (such as the situation of the elderly, young people or intellectuals), while others were related to some more specific activities (such as the computer program, the commercial links between firms or the solving of problems caused by natural disasters). We asked our respondents whether they thought that in the above areas there was a need for the 'attention' of the district PC.[9] If according to the majority of the respondents in the areas listed above, none of which referred to specifically political issues, there was no or only slight need for the attention of the district PC, then it would be true that these activities were only remnants of a distant past. But if the majority affirmed the need for attention concerning issues like the profitability of the firms, work discipline in these firms or the situation of retired people or women of the area, then the reference to the past would not be sufficient in itself.

Out of the 202 respondents in our sample, three refused to answer this question, 15 left out one, and 13 others a few of the sixteen items. Thus, we had 171 full answers. First, we combined all the answers and tried to assess how many areas our respondents chose on average. For this, we could only use the full answers. Out of these, there were only 27 (16 per cent) who indicated not more than four areas; a further 65 (38 per cent) chose five to seven items; 55 (32 per cent) of respondents thought the attention of the district PC necessary in eight to ten areas, while the remaining 24 (14 per cent) chose more than ten areas out of the sixteen possible ones.

Let's see now the other side of the coin, the distribution of answers stating that the district PC should not deal with these areas.[10] According to 16 persons (9 per cent), there were no such areas; a further 57 (33 per cent) indicated only one or two, while 51 (30 per cent) indicated only three or four such items. There were only 16 persons (9 per cent) who thought that the district PC should not deal with seven or more out of the sixteen areas listed.

According to the overwhelming majority of the present members of the apparatus, in the areas listed there was in general a need for the attention of the party, no matter that these areas belonged to the jurisdiction of social or state organs, even according to the official view. What we found was thus not just a survival of practices long abandoned. The need to know about and consequently to intervene in everything was deeply embedded in the thinking of apparatus members. They simply took it for granted that the district PC was competent in most of the matters listed.

It was only on second thoughts that a few of them realised that something was wrong here; that these things should not be done (or at least said). In this respect, the reasons given by those who refused to fill out this part of the questionnaire is particularly interesting:

We must deal with the political aspects of all these! (And with a thousand other related political issues). I can't assess our work in this way! We must deal with 'the' politics. To provide arguments and information, to discuss and to indicate the tendencies, movements, the mood, the ideas, the evaluations toward the top.

(V.10)

This is a bad question. On the level of phenomena, there is a need for attention. The question is, what should happen after? I think the questions that may be solved at the local level should be solved by local economic and state organs. The task of the party is, for example, to realise that new education or health legislation is necessary, that the economic administration must be restructured, etc. The need for these changes may be realised in time at the district level.

(V.11)

These are not PC matters, but any of them may become one!

(B.1)

These three respondents, then, out of the 202, stated the need to separate political and non-political issues, and thus refused to give a concrete answer to the given question. The curious thing is that two out of the three were among those seven who, for some reason, sent in their answers later, through the mail. They had more time to think about the answers, and to question in themselves what, on a first reading, might have seemed obvious. This hypothesis is supported by the fact that, out of the seven, there was another one who, though answering the question, in thirteen out of the sixteen areas marked that the district PC should not deal with them (that was by far the highest value); did not think that this attention was necessary for any (there was only one other such case); and on the top of the page wrote the following: 'Mostly tasks of state-policy' (F.11).

One possible interpretation is that, at the time of our research, it was quite usual to talk about the separation of state, social and party tasks. It was not thought proper to state that the above areas should be under party control. But in the everyday activity of the district PCs, even if by changing methods, the same attention was still preserved. The respondents took it for granted that the activity of the PCs should extend to these areas in principle. A long 'ringing' time was necessary for them to realise the contradiction between everyday practice and the new ideas.

If there were new intentions at all. Because, as we found out in some interviews, some people interpreted this question quite differently:

About the place of the party, whether the party should or should not have a say in some questions, whether the party has an impact on the council – there was a question like that. Well, these are wishes. . . . I think that is the way it should be done, and it does not necessarily reflect reality, or the party ['s opinion].

(G.E., secretary)

Thus, we must go further, beyond the immediate explanations, if we want to find out the reasons behind these interventions, to reconstruct the specific logic underlying the desire to intervene in everything. We consider that it is justifiable to put the question in this specific way. The opinion according to which these substitute activities are just mani- festations of a universal will to power is as empty, because overtly general, as the similar view that there is no point in looking for a reason when there was simply no such thing here. Neither of these answers the question as to why these and not other activities were performed.

In discussions about 'substitute activities', two different things were drawn together. In one sense, 'substitute activity' meant that the PC took over the tasks of other organisations; in the other, it stood for seemingly useless, routine activities like the execution of endless resolutions about insignificant and distant topics (fire prevention, solidarity with the Third World, etc.). But if we consider as their common goal the maintenance of morale in order to avoid a lessening of the readiness to fight (this alludes to the military character of the party cells), or to internalise the constant, omnipresent attention and vigil- ance, then both types of substitute activities may be considered as functional. If they succeed in internalising supervision, they pay off.

However, what we have stated earlier about the lack of success is valid here as well. Something was misfiring, the supervision did not become internal for the majority in the intended sense. People did not become active enough, refused to 'multiply' their efforts and energies. Moreover, often the 'results' were the opposite of the pronounced goals: instead of becoming active, of working efficiently and imaginatively, people become passive and careless.

A formal automatism

At this point, it may be proposed that this ever-present attention was just a natural consequence of an organisational issue, the growth of bureaucracy. However, this argument falls on two different levels. First, the general theory of bureaucratisation is as empty, being too general, as the reference to a will to power. Second, the Weberian concept of formal bureaucracy as an organisation based on expertise and adherence to formal, written rules does not cover the organisation and functioning of a party apparatus at all. Of course, a number of signs of bureaucratisation are present:

Q: Still, you used the words: 'one loses oneself'. What did you mean?

A: Partly, whether one acknowledges it or not, this is obviously a very bureaucratic and very strictly hierarchical organisation.... There is a formal organisation which has a formal automatism and a codified rule, where one has to maintain the rules of the game. Then there is a softer part, where the leader [the first secretary] defines the profile and the mood of the apparatus....

Q: Are you subordinated to that one person?

A: Not just to that one person, as there are mediators here, the [district] secretaries. It is very important whether the secretary can serve as a 'shock-absorber' or not.

(A.L.)

From this, three elements are particularly relevant for us: strong hierarchical subordination, the presence of a formal rule that is different from the codified one, and the quasi-omnipotence of the first leader. The use of the word 'bureaucracy' is thus somewhat confusing here, as this term means, after Weber, a formally rational organisation, an identity or at least convergence between actual practice and codes.[11] This view may be supported by the following quotation as well:

Bureaucratisation – it depends on what we mean by this. If it stands for rule by office, then it is valid for the party. If for the all too frequent paperwork, then even more so. Unfortunately, the professional element, say, in administration, is far less present.

(G.D.)

We may add, thus, as a fourth element, that in the organisation professional expertise was not necessarily required.

The reference to bureaucracy or bureaucratisation is also questionable as, from their inception, the communist parties led a constant struggle against bureaucratisation. Time and again, it was the party that stimulated and led the fight against the bureaucracy. One may say that this struggle was unsuccessful. And exactly because of this fact, the reference to the bureaucratisation of the party itself was always a very sensitive topic. It was easy to create attention, to score points by denouncing the party as a bureaucracy. But we think that instead of toying with the idea of 'bureaucratisation', the stakes in this struggle should be understood in their positivity, analysing the constant struggle against bureaucracy and the antipathy toward expertise, and the resurrection of a hierarchical, quasi-bureaucratic structure as sides of the same coin.

Furthermore, there is one characteristic of the party that definitely represents a deviation from the requirements of formal (or any) bureaucracy: the specific importance attributed to personal connections. Of course, in every bureaucratic organisation, all routine activities, even formal ties, appear in the form of face-to-face human relations. But in the ideal-typical form of bureaucratic organisation, these ties are passing, accidental phenomena, something that should be eliminated or at least reduced to a minimal level (that's the project of Taylorism); or that, on the contrary, should be used for the more efficient government of the employees (as in the 'human relations' school). But in the case of the party, the emphasis is elsewhere. Personal connections are the central elements of the whole organisational structure and the decision-making process. The effective structure and working of a party committee are based on personal ties. It is the formal organisation that is built up on personal ties, and not the other way round. Instead of bureaucracy, concerning the internal organisation of the party, one should talk about a principle of authority and unconditional obedience:

> This is a completely, I hate to use this word, Stalinist model, because this is not just restricted to the name of Stalin, though it can be connected to it, but it is like that independently of him. This is something based on a principle of authority. That we state some things, and one should accept it, because the PC said so. Now the whole machinery is basically built on this.
>
> (J.A.)

All this would suggest that, instead of using the model of bureaucracy, we should rather talk about a military organisation, a fighting machine, as one of our interviewees explicitly stated it, responding to our question whether current party organisation was related to the period of illegality:

> The organisation during the years of illegality was quite different. Rather we preserved the structure of the coalition period [1945–8], the fights when we kicked the other parties out of political life. We inherited the structure of the period when it was really a war-like goal to get this country in shape. To start something. That required a large concentration of will-power and force on the part of the party. It was possible only if the party worked with a soldier-like punctuality and

discipline. Now, the biggest problem of the army is peace. There are no tasks. We are a combat-troop, and there is no war. . . . So, for the present problems, the party is like a bull in a china shop. It attacks everything, wants to fight, to battle, and so on, when the problems have been quite different for a long time.

(G.D.)

According to the well-known saying of Clausewitz, war is the continuation of politics. In his famous book Michel Foucault turned this statement round, and said that politics is a continuation of war: politics is nothing but war waged with different means (Foucault 1979a: 168). Is this the case concerning the party? Is the party such a paramilitary organisation that found itself a task in times of peace, but now wages its continuous battle, its activity spreading to all elements of day-to-day activities without any point or success, and is engaged in 'substitute activities'? Our interviewee sets forth this view, and in detail:

I perceive that the district PC looks and adjusts itself to above; tries to interpret the directions given from above and find its own tasks there. The other part is that it forces its apparatus to bring these tasks before the elected bodies, no matter how much sweat this entails. In other words, it does not happen that practice raises a problem, and we say let's solve it, but we create a problem for ourselves. We are not pressed, nobody is knocking at the door, not even in an abstract sense, that please, this is real life, let's deal with it. All this does not concern us. Not because we are stupid, but because nothing can surface as a political interest. We are not even concerned with political matters, but with financial ones that have nothing to do with politics. Or it must be really distorted to be qualified as political. This raises the question of the competence of politics: why does something become a political question, and to what extent is it political?

(G.D.)

Really, the answer to this question can no longer be postponed. When will a problem be termed 'political'? How will something be 'raised' to the level of politics? And an answer that would define the party as a military machine, along the lines expressed above, in light of later events does not seem convincing. If all that had been necessary for the party to become efficient and mobile was political struggle, then the years 1988–90 would have led to a resurrection of party vigilance. Nothing like that happened. The specific 'politics' of the party cannot be reduced to war, not even at the limit.

This chapter started with the claim that, in principle, a district PC deals with all sorts of political questions. The whole discussion was conducted on this assumption. However, a detailed analysis of the activity of the district PCs showed that it by far surpasses the area that in any sense can be considered as political. We did not state this from a normative basis; we were not starting with a 'theory' about the 'true' meaning of politics. But a number of the activities carried out by the PCs exceed the boundaries of any possible definition of politics. This became obvious even for those who accomplished these activities, and it was reflected by the fact that, in the last period of the rule of the communist party in Hungary, a desperate attempt was made to transform the party from an administrative party into a political one. In this chapter, we have attempted to gather the reasons given for the interventions at the level of concrete activities. In the next, we shall turn to and attempt to reconstruct the concept of politics underlying these justifications.

4   What is 'politics'?

When you have thus formed the chain of ideas in the heads of your
citizens, you will then be able to pride yourselves on guiding them and
being their masters. A stupid despot may constrain his slaves with
iron chains, but a true politician binds them even more strongly by
the chain of their own ideas; it is at the stable point of reason that he
secures the end of the chain; this link is all the stronger in that we do
not know of what it is made and we believe it to be our own work;
despair and time eat away the bonds of iron and steel, but they are
powerless against the habitual union of ideas, they can only tighten it
still more; and on the soft fibres of the brain is founded the
unshakeable base of the soundest of empires.

(Servan 1767, quoted in Foucault 1979a: 102–3)

In this chapter, our goal is not to give a definition of 'politics', neither is
it to review the enormous literature that has pondered upon this
question at least since *The Politics* of Aristotle. It is only to distil the
sense of politics that governed the activity of political workers. In our
study, following the perspective of Foucault, we were not concerned
with the 'opinions' of apparatus members, their subjective views about
what they were doing and why. Neither did we consider the statements
made by them as reflections of an ideology or of a false consciousness.
Rather, we tried with their help to reconstruct the rationalities that were
embedded in their activities, that were working, as it were, behind their
backs. We were ourselves surprised to realise to what extent they were
willing to take part in such an unusual exercise.

A FEW DEFINITIONS BY COMMUNIST-PARTY WORKERS

When confronted with the incredible scope of the activities of district
party committees, we tried to find out how such activities could at all be

justified by those who were carrying out these activities. The recurrent answer was that these were – or may have become – 'political' questions. But the question of the exact meaning of 'politics' posed many problems for our interviewees, which is not surprising as it is very difficult for anyone to reflect on the reasons for one's own actions. In order to get around this obstacle, we'll first review a few definitions. Let's start with the following:

> [The most important political goal] is what best expresses the social interest, or the interest of the district. So, it is the one that takes into account the material possibilities, the personnel possibilities, the interests of the people, their opinion, etc., etc.
>
> (B.C.)

This definition is quite well known, and hardly goes beyond empty generalities. However, the next sentences of the same interview provide some details:

> Q: And if these cannot be reconciled?
> A: If these cannot be reconciled, then there is conflict, and I think it should be presented to a body that can be called upon to judge the case. Now this has never happened before; all I am saying is that, in theory, it is possible.
>
> (B.C.)

These remarks do not specify the exact meaning of the 'social interest', but show how 'politics' was handled by the district PCs. First, there is an attempt to deny the very existence of conflicts. Second, the approach contains a presumption that possible conflicts should be judged by an 'objective' forum.

The next definition is still fairly general, but gives us a different angle:

> Political activity is a conscious will that is in some sense oriented toward the alteration, the formation of basic social relations. . . . One may, of course, take it in a broader sense and define it as an activity aiming at the formation of interpersonal relations in general, but that would be such that it would include everything, beginning with social encounters.
>
> (H.O., secretary)

This definition contains more than empty words or dreams. Rather, we have here the document of a general orientation, a proof of the all-inclusiveness of the activities of a district PC, a will to claim competence for all aspects of social life. This is made more explicit later:

Q: How could you define your work, your political activity? ... In your daily work, what is the extent, scope and content of political activity? What means are at your disposal?

A: ... Given my position, I have a conclusive impact on the way things are organised in this district. The rules of the game, the systems of conditions. I try to mould them, to create such 'one-way systems' that would force things in the directions I consider to be right in particular cases. I am not stating it more concretely because this is a universal function, and so extends in practice to almost all the areas of life.

(H.O., secretary)

At the level of district secretaries, the formation of rules and the definition of conditions and framework of life for people living or working in the area are part of day-to-day activity. And this activity extends everywhere, is *a priori* unlimited.

The next detail helps us understand how such a general activity, such an unlimited licence, may be justified:

Another thing – I believe that this party has a mission. That *this* party has a mission.

Q: How could you summarise this?

A: It is the task of this party to lead this country, this people. To lead in a political sense, and not taking by the hand. To lead it, to see beyond petty interests, to see beyond the one-year horizons on the basis of some sort of complex analysis of reality in order to help, to promote consciously the development of this society and this economy.

(H.O., secretary)

As in the earlier case with respect to 'social interest', this definition of politics implies a goal that is defined outside and above individuals and groups; a goal which should thus be discovered and realised, not formulated and created. This has certain implications concerning the methods to be chosen:

I think manipulation should not be used merely in a negative sense. In a sense, everything that is used as a tool for making people accept something is manipulation. I think the major difference between true and false democracy stands in the ends that these means serve. The major point here is the realisation that our interest is to maintain and carry on this development, in a complex sense.

(H.O., secretary)

In this case, the position taken is that the object of social development serves as a justification for the necessity of 'political' activity. In the next section of this chapter, we'll take up this point in more detail. But let's return to everyday activity in order to specify the meaning of politics at that level. First, let's see a few statements defining the aim of political activity with respect to economic life. Even this restricted question posed considerable problems to our respondents:

> Now, after a year and a half, I don't have the slightest idea what the scope of the economic activity of such an intermediate level party organ should be. I don't have the slightest idea.... In economic policy, a number of questions seem to hang in the air.... We should deal with questions – that's what we are told – that have political aspects. That is, with questions that are rooted in or can be traced back to the economy, but that have political implications. In principle, it is quite clear, but whenever you actually start a concrete study, either by writing reports, collecting information or talking to local party secretaries, you either repeat empty generalities, or become involved with practical questions – practical economic questions, not questions of economic policy, but questions of economics in the classical sense that you cannot escape. The balance between these concerns is so delicate that I don't know how to find the middle way.
>
> (G.C.)

We can get around this problem of definition if we stay close to the actual scope of these activities. The following details provide us with a much needed connection between the description of activities and their justification in terms of political aspects:

> As to the decisive impact the local PC has on the economic life of the district, I think that our activity should extend to – and I believe it does extend – first, mobilisation for the realisation of certain goals, and second, collecting information about actual results in all areas, and its application at other places.... We are paying attention to the activities of enterprises. This can be divided into two issues. The first is the cadre question ... the supervision of individuals belonging to the competence list of the district PC. This is obvious. The second is the supervision of the firms' economic activities. This does not happen because we want to intervene in everything, but in order to point out possible problems. If these problems have already been solved at another place, then we may help. And political problems may also emerge in certain areas. For example, if at company Z 300

people are to be laid off, then this is a concern for us. That's why I was talking about 'paying attention'.

(J.L.)

Thus the boundaries between politics and economics, difficult to draw at any time, have become indiscernible. Any element of concrete economic activity concerns the district PC as it may become political; it is potentially political. This coalescence is obvious for the political workers: 'At the firms, party activity is not really separate from economic activity' (A.T.).

The circle is closed, the attempt to define political work takes us back to intervention in economic life, to continuous substitute activities. Let's recall part of a statement that has already been quoted: 'We are not even concerned with political matters, but with financial ones that have nothing to do with politics. Or it must be really distorted to be qualified as political' (G.D.). Even if the separation of economics and politics proves to be impossible, the details of the activities of the PCs may lead us closer to the searched-for rationalities of politics embedded in these activities:

I do not separate party affairs from economic affairs. If there is a chance to help them in economic matters, for example, to connect them to another firm, I will do it. I feel I have to do so. So I won't say that it is not the party's business.

(A.T.)

This detail is important for two different reasons. First, it involves a new element in our definitions, according to which it is the role of the party, or politics, to 'connect' – in this case economic units. Second, it is implied that all this happens because otherwise it would not happen at all, because there is a lack of self-governing people.

In the following case, the district PC is not just linking individual agents, but is rather presented as the 'cement' that binds society together, that prevents the disintegration of communities:

One should be aware that in such a college – especially after the new laws gave them independence – with the low salaries, the teaching body is always ready to break up into different elements. Thus, it loses its stability, neglects its own education and is only concerned with hunting extra income, etc.

(M.B.)

The next interviewee tried to justify political intervention in economic life from a different perspective:

> Political information does not necessarily have to contain the inform-
> ation that the factory has produced 85,000 pairs of stockings, but it
> should include the following questions: what are the problems con-
> cerning the production of stockings, and to what extent does all this
> have an impact on the morale, on the political morale of the workers?
> ... The district PC has to deal with the profitability of local
> businesses only because ... if a firm is profitable, then under normal
> circumstances workers there must have better morale than in firms
> suffering a loss.
>
> (G.E., secretary)

And the creation of the right morale is necessary in order to mobilise,
activate people:

> We have to create the morale necessary for positive action. To return
> to an economic example, one may well talk about wages and
> accomplishment, etc. But if I create a morale among workers that
> means they really need and really acknowledge good performance
> among themselves, then they themselves will begin to require it and
> will be able to achieve it.
>
> (G.E., secretary)

What then is this 'politics'? What questions are deemed political by the
communist party workers themselves? What should be the scope of the
activities of a district PC? Using the above definitions, the following
answers can be proposed:

1 Conditions

First, the scope of politics is extended to the basic forms of all social and
human relations. Thus, it extends to all 'conditions'. Within it, two areas
can be separated that require different treatment. First, all questions
concerning social relations and the rules of the game are defined as
political, and belong only to the higher levels of decision-making. It is
taken for granted that their formation does not require democratic
participation or open public debates. Therefore, they are to be conducted in secret. Second, 'conditions' refer to the circumstances of
day-to-day life. These may become political questions if problems arise
that have an impact on the morale of the population. The solution here
requires open intervention, thus public knowledge about the activity of
the party. Though even here we can talk about hidden activity, carried
out in the background, in order to prevent problems from surfacing.
This preventive activity more often than not is identical in practice with
suppression, even repression.

2 Connections

Second, the sphere of politics includes social and human relations, the different types of cooperation between firms and institutions, and the maintenance of the coherence of these organisations. Creating and maintaining links thus become matters for politics. As our interviewees stated and implied, without the party people would not be able to find each other, to make contact with each other, or to maintain their links. It is the task of the party to help firms find each other, to share their experiences, to solve their common problems, to create communities and to prevent the dissolution of the existing ones. Earlier we saw that it was the task of the party to establish, maintain and change the whole set of external conditions. Here, we must add that it must also make the actual connections themselves. The party has to be not only the ground, the sole under our feet, but also the cement to keep us together, to prevent the individual units from closing in on themselves or the centrifugal force of individual interests from breaking the existing connections.

3 Conditioning

But politics extends even beyond this; one may say that it goes 'deeper', as, in the third phase, the behaviour, activity and thinking of individuals themselves become a political issue. The main targets of political action, and the means as well, are individuals. In a first approximation, the policy-makers are interested in the morale of the population. Political information must include whether people are satisfied and happy or not, whether they are aware of the results. But this is not just a goal in itself. Morale is important because only a satisfied, happy person can act and work properly. Morale is thus a mobilising force. And, from this perspective, we may perceive a change of emphasis. The question is not just to assess whether people are satisfied or not; they must be so. Thus politics is extended to the active formation of morale, of the way individuals form their perceptions. The party has to ensure that people are happy with the results and are ready to carry out future tasks. At the time, our respondents emphasised that the formation of opinion should not be done forcefully, but they themselves admitted that this was not always the case. However, from our perspective, it is not the violence or the subtlety of the methods employed that is interesting, but the direction of political influence. And here the emphasis is not just on the formation of morale or perception, but on the control of activity itself. The party, through its 'extended hands', the political instructors, must ensure that people work and live properly.

We reached the same result when discussing the definitions of politics as when we were earlier analysing the activities of the district PCs. Thus, it is not accidental, nor surprising or dysfunctional that the district PCs supervise and influence all the different aspects of day-to-day existence. After all, all these activities appear to apparatus members as, at least potentially, political ones.

WHY WAS POLITICS DEFINED IN THIS WAY?

The spread of the activities of district PCs, which to us, at the end of the twentieth century in Europe, no doubt seems pathological, was thus not accidental, but connected to the way apparatus members conceived the nature of their political task. Still, if we want to come to terms with this phenomenon, we should continue our search, and try to find the grounds on which such a definition of politics could ever have been made. In order to get closer to an explanation, let's first review two dualities that are key aspects of the concrete activities of party committees: the dual character of the power exercised by the party, referring to negative (repressive) and positive acts, and the dual goals of satisfying the aims of the high decision-making organs and the needs of the population at large.

On the one hand, the relationship of the party to everyday life is based on a strange duality, a combination of positive and negative power, of destruction and repression on the one hand, and construction and assistance on the other. These two modalities presuppose each other, but can neither be explained by nor reduced to the other. They are based upon something else. Everything points toward the existence of a single factor, a text, a programme already written, a truth waiting to be discovered; a mission to be accomplished. The repressive organisations are not just executing orders and liquidating enemies, but helping to realise 'the' truth of history, the elimination of 'the' enemies of progress and the future. And the same is especially true in the case of positive actions. Thus, the real world becomes a mere phenomenon, the manifestation of underlying essences. Neither the negative nor the positive aspects of power could function without the connections made in the 'soft fibres of the brain'. This specific negative and positive, thus dual, power is based on the positing of the 'truth', the truth of 'progress' and 'development', and the sense of mission concerning its realisation.

On the other hand, we may look for the reasons for this extension of politics at the intersection of two axes. The first is the distinct sphere of high politics; what in daily usage in Hungary was simply termed 'politics'. This dimension included the top level of the party and state hierarchy. Along this dimension, the sole task of the district PC was to follow the given line. The justification of the whole process and of the struggle for exclusiveness was given by the claim that the party was not just 'politicising' in the sense of reconciling the interests coming from below, but realising a historical mission. The task of the party was to meet the requirements of historical development. This constituted an attempt to objectify politics, by reducing it to the reading of a book that was already written.

This approach, on the one hand, justified the maximalisation of the amount of power to be appropriated and used by the centre. On the other, it precluded the very possibility of democratic control, as the question of responsibility was postponed to the 'tribunal of history'. The crucial point here is not simply that this power was uncontrolled, but that it was specifically constrained and tied up, internally, and not externally. The exercise of power over others was made an obligation and not a right, something one had to use in order to promote the universal cause of development. With this, the millennial purpose of Christianity and moral philosophy to limit power on the basis of ethical grounds loses its meaning. Moral questions could emerge in the context of power as a right but not when power itself is conceived of as an obligation. Ethics is possible only if there is a freedom of action. If the users of power fulfil a historical task, they do not possess a degree of freedom. This chain of thought can form a structure of power with specific methods for its exercise that may take on a life of their own without the question of external, democratic or internal, ethical control ever being raised. The belief in development and progress, in the mission of the party, is not just an ideology, but the ground, the bastion on which this whole project is based. It is this belief that moves the members of the machine.

The other goal is related to the population, to supplying their needs and ensuring their happiness. The important point is not the independent existence of these two goals, but the specific way in which the party connected them. The power it exercised was not arbitrary, but related to the happiness of people. But this purpose was not simply concerned with concrete individuals, but was related to the specific dimension of the public interest. The party's field of action was thus given as the common dimension of social progress and individual happiness. It motivated people in order to orient their activities toward this common dimension. The party was supposed to promote all public goals that made people happy, and was supposed to work on the satisfaction of all human needs that were at the same time social ones. The mission the party found for itself was the ever more perfect and conflict-free fitting together of these two goals.

On the one hand, the party's activity is linked to the objective characteristics of progress. Here the main task, the mission of the party, is the realisation of the exact path, where the study of the Marxist classics can provide hints; and the specific task of local party organs is restricted to the faithful execution of the resolutions made at the top. On the other, the party must recognise the real needs of the population, and the promotion of the satisfaction of 'correct' demands. The two goals are connected as they are both related to the public sphere – the first on a theoretical, the other on a practical level.

Here with respect to both questions, we also find a reason why the sphere of politics seems to exceed all conceivable limits. First, the task of politics, according to the etymological sense of the word, is the handling of affairs belonging to the 'polis', the whole community. What we have encountered here is not just the impact of a political party or an ideology but the redefinition of the 'public sphere'. Or, more exactly, in our case it is a political party that extends its activity to all areas that were defined or redefined as 'public', but that had been functioning earlier not according to a political rationality, but another – economic or social.

Second, at the level of concrete activities, political work as embodied by the tasks of a district PC is the coordination or harmonisation of the theoretical and practical concepts of 'public'. The party's goal is not simply to represent a line discovered by scholars and augurs – even if there is a definite tendency, acknowledged time and again, to commit such mistakes – and, obviously, it is not just the satisfaction of the demands of the population, which would be mere social democracy. The party rather must reach the two goals at the same time, by the co-harmonisation of the two tasks. The party must not only discover the way, but also motivate people to realise the true path, which is only possible through an – at least partial – meeting of demands. In the words of one of our interviewees: 'I think that [the district PC] represented the interests of politics [i.e. the higher organs] and the population. The two are not the same, but they can be represented in a parallel manner' (J.L.).

We wondered whether political workers would agree with this statement, and included it in our questionnaire as one of fourteen items in a question. Here, we listed statements taken out of the pilot study, and asked our respondents about the extent to which they agreed with each of these sentences. The exact wording used was the following: 'To what extent do you agree with the statement that the district party committee represents the interests of politics and the population in a parallel manner?' More than half of our respondents, 54 per cent, agreed with this claim; a further 31 per cent agreed with reservations; and only the remaining 15 per cent did not agree at all. Of the fifteen items of the question, there were only four where the proportion of those agreeing with the proposition was similarly high (above 50 per cent).

This 'parallel representation' was again not just an ideological slogan, but the guiding principle of the day-to-day life and activities of a district PC. In its daily work, the party had to act in a dual role, helping, guiding and educating. It had to mobilise the population to the attainment of goals, it had to teach them. To ensure this people had to be able to recognise and accomplish the activities that served the 'public', and to formulate their own goals in dimensions that belonged to the public sphere thus defined. This task required permanent and detailed supervision and help. The harmonisation of the individual and the public was not just an ideology, a theoretical goal, but an activity that could not be formally defined and that required infinite patience: it was a permanent feature. For the accomplishment of this task, it was not enough to have a distant centre, an all-powerful government, as the latter could not be present everywhere and provide help and guidance in every question; and, quite obviously, it was not enough to rely upon the usual ways of doing things, as that would not provide a social optimum, an efficient way of harmonising individual and public concerns.

Perhaps the best way to define the functional, programmed role of the activities led by a district PC is that it was not just to serve the interests of 'politics', and obviously not just to serve local needs, but to minimise the distance between the two. The district PCs had to inform the top leadership so that the latter would be able to meet the needs of the population. At the same time, they had to direct the work done in the district according to the needs of the whole, where this whole was more than the aggregate of its parts. Finally, the key role of the district PC consisted not in the actual performance of tasks, but in assuring that everything fitted together as a matter of principle. At the level of built-in programmes, the role of the district PC was conceived of as a tool of a civilising mission led in the name of the common interest; at the final count, in the interest of all mankind.

Lurking in the background of all attempts to come to terms with the reasons behind the activities of the district PCs and the specific meaning given to politics is the belief in the historical necessity of progress.[1] Behind intervention into the smallest details of everyday activities, behind the perceived need for these interventions, lies a strange combination of denial and affirmation of reality. The denial consists of a rejection of the given state of things, of all that has transpired, and a doubt in the ability of those present to realise such goals and perform their duties. On the other hand, there is a sincere belief in a 'true' – if hidden – reality, in the possibility of realising true potentials, through the discovery of 'true' needs and interests. It is this sense of mission and a confidence in the ability to discover this deeper truth that confer the right to power on those who exercise it; moreover, it makes them blind to the simple fact that the exercise of power may be dangerous or problematic.

Thus, from our interviews we got back the well-known ideology of communism. What is interesting in all this? The mere fact that the realisation of these goals does not happen by itself; it requires constant enforcement, supervision and activity. The theoretical discovery of the basic goals is not sufficient; they must be put into practice. The harmonisation of common and individual interests is a concrete task; the 'true' reality, the goal of history, must become part and parcel of everyday life; potential must actually be pried from its inner recesses; the perfect fit between the individual and the social must be realised at the level of activity, behaviour, attitudes and values. Thus, it follows that politics cannot be restricted to the top level of central decision-makers. In this case, the loftiest goals would remain hollow; daily activities must be permeated, potentials revealed.

We began this chapter by quoting a French author, a member of the Ideologues, the successors of the Enlightenment. This quotation also partook of utopian thought, a circle of ideas whose main target was the realisation of the perfect society – a city without sickness or sin – merely through the impact that ideas concerning the 'good' would have on the mind. Well before the emergence of so-called 'utopian socialism', these views envisaged unrealisable utopias.

We think that bolshevik-type state-parties surpassed the earlier, utopian ideas in two respects. On the one hand, their belief in progress and sense of mission provided the mobilising force, the initial impetus. The centuries-old intellectual project of encasing the world in a single, perfect discourse was reinvigorated with the idea of progress; it became related to earthly goals and was given targets for action. On the other hand, this discourse became connected to certain 'means' necessary for its realisation: the formation of a regular apparatus of teachers and soldiers, or rather teacher-soldiers. The importance of the permeation of daily-life activities, of grasping the routine elements of behaviour, was realised even by Servan and his contemporaries, though they were unable to provide a detailed programme for its realisation.

But something went blatantly wrong here. It is obvious today at the level of daily reality, with the sudden, shameful collapses of all such systems. For a substantial part of the population in the region, it went wrong throughout the whole period. And it may indicate that something was wrong at the level of the fundamental moving principles. In the discussion above, we tried to make sense of a very peculiar definition of politics. We were able to distil some degree of consistency. But we also stumbled upon a basic logical error, a fundamental contradiction, the coexistence of two principles that are fundamentally incompatible, that cannot be reduced to any type of 'dialectical synthesis'. On the one hand, the party was based on an optimistic world-view, an underlying faith in progress, belief in the unfolding laws of history, a faith in 'man', his abilities and potentials. On the other, its concrete activities were motivated by an opposite perspective: a perceived need to intervene in everything, a conviction that men are lazy, need constant supervision and stimulation; a pessimistic outlook that sometimes bordered on a theory of degeneration.[2] An incompatible dual reasoning lay behind the need for intervention in the minutest details of daily activities: the attempt to create the prerequisites for progress, to lay down automatic systems inside individuals that would be the guarantees of further development; but also the conviction that constant supervision is necessary in order to prevent inherent tendencies of disorganisation and chaos from surfacing. In the last chapters of the book, we'll return to this point in detail. To close this chapter, we'll only give one concrete illustration for these incompatibilities and their consequences by analysing the different meanings with which the word 'efficiency' was invested in our interviews.

WHEN WAS A PARTY COMMITTEE WORKING EFFICIENTLY?

'Efficiency' was a slogan so wide spread in Hungary from the 1960s that it is difficult to make any sense of it at a general level. Thus, the frequently made statements that the district PC must work 'efficiently' do not catch the attention. The following sentence hardly goes beyond this, but still provides something to hold on to: 'We have a resolution that public institutions in the district should work in the most efficient way possible, by making full use of their capacities, because that is the social interest' (B.C., secretary). This definition concerns us from three different aspects. First, it links efficiency directly to the social interest. Second, the criterion of efficiency is related to public institutions in general. Third, it puts the emphasis on the input side as the full use of existing resources. This is a highly peculiar perspective, quite different from that of the meeting of demands, or of the best possible coordination between needs and possibilities. Translating the above definition into the language of economics, we may say that the logic of economic maximisation is turned upside down: instead of a maximisation of results, given the capacity constraint, it maximises the use of given capacities, without even mentioning the satisfaction of needs. All of which points to a hidden purpose: the redirection of existing resources to a goal overriding the satisfaction of the demands of the population.

But we wanted to get further and discover the exact meaning of efficiency concerning the activities of district PCs. This question, like the one about the meaning of politics, was not very popular. One of our respondents, to his credit, struggled with the answer several times:

Q: When does the district PC work efficiently?
A: Well, obviously not if all desires are met, as it is simply not possible. But when in the given period, the capacities are properly used, compared to the possibilities. This doesn't mean that I get some extra money and build an eight–floor culture centre – which would be much needed and a nice dream, but everybody knows that it is not feasible. But if the existing institutions can still function, working properly according to the needs of the population, the environment, and also of the firms and the public institutions.

(M.B.)

Compared to the earlier definitions, both the similarities and the differences are remarkable. As a sign of new times, we encounter here the real satisfaction of needs as part of the definition of efficiency. But the emphasis is still on capacity utilisation. The question is still the following: what is the smallest possible amount of resources that would be sufficient for the proper satisfaction of demands and would *still* enable public institutions to work?

Here, a solution may be found to the dilemma concerning the role of the party in meeting the demands of the population. Why is there a need for political action here? First, it is the role of the party to evaluate the demands, to assess whether their satisfaction is really in the public interest; and second, according to the definitions of efficiency given above, the party should work toward the proper satisfaction of those demands deemed to be acceptable.

A few examples may help in clarifying the links between this meaning of efficiency and politics. As a first example, we may refer to the point that was already made concerning the trouble caused by the new economic measure of profitability for the district PCs.[3] If the work of firms is evaluated on the basis of this criterion, then the district PC has to be engaged in strictly economic problems, and its political work becomes either superfluous or self-defeating.

In the second case, the question is whether the district headquarters of the pioneer movement should be opened to the public in order to make the services offered available to a wider range of the population. This goes against the wishes of present users:

Q: In this case, for example, where does the political goal come in?

A: Well, the political goal comes in as there are a number of cultural activities that the population or the youth of the district want. Given the current possibilities, the cultural institutions cannot meet these demands. The pioneer centre would be able to meet these demands, but it cannot make such decisions. Thus the political goal can only be to meet the demands, to create the possibilities without taking anything from public money. Under the present circumstances, this wouldn't be possible anyway.

(M.B.)

The final example provides a new angle on the interpretation of efficiency. One of our interviewees mentioned efficiency with regard to the link between the party and the council:

The district party has an impact on the efficiency of work done at the council. That is its goal.

Q: And how can you separate the executive powers of the council from the political influence of the party?

A: The role of the council is to organise the life of the area; and the political impact lies exactly in the measurement of its accomplishment, on the mood of the population that enjoys the results.

(G.E., secretary)

Here the emphasis is put on the other side of the equation of efficiency, on the successful meeting of the needs of the population; on satisfaction. This leads us back to a detail of the same interview, quoted earlier, about the connection between satisfaction and mobilisation.

As a conclusion we may state that, in the definitions analysed in this chapter, several different rationalities get mixed together. According to the first, the party must be everywhere so that things work normally. This is the attitude of a conqueror toward a subjugated population.

According to the second, all possible resources should be withdrawn from the sphere of civil population and redirected to areas under the direct control of the political leadership. This again is a sign of militarisation. In both cases, the direct reason for this activity is given by the threat of an enemy: in the first, the enemy is internal, in the second, external. The third logic refers to a self-proclaimed civilising mission, the education of the whole population in proper and at the same time efficient forms of behaviour: those that help the joint satisfaction of social and individual concerns. The fourth logic, where the competence of the party ends even in principle – but toward which the road was built by the party – is that of economic rationality. The party prepared the way for this one-dimensional definition of efficiency, indirectly, by reducing and constraining all activities into the single dimension of the 'common' or the 'social' as given by the all-encompassing definition of 'politics', thus creating a *'tabula rasa'* that is not completely alien to some of the basic assumptions of modern liberalism; and directly, by introducing the measure of profitability in a succession of reforms. But with this, the party eliminated its own grounds of existence. The party apparatus was not so much a ruling élite that attempted to maintain its own privileges and easy life as a mechanism of government that worked extremely hard, in a seemingly purposeless way, to make itself eventually superfluous.

Up till now, we have been talking about the tasks a district PC was supposed to perform, and the basis on which such activities could have been founded. The whole discussion was based on the perspective that these tasks were not general and abstract concerns, but elements of daily life in the countries of 'formerly existing socialism', programmes and techniques realised in concrete practices. Therefore, there was a need for concrete individuals who could be entrusted to carry out these activities. The carrying out of these all-encompassing tasks – the continuous gathering of information on a daily and minute basis, the supervision of all activities that were deemed to be of public concern, the actual fitting together and co-harmonisation of individual and society – required the constant presence of a regular apparatus, the formation of a 'standing army' whose basic task was to help and teach the population in matters of daily life in times of peace.

5 The background and value system of party workers

> In order to judge – and in contemporary history or politics judgement is identical with action – we need to know, and this requires the knowledge of everything that is knowable. What is this 'knowledge'? Statistical, mechanical, scholastic knowledge gained from books – historical knowledge – intuition, a contact with the living and moving world, an ability to reach each and every individual.
>
> (Gramsci, *Prison Notebooks*, 1930–2, in Gramsci, 1975)

The district party committees as well as the higher party organs should be at the head of a detailed account of their members, but these data were inaccessible for scientific research in Hungary. Thus, though our study was restricted to the district-level apparatus of Budapest, the conclusions may be used as an indication of the general characteristics of the former political apparatus in Hungary.

DEMOGRAPHIC CHARACTERISTICS

The results concerning the major demographic characteristics were somewhat unexpected both according to age and sex. According to age, it was surprising to find that the apparatus is very homogeneous and relatively young. The overwhelming majority, about four-fifths of the 201 respondents, were at least 30 but less than 45 years old. There were only a handful of 27–29-year-old party workers in our sample, and the few above 45 were mostly secretaries or retired workers doing a part-time job. The statistical results correspond to the statement often uttered in our interviews that the apparatus was relatively young and that most members retired from the apparatus after a limited time.

If we look at the distribution according to sex, it may again be surprising that the percentages of males was not much higher than 50 per cent: 56 per cent of our respondents were men, while 44 per cent were women. However, it is true that the picture would be somewhat different had we looked more closely at the differences according to position. Among district secretaries and in the departments of economic policy men predominated. Most women worked in more or less administrative jobs, like those related to the preparation of information reports, or cadre administration. But segregation was far from being complete.

FAMILY BACKGROUND

In our questionnaire, we included several items to map the childhood and family background of political workers. We were interested in the type of family motivation received, both in material and spiritual terms, and in the circle of recruitment.

We tried to get in the questionnaire a fairly detailed picture about the professional career of the parents of our respondents. If we consider the first job of these parents, in most cases we find a working-class background. The first job of 69 per cent of the fathers and 65 per cent of the mothers was of a blue-collar type.[1] The first occupation of only 18 per cent of fathers and 8 per cent of mothers was professional or managerial. However, the results on the mobility of parents were more interesting. If we look at the most recent job of parents, the percentage of blue-collar work is decreased somewhat (to 53 per cent in both cases), while the percentage of professional or managerial jobs is doubled (to 35 per cent in the case of fathers, and to 17 per cent of mothers). This points out that, though the majority of party workers came from the working classes, a substantial part did have a middle-class or intellectual back- ground. About a half of these families were first-generation intellectuals.

Recruitment seemed to be more closed when we looked at the party membership of parents. According to this variable, 45 per cent of the fathers and 23 per cent of the mothers of the political workers were themselves party members. Moreover, in a considerable number of cases, this membership went back a long time – 28 per cent of fathers and 12 per cent of mothers joined the party before 1948. This lends support to the claim often made in our interviews and in some questionnaires that a considerable number of the members of the apparatus received strong parental motivation for such a job.

We also tried to get a picture about the childhood of the respondents, as far as it was at all possible with the methods of survey analysis. On the one hand, respondents had to place themselves on a nine-step ladder according to whether their family was relatively poor or affluent during childhood. On the other hand, in an open item, we encouraged respondents to supplement this assessment with a few words of their own. Here we were especially concerned with testing a hypothesis that a troubled childhood may have helped people to formulate a life strategy oriented toward a career in the party apparatus.

If we look only at the results derived from the nine-step ladder and compare them to the results obtained from the 1977–8 national representative sample, then the hypothesis may seem to be given some support.[2] The members of the apparatus place themselves systematically lower than average Hungarians. But it is very doubtful whether these results can be taken at face value as, surprisingly, the largest differences are at the highest steps of the ladder. For example, out of the 202 respondents, nobody placed himself or herself at the top, and only 4 per cent of the total in the top three steps, as opposed to the 10 per cent of the population in 1977–8. However, as it is clear from the data, a number of parents occupied leading positions in the 1950s and 1960s, putting them at a considerable advantage compared to the population at large, especially because at that time there were hardly any other possibilities for social or economic advancement. Thus, instead of talking about the relative lack of privilege of apparatus members during childhood, we should rather talk about cognitive dissonance, where the actual situation (often providing considerable advantages) conflicted with the requirements of ideology (working-class, underdog background).

This hypothesis is also supported by the fact that, in our earlier study, we found that real differences between the population and the party élite were to be found at the bottom steps of the ladder, due to the fact that a considerable percentage of the party élite recalled their childhood as being extremely difficult and unhappy. However, with present party workers this is not at all the case. In the two bottom steps, there were no differences compared to population averages (6 per cent opposed to 7 per cent, and 9 per cent opposed to 8 per cent for the two bottom steps, respectively). Also, the answers given to the open item clearly indicated that the expectation of an abusive and mistreated childhood was simply not borne out for present apparatus members. Even though the wording of the question was oriented towards the material circumstances of childhood, a quarter of the respondents (40 per cent of those who put down anything at all) said voluntarily that they had had a very balanced childhood, rich in affection and love. There were only two of them who mentioned childhood deprivations in terms of family neglect or lack of affection. Thus, even if earlier the expectation may well have been of a childhood full of deprivation and a subsequent rise due to the party, the ideal for party workers in 1988, at least as they projected it back toward the past, was a 'poor, but happy' image of childhood.

PREVIOUS CAREER: EDUCATION AND OCCUPATION

The way the whole problematic of education was posed and handled in daily life in Hungary tells a lot concerning both the characteristics of bolshevik-type communist parties and the activity of the apparatus itself. On the one hand, there was the picture of a workers' party and a subsequent accusation concerning lack of professional and managerial abilities; a picture which gave strong support and backing to different sorts of technocratic approaches and ideologies trying to base their own project for the transformation of society and nature on the failure of the bolshevik project. On the other hand, there was a strong demand for formal education both for and on the part of political workers.

In the 1980s, this training was not restricted to different political schools, and a college degree did not necessarily refer to evening or correspondence courses either. According to our results, more than half of the apparatus did possess a degree; 27 per cent finished a university course, and 30 per cent a polytechnic.[3] Everybody had a proper secondary-school education. In our sample, there were only three persons who completed only a high school designed to turn out skilled workers. Sixty-five per cent of those who finished university and 37 per cent of those who finished a polytechnic course got their degrees as full-time students.

Here we also studied the additional question whether there were some changes across time in the education of apparatus members, whether the younger cohorts were more educated than the older ones. Surprisingly enough, even though the differences in age within the apparatus were small, large differences were found between the formal educational attainments of the younger and the older generations of the 1988 apparatus. While only 38 per cent of those who were older than 45 years had a degree, this percentage was steadily increasing in the younger cohorts, and jumped to 81 per cent for those who were under 35. This difference was almost exclusively due to the increase in those having a polytechnic degree; the proportion of those completing a university degree was a stable 30 per cent.

As it was exactly in the case of these polytechnic graduates that the proportion of full-time students was relatively low, it was interesting to check whether the increase in schooling was accompanied by a similar increase in those who had completed higher education on a daytime basis. Thus, we analysed the interaction between age, education and the type of degree. Our results showed that, in the case of younger members, the number of those who got their degree by correspondence or evening courses has declined. For those above 45, only 38 per cent obtained a degree, and only a quarter of these on a daytime basis; while in the youngest cohort, 55 per cent of the total sample got a college or university degree on a daytime basis. This difference is only reinforced by the fact that the members of the younger generation have still more chances of acquiring further education.

The process of 'intellectualisation' and its speed can thus be documented even in our fairly homogeneous sample. The attempt to bring professionals into the apparatus was manifest. Instead of talking about the low educational qualifications of the political workers, we should rather speak of over-education in terms of formal schooling, as they were spending a disproportionately large part of their lives at school desks. Not a few of them possessed two degrees, to which one may add the years spent at political schools – the completion of the political academy course took four years, while that of the Marxist-Leninist evening university, if one also finished its special branch, may have taken seven years altogether. So it is not at all surprising that we get strange numbers if we calculate the number of years members of the apparatus spent in formal training.

If we consider only years spent in state education, then 58 per cent of our sample spent more than fifteen years in schools, though the completion of a college degree usually takes only fifteen years from the beginning of primary education, and 25 per cent of them spent more than seventeen years. If we add the years spent in political schools, the results are even more telling. Sixty-nine of our respondents failed to mention any political schools. It is very probable that most of them have also completed such an education, but restricted the answer to state education. Still, keeping this distortion in our results, a full 80 per cent of our respondents spent more than fifteen years at school desks, and 25 per cent more than twenty years altogether. If we leave out those who have not put down any political schools in the questionnaire, then these numbers become even higher: 85 per cent, and 35 per cent, respectively.

Thus, it is possible to document the fact of over-education, of the postponement of the completion of schooling beyond any meaningful limits. This hunger for studying represents a highly specific version of the 'will to knowledge': a permanent education, yes; but one constantly carried out in a hierarchical-disciplinary framework, involving the coexistence of a single written text treated as sacred – 'the' textbook of the course – and a teacher-student relationship which is at once personal and authoritarian as a matter of principle, independently of personal dispositions.

Let's now follow up the professional careers that correlate with the educational background detailed above. Our first question here was the same as in the case of the career of parents: to what extent can we talk about the closing of the channels of recruitment? Given the homogeneity of our sample, the differences were again surprising, though most of them were restricted to the youngest cohort. If we consider the first occupation, then among those who are 45 or older, 62 per cent began as manual workers; in the case of those between the ages of 35 and 45, this proportion is down to 49 per cent, while in the youngest cohort it is 25 per cent. Similarly, the percentage of those who started as professionals or managers has increased: from 16 per cent to 25 per cent, and then to 42 per cent.

Looking at the most recent employment of political workers before entering the apparatus, we encounter two interesting features. First, even before joining the apparatus, future members showed a high degree of mobility. The number of those who joined the apparatus directly from the shop-floor is negligible: in the case of the oldest cohort, it was 24 per cent; in the younger ones, it falls to 16 per cent and then to a mere 4 per cent. A parallel increase may be noticed for those who joined the apparatus from professional or managerial positions: even for those above 45 years old it is 56 per cent, while for the youngest group it is a full 80 per cent.

However, we must be careful here, as this 'professional' position may cover very specific areas. Thus, for example, every fifth political worker joined the apparatus from the KISZ, the communist youth organisation. If we adjust the above numbers for this factor, and also leave out others who filled positions in other apparatuses (trade unions, pioneer movements, etc.), then in all cohorts the percentage who joined the apparatus from professional or managerial positions was about the same: 40 per cent. In the younger cohorts the shift is toward those whose first position was professional from those who themselves had made the transition from blue-collar to white-collar work; and from 'worker cadres' to 'apparatus cadres'. This represented a double restriction on mobility: on the one hand, the requirement for formal schooling at the beginning of a career became stronger; on the other, the alternative possibility for mobility using a politically oriented career lay through positions filled in different apparatuses; a working-class origin was less and less of an asset.

Finally, an important part of the career of would-be party workers was earlier work done in the 'movement'. Most of them joined the party at a very early age: 71 per cent had become a member at the age of 25, and only 7 per cent were older than 30 when joining the party. The younger members of the apparatus joined the party even earlier: in their case, 77 per cent became a member at the age of 25 as opposed to the 64 per cent of those who were older than 35. These results were only reinforced by the data received for membership of the communist youth league: 70 per cent of those who are or were members of KISZ had already joined the organisation at the age of 15, and only a mere 6 per cent after the age of 18. Here again, these results were even more characteristic of the youngest cohort: almost 80 per cent of those under 35 joined the KISZ when they were 15 years old.[4] And the majority of our respondents did not stay mere members: 65 per cent of them have become secretaries at the local or a higher level of KISZ.

Thus, the members of the apparatus could be characterised by an early engagement both in terms of KISZ and party membership. Or, to put it in a different way, those people who failed to join these organisations at a very early age had only a slight chance of ever becoming members of the party apparatus.

PERSONAL CHARACTERISTICS

In our questionnaire, we also asked our respondents about their preferences as regards values and personal characteristics. As a part of this, we used nine seven-step ladder scales of human properties, developed especially for the study of political élites.[5] The end-points of the scales were two opposite characteristics – confident vs. insecure, or emotional vs. unemotional – and respondents had to place themselves according to which end they felt themselves close to and to what extent. As all nine pairs contained a negative and a positive pole, the distorting impact of expectations and self-evaluation is obvious. Still, in itself, reproducing party workers's assessments of their personal characteristics may be interesting.

If we look at the top or the top two steps of the ladder, three properties stand out. Political workers consider themselves to be particularly flexible, emotional, and sympathetic. In the case of these three attributes, about 30 per cent of the respondents placed themselves at the top, and altogether 70 per cent at the top two steps. A strange group it is for members of the apparatus of a political party. One would expect decisiveness, independence, rationality or confidence to be more important requirements than being emotional and sympathetic. Of the four listed in the sentence above, the first two (decisive and independent) approach the leading trio if we add up the three top steps, but, in the case of the other two, the difference remains considerable. Only 8 per cent of our respondents considered themselves to be very confident, placing themselves at the top step; and adding together the first three steps, we only get 75 per cent as opposed to the near or more 90 per cent of the five leading characteristics. Concerning rationality, the situation is even worse: the latter number is only 64 per cent. Finally, in the case of two pairs, the results are ambiguous. The first is the calm–anxious pair, where the distribution is almost equal. A lot of party workers considered themselves very calm (17 per cent), while a large proportion, 26 per cent, openly acknowledged being anxious. In the case of ambition, only 46 per cent of our respondents stated that they considered themselves to be ambitious rather than not ambitious. This result, on the one hand, supports those of earlier value studies about the negative connotation of ambition, especially among the more educated strata of Hungarian society;[6] on the other, it points to a possible source of this sensitivity.

These results can be summarised in the following way: the characteristics party workers claim they possess most are not those related to the achievement of certain results, but those which imply person-to-person relations. It is the reaction to others, flexibility, sympathy and feeling that proved especially important to them rather than rationality, confidence or decisiveness. In the case of the latter two, it is interesting in itself that apparatus members rank themselves higher in the case of decisiveness, or certainty expressed toward the outside, than in the case of confidence, or inner certainty.

For a better understanding of the structure of personal characteristics, we have applied factor analysis to our data. We obtained three factors, all of which could be interpreted in a fairly straightforward manner. The first was the usual general factor, explaining 26 per cent of the total variance, meaning in this case that there is a general tendency among respondents to place themselves higher or lower in every scale. Only one of our pairs, the calm–anxious pair, was missing from the general factor, indicating that self-evaluation on this item is not related to general self-evaluation. Among the other eight items, it was decisiveness and confidence, and to a lesser extent flexibility and independence, that received the highest factor loadings here; in other words, exactly those characteristics that may be considered to be the most 'political' ones. The properties that proved to be so important for party workers, emotion and sympathy, had a smaller impact on the variance of responses in terms of general self-evaluation.

Our second factor, explaining 19 per cent of the total variance, contained exactly these items as one side of a polar factor. On the other pole, we found rationality and calmness. Those who considered themselves to be emotional and sympathetic had a tendency to judge themselves as anxious and irrational as well. Party workers could thus be best divided – considering types and not strength of self-assessment – in terms of personal properties according to temperament: 'warmth' (emotional sensitivity) or 'coolness' (lack of emotionality); which is fairly surprising when talking about political workers. Finally, in the third factor, ambition and flexibility were contrasted with anxiety. In order to fulfil ambitions, flexibility was required; but those who pursued this strategy had to put up with a higher level of anxiety.

Factor analysis thus refined the earlier picture in three different aspects. First, feeling and sympathy were very important for the overwhelming majority of political workers, more or less independently of the general level of self-evaluation, but there were considerable differences among the apparatus in terms of 'emotional' and 'indifferent' types. Second, overall self-evaluation was most related to active, 'political' characteristics like being confident and decisive. Third, the central role played by flexibility may have been caused by its being at the juncture of two different axes: on the one hand, it was close to care, attention and adjustment toward others, characteristics that had proved to be so important for party workers; on the other, with its affinity to smoothness and the capacity for self-accommodation, it provided an acceptable alternative to ambition.

CHILD-REARING PRINCIPLES

The results obtained by the analysis of child-rearing principles support and supplement the previous discussion.[7] Comparing the value choices of party workers with those of the total population, we were first struck by the homogeneity of the value rankings of the former. Party workers uniformly accepted certain values and rejected others. The five child-rearing principles they considered to be the most important accounted for two-thirds of all possible choices; thus, the remaining eleven values of the set had to fall in the remaining third. In the case of the representative sample, the five most important values accounted for merely half of all choices, and even in the case of a relatively homogeneous control group, those having completed some higher education, this percentage did not reach 60 per cent. Similarly, if we take the five values that are considered to be the least important, in the case of party workers they only represent one twenty-fifth of the total choices, while for the sample it is one tenth, for the control group one twelfth. We may thus conclude that party workers both choose and reject the same values as a group, much more so than other social entities.

But what were the values considered to be important and unimportant by party workers? How did their value system differ from those of the general population or groups with a similar education or age? Of the five values that members of the apparatus considered to be particularly important, four were given far more weight than they were by the population at large or any of the control groups: these were independence, responsibility, hard work and tolerance. The only exception was honesty, where the selection rate was somewhat below the average. Apart from the four listed above, two other values were also relatively important for them: decisiveness and imagination. It is interesting to remark here that in the case of all values that were especially important for the party workers, with the exception of hard work, the importance steadily increased in the representative population sample with the level of formal schooling; but even among the most educated strata of society it did not even approximate to that given by the party workers, though their level of formal schooling was much lower, 43 per cent of them not having a regular degree. It seems thus that party workers were in the vanguard of the 'intellectualisation' of society. This was especially so in the dimension of active, individualistic, 'protestant' values like independence and responsibility – these two were ranked by the vast majority, four-fifths, of party workers among the five most important values – but also in the case of 'post-industrial' values like tolerance and imagination.

We get similarly characteristic results by reviewing the values that party workers considered to be especially unimportant. In the case of a homogeneous set of values, this difference is particularly striking: these are the 'traditional-disciplinary' values of obedience, politeness and good manners. These values were among the most important ones for the least educated groups of the population. For those who have finished at least a high school, they recede to the back of the list; only 20–30 per cent consider these values to be important. But for party workers, these were simply erased from the value system: politeness was chosen by only 15 per cent of the respondents; good manners by a mere 3 per cent; and nobody out of the 200 respondents answering this question included obedience among the top five choices. This value orientation based on surface-level, external control has lost all its validity for political workers.

Besides this value group, there were two other values that were relatively unimportant for party workers: frugality and self-control. The first was relatively neglected by the most educated groups, and even more so by the members of the apparatus. The second, on the other hand, was important in general for professionals; less than average for party workers.

Given the specific 'intellectualisation' of the value system of political workers, it was worth assessing whether this could have been restricted to a certain part of the apparatus. To our great surprise, we only found minor divergences in value choices within the apparatus according to educational levels or occupational careers. Thus, politeness was somewhat more important for those who began their career as manual workers but even in their case the selection rate was below that of the college- or university-educated group of the representative sample of the whole population. The differences were similar in the case of imagination, while the choice of self-control was quite peculiar: it was especially important for those who started their careers as blue-collar workers and was at a similar level to that of the most educated strata of the whole population; while those party workers who started as professionals considered it to be less important. The taking up of a job as a party worker thus assumed – or created – a high degree of homogeneity in terms of value choices, independently of previous qualifications.

We emphasise four elements from the previous discussion concerning the value system of political workers: the special importance accorded to the 'protestant' values of individualisation (independence, responsibility and hard work); the complete absence of disciplinary values based on rigid, external controls; the peculiar, 'post-industrial' combination of human relations and imagination; and finally the fact that the ethical values related to inner composure (honesty, self-control) are less important for party workers than for intellectuals in general. Thus, for political workers, the importance of values related to both rigid external control and self-control has decreased, while at the same time the importance of values related to activity and relations toward others has increased.

6   The tasks of political instructors

> The providence that's in a watchful state
> Knows almost every grain of Plutus' gold,
> Finds bottom in the uncomprehensive deeps,
> Keeps place with thought and almost, like the gods,
> Does thoughts unveil in their dumb cradles.
> There is a mystery – with whom relation
> Durst never meddle – in the soul of state;
> Which hath an operation more divine
> Than breath or pen can give expressure to.
> (Shakespeare, *Troilus and Cressida*, III.3)

The main body of a district party apparatus consisted of political workers. They were full-time party employees, and their job was to execute the tasks a district party committee was called upon to do. During the period of our research, the political workers of a given Budapest district party committee had primarily two different tasks: they worked partly as 'instructors' and partly as 'collators'. The latter job required the performance of certain specific duties, like the preparation of reports, the management of administrative or disciplinary matters of the committee, etc. Its highly standardised, bureaucratic activities were carried out in-house, within party premises. The duties of an instructor involved extra-mural tasks, in the primary party organisations (PPOs).

The term 'instructor' was almost completely unknown in the past both for Eastern Europeans, even political or social scientists, and Western academics. For example, in the standard textbook on the Soviet communist party, the word is not even listed in the index, and is only passingly referred to in the text (Hill and Frank 1981: 62). To become familiar with their activity, let's first quote in length the definition given by the official *Dictionary of the Party Life*:

Instructor: a party worker whose task is to spend the larger part of his work time at the primary party organisations in order to assist them in carrying out the resolutions of the upper organs with information, suggestions, advice or the propagation of the methods that proved to be efficient in other local organisations, and to ensure the collection, analysis and upward transmission of local experience. In their work, instructors cannot take over the area or the responsibilities of the elected bodies or the leaders. They present their opinions or advice in the form of suggestions – these may be considered and used by the primary party organisations, but may also be ignored. Instructors can issue commands only if they witness practices contrary to the politics or resolutions of the party, or to the rules of organisation.

(Barsi 1985: 56)

Before going into the concrete activities of the instructors, let's first look at this definition in detail. Though, not surprisingly, it contains mostly empty generalities, some things are worthy of attention. First and obviously, the activity of the instructor is restricted to the party organis-ations and involves no right to deal with economic, social or administrative problems beyond the party cells. Second, the actual work done by the instructor is divided into three parts. Two of them involve merely intermediary roles: the instructor supervises the execution of the resolutions of higher organs, thus working from the top down; and transmits his experiences at the local units, thus working from the bottom up. These two tasks can be defined easily, but the third one possesses a much wider range of possible interpretations: the instructor is physically present in the individual party cells, or local organisations, continuously helping their work, giving suggestions and advice concerning their everyday activities. In this, except for questions related to technical or administrative party matters, he has no legal authority, and his status as an instructor gives him no competence over the specific areas he is supposed to instruct. The local organisations are free to accept or reject his suggestions.

Except for one thing. If the instructor perceives that the practice is contrary to the official policy of the party, he has the right to intervene directly. So, while, until that point, the instructor did not possess the right nor the competence to intervene even in the work of the PPOs, suddenly he becomes a dictator with complete powers, and in this case those are not restricted to the local party organisations. There is only one requirement to make the intervention of the instructor legal, even necessary: to declare any activity, action, practice or problem 'political'. Up to the last sentence of the definition quoted on page 93, anything concerning the instructor had only to do with the local party organisations. In the last sentence, related to 'political' questions, this qualification is missing. Perhaps this is only because it is taken for granted. But even in this unlikely case, the omission is still revealing.

Given the description above, it is still hard to imagine what the practical work of an instructor at a local party organisation consists of. The instructors themselves felt the same way, even after spending several years on a district party committee:

> So that's why I say that in my opinion this job is hard to grasp and very difficult to define.
>
> (T.N.)

> Q: And your work as an instructor?
> A: Well, this is much more complicated and more difficult [than the collator position]. I say that this is a lot – a very complex matter. And the more you do it, the more difficult it becomes.
>
> (I.K.)

This is only reinforced by the fact that the instructors are not given concrete directions concerning their job at the beginning: 'If one is lucky and meets his predecessor, and goes out with him to get acquainted with the partners, then it is somewhat easier' (J.A.). This practice is surprising at first view, and a number of instructors perceived it as a lack of care, as complete abandonment on the part of the PCs. This would have been a very surprising thing indeed, as the party showed extreme care in the selection of its instructors. Given the everyday activity of a district party committee and the definition of politics, instructors had a key position, as they linked local organisations to the centre. Without them, this whole structure would cease to exist; the leadership and the members would be disconnected. The function of the instructors, then, was crucial from the perspective of the party, and most of them were well aware of this:

> [Political instructors] are the group of party workers most at the centre.
>
> (M.B.)

> Q: Thus the work of the instructor assumes the qualities of a politician?
> A: I would even risk saying that it is the most political. As I frequently meet the party secretaries of businesses, or the workers there, and since I transmit information in all directions . . . [I] am the first filter who can distort information.

Q: Had you had any training [when entering the apparatus]?

A: Yes, well, let me tell you what the instruction was that I got when I entered the job. It was that we have to be aware that we are not the creators of politics, only its executors. Now I found it funny as, at the level where we move, we are really the creators as well.

(M.B.)

[The instructor is] at the borderline, at the transitory zone where members and the upper leadership of the party meet.

(A.T.)

The instructors thus played a central role in both the transmission of information and in handling the encounters between the membership and the leaders. Therefore, their position was bound to be filled with tension, especially at the time of our research when such conflicts increasingly came to the surface.

One final comment to close this introductory section. In the preceding, we often quoted statements concerning the basic importance of the work of the instructors and their central role in the whole party structure. This ought to be surprising as, in our everyday life, one all so often heard about the party, but had not even the slightest knowledge of the instructors. But let's not be misled here. One of the most intriguing characteristics of the work of instructors – and one which deserves further analysis – was that it could not be seen. Instructors had to be present everywhere, know everything and still stay in the background. Their activities were unknown not only to the man in the street, but could provide surprises for the leaders of the local party organisations or the members of the elected bodies:

Now I am at a level of information where one or two sentences are enough. I know who left which school, and where he went to. I even know as far as that – not in everything, but there are things like that. When the party secretaries told me who had left their school, I already knew where they had gone. And then they were surprised. It is not that hard to follow things like that.

(V.K.)

Q: As a member of the elected body, how did you see the work of the instructor?

A: I haven't seen it. I haven't seen it at all. I have only seen – as I told you, I was working at the local council – that the instructor sometimes appeared at the party meeting and said something according to the rules of protocol. Because if he

happened to be there, he had to say something. That's what I
have observed. There, at the local organisation, I was not
aware at all of the activity of the instructor.

(M.B.)

Let's then give an account of the work of an instructor: how did he/she
attempt to realise the tasks a district party committee was supposed to
perform?

THE REPRESENTATION OF THE 'PARTY' IN THE LOCAL ORGANISATIONS

The basic task of the instructor was to supervise the everyday activities
of the primary party organisations, to assess whether they were working
in accordance with expectations, whether they properly represented
resolutions, the 'party line'. But the term 'representation' is a bit
misleading, as it does not express the specific nature of the power
'embodied' by the instructor, in the strict meaning of the word.

You are the party

The instructor was not just a spokesman, not just the reflection of an
image: he was the 'party'.

When you go out to a local party committee, there you are the party.
What can be the trouble here? If you really believe that you are the
party; if you become convinced of this. The two things must not be
confused. That you represent something, or you really believe this. In
the last few years it has no longer been observed, but four years ago
the director of an enterprise went out and met the 28-year-old guy at
the gate . . . that certainly gives you a fantastic confidence in yourself
and an ability to make decisions; at least the appearance of an ability.
You think you have an influence on important things, and that you
make decisions. In a number of cases it is quite true. But if you cannot
make a distinction between what is due to your position and what is
due to you as a person, it can lead to tragic misunderstandings.

(A.L.)

This statement is repeated almost word for word by another interviewee:

It is interesting, this job, as there is a big trap here. Somebody comes
to work here, and after a while he goes out to the local organisations,
to the meetings, and gives his opinion about the work done, passes on
the expectations from above, etc. And they all listen carefully, make

notes and don't object to anything – although lately there have been more objections. But it is still not characteristic. Thus, there is still a – although decreasing – glamour about the district party committee at the local organisation level. If you go out there from here, then you are from the party committee, and whatever you say they accept as such. Then you believe what a clever guy you are, saying things which nobody can object to. But this is not the case; this is the trap. A lot of people believe after a certain time that they are the 'clever guys'.

(A.T.)

The above details are important for at least two different reasons. First, they testify to the almost dictatorial power of the instructor. But we are talking here about a very peculiar type of dictatorship. First, it is not identical in nature to the current, pejorative notion of dictatorship which is defined as arbitrariness and an abuse of power. Of course, like all power, the power of the instructor can also be abused. But in his case dictatorial powers refer to an ideal-typical, positive form. This is not in the classic, Roman sense as shown, for example, in the well-known case of Cincinnatus. There, the dictator received full powers in a highly irregular situation, for the accomplishment of a concrete task. Within these limits, everything was entrusted to him. The instructor is also a dictator in a certain way, but, at important points, in a way opposite to the Roman model. First, his term is not specified for a concrete task and an irregular situation, but is permanent and unlimited. Second, in the final count, his powers are not derived from himself, but from the party. He is not given dictatorial powers because he is personally trusted as the only individual able to resolve a given difficulty, but because the 'party' is embodied in him.

Second, in order to perform these tasks, instructors must possess certain well-defined characteristics, and not everybody can possess these requirements. They have to meet the challenge, must prove themselves to be fit for the trust invested in them by the party. They have already completed the first part of the test as, from a wide range of possible candidates, the district party committee has chosen them. This choice was never accidental. The question of 'recruitment' or 'cadre replacement' was given high priority in the work of a committee. The 'cadre development list' contained the names of all possible candidates for the job, and the important changes in their lives were all registered there. From time to time, they were called on by the PC and asked whether they were willing to work there now or in the near future.

Potential candidates were carefully scrutinised before actually being selected; thus their control and supervision in their work at the PC was no longer deemed to be necessary. Those who had come so far did not need to be looked after; they could serve the 'cause' independently. The second part of the test did not refer to moral problems related to the use or abuse of their power; the careful mechanism of selection had *a priori* excluded this possibility. Had problems of this type occurred, the mechanism for the selection of cadres would have failed, which was considered as a contradiction in terms. And in case of any problems, in the final instance there was the possibility of internal disciplinary action.

I am my own master

On meeting the above requirements, the instructors attained a unique position. They were no longer under continuous supervision:

> In all questions related to the work of an instructor, I am my own master. Obviously there are things for which I am accountable, orders I have to carry out, but beyond that, the contact I keep with organisations – how I make the connections, what their nature will be – is completely up to me.
>
> (J.L.)

Thus, the second part of the test did not refer to moral qualities, to faith, enthusiasm, fidelity towards the party, but it had to do with the work to be accomplished. The instructors were deemed worthy of independence, and had to construct their field and methods of action completely on their own. They were thrown into the ring, and there had to find their own way.

Completely left alone

Their independence in this respect was so complete that they often thought that they were 'being left alone':

Q: May I say that, when you go out to a local party organisation, then to the questions posed there – whether they are general questions or related to daily political issues – you give your own answers, without any precise guidelines? Is this a free game?

A: It is a completely free game. For a number of questions raised I cannot even say that this is the point of view of the party or of the district PC, or that it is their suggestion or advice. You try to place the question in context and begin to improvise. Then you say what you – not just what you are expected to say. This is a dual situation as, on the other hand, you do not want to get into conflict with the local leadership, that is, to say something very out of line. It may also happen that you know the party line, but members categorically refuse to accept it. These are the most extreme cases when one begins to steer a careful course, to say things and not to say them. After all, you cannot say that your opinion is the same as the members'. It is here that I feel the political workers are completely left alone.

(G.C.)

In this situation the 'testing', the 'measurement' mean two different things. On the one hand, the instructors have to find their own way to accomplish their task, without a detailed job description (which cannot be provided anyway). Outside, at the local organisations, all they can (and also must) refer to are general guidelines that in concrete cases only express empty generalities. On the other hand, they have to convince their colleagues, the members and especially the local leaders, that they are able to represent, to embody the 'party'.

This attitude, the myth of the embodiment of the 'party', has a very strong impact on both sides, both as a requirement of members toward the instructors, and of the instructors toward themselves. The latter cannot take in-house debates or their own doubts out to the local organisations; they are not even allowed to show or to allude to these. Moreover, they are even convinced that this is right:

One is permanently in a dual situation as inside, up here, we are furious, we quarrel with each other, we grumble. But if one goes out, one tries somehow to keep quiet about what one knows and what seems likely to happen. He/she tries to represent and not complain that now, after all –

(J.A.)

The first difficulty of the instructor's work is thus to make outsiders believe that he/she is able to represent, in principle, the PC, to embody the 'party'. The second trouble comes with the practical tasks of representing the line, especially when it is different from or even contrary to the conviction of the instructor.

I do make compromises

Here we encounter one of the greatest, unsolvable, inherent sources of conflict in the instructor's work. This job could be done successfully only by individuals who deeply believed in what they were doing. The main job of the instructor was to mobilise, to convince others, to get them to act and work, and those who were themselves not convinced of the truth and importance of all this were not able to perform the task. But such a deep internal conviction may in concrete cases go against the given party line. The more an instructor 'believes', the more he is suited to perform his job, the stronger is this conflict.

This problem of taking up conflicts or accepting compromises and the question of limits to be drawn here often cropped up in our interviews:

> This question about whether to make compromises concerning one's convictions – I have been thinking for a long time what to say. Because if I say that I deny this as a matter of principle, then I should answer accordingly. Still, I have to admit that it does happen. It occurs in a number of cases that a party worker has to represent the policy of the party – that's why we are here, to proclaim the policy of the party in its entirety, and to make people behave accordingly. Thus, it may happen that I myself am not deeply convinced that it is right; still, I have to do my job. So I actually do make compromises. Therefore, the correct answer would be that it does happen [that I make compromises], but it is against my principles. Something like that.
>
> (E.T.)

> Now how can one survive with such a state of mind? I think I did make compromises, obviously. It was said that politics is the art of the possible.
>
> (H.O., secretary)

> Q: Were you able to adjust the people here to yourself, or they –?
> A: It was extremely difficult. You toy with the idea that you can preserve your integrity, but I am afraid that it is not true. I was not able to preserve everything, though I certainly did keep a lot. It was awfully difficult to accept [being there]. It is very difficult even now.
> Q: To accept what? Could you tell it? What annoys or irritates you the most?
> A: Not that it annoys me, but it is very difficult to accept the situation of having a dual opinion. It's a dreadful thing. It means that here, at the group where I work, the atmosphere is pleasant, I'm on good terms with my boss. Here anything can be said, we debate a lot, but this was the case even in 1984. But most of this cannot be taken outside. After a decision is made at a certain level, you go out to a local organisation as a member of the apparatus. There you can be progressive, but

within limits. For a number of reasons. There are a lot of strange things. After all, you fulfil a transmission role, and in two directions. You have to represent the line, you cannot say the opposite. For example, you can argue here, but you cannot do it in front of a local party organisation. You simply have no right to do that.

(A.L.)

I am willing to make compromises, but refuse to lie.

(A.L.)

We included this issue in our questionnaire as well. We listed in a block eight situations that might arise and cause difficulties during work, and asked our respondents about the extent to which they considered these situations as difficult.[1] Out of the eight, the situation 'having to compromise your convictions' was judged to be the second most difficult; 63 per cent of our respondents claimed that this situation was difficult, and only the possibility of being short of information was deemed to be harder to cope with.

Let's stay here, on the question of information. A key part of the activities of the instructors consists in transmitting local experiences toward the centre, the district leadership or the central party organs. In this, the collection of all sorts of information occupies a central place. 'Information' is a key word anyway, related both to the work of instructors and the district PCs. Problems about the collecting and supplying of information came up time and again in our interviews:

Q: How important is it [for your work] to be provided with information?
A: It's extremely important. That would be the most important thing. With all sorts of information.

(G.C.)

THE MACHINERY OF INFORMATION COLLECTION

While making and reading the interviews of our pilot study, we were struck, on the one hand, by an insatiable hunger for the collection and processing of information, spreading to all conceivable parts of human and social existence, and on the other by recurrent complaints on the part of political workers about the scarcity of information they had to put up with. We were trying to assess the generality of this complaint, and included in our questionnaire some items covering this topic. Thus, we asked our respondents how difficult they considered the situation of not being provided with sufficient information, and whether they agreed with the statement that 'the instructors often do not receive the information necessary for the performance of their duties'. The results showed that the interviews of the pilot study did touch on a crucial issue.[2]

Taking the latter item first, 54 per cent of the respondents agreed with the statement, and only 20 per cent denied its validity (the rest 'agreed with reservations'). Of the fourteen statements listed, the assessment of this was one of the most equivocal. Moreover, 20 per cent of the respondents indicated the 'strongly agree' alternative, which, if an item that proved to be a truism was omitted, was the highest proportion, confirming that the lack of information did create a lot of trouble for a considerable number of our respondents.

The analysis of the former item gives similar results: 39 per cent of political workers considered the situation of not being provided with sufficient information very difficult, and a further 30 per cent somewhat difficult. Thus, all in all, 69 per cent of the respondents found the situation of being short of information difficult as opposed to a mere 9 per cent who stated that this situation was not difficult for them. Out of the eight situations listed, this issue proved to be the most problematic.

We may conclude that the majority of our respondents agreed that instructors lack items of information crucial for their work, and this situation presents considerable problems. To understand the central role of information, let's overview the mechanism and the purpose of information collection and exchange.

It is based on your curiosity

As the activity of district party committees spread to all possible aspects of economic, social and political life in the district, the gathering of information was also supposed to cover everything. The instructors, through direct personal experiences and connections, or with the help of information reports prepared by local party organisations, had to give an account of everything that was happening in their area – be it market prices, the crowded conditions of daycare centres, the situation of the elderly, traffic problems, the opening of pubs, etc. etc. The instructors were above, or rather beside the law; there were no limits to their search and thirst for information in the field of economic or administrative activities or even personal life:

Now access to information, that includes all sorts of information related to the economy; no changes were made here.

(T.N.)

I can go to the department of culture [of the district council] at any time, look at the plans of the schools, examine the regulations concerning their organisation and activities.

(V.K.)

But it was completely up to the discretion of the individual instructors how they met these requirements, how they gathered and processed all information deemed to be relevant:

There are no data there that you will not receive if you ask for it. Thus it is based on your curiosity: what type of materials you demand, what you pay attention to, what you decide for yourself.

(A.T.)

Instructors had the full right to any items of information; nothing could be hidden from them. On the other hand, it was their duty to know about everything. They could not neglect or withdraw any piece of relevant information; they had to transmit everything. In the words of one of our interviewees: 'No apparatus member has the right to neglect a single item of information. He must report all information – not individually, of course, but in a systematic way' (D.F., secretary). The task is indefinable, overflowing, impossible to accomplish. One just cannot perceive, gather, process and transmit all information. This impossible task is termed and turned into a duty. This explains, in itself, the insatiable hunger for information and the permanent, frustrating feeling of always being short of it.

They ask you how you feel or what is your opinion

At any rate, even if the requirement was the submission of all information, there had to be some guidelines for selection. The main criterion was whether an item of information could be considered 'political', as the task of instructors was restricted to the collection of information that was – at least potentially – political. But the scope of 'politics' in this system was extremely large: it included the maintenance of order; the proper performance of economic or public activities; efficient work, the strive toward better performance; and finally the mood of the population. Information reports thus had to contain all these items together.

Instructors dealt with two different types of information. One was the signalling of specific events and problems, the other the monthly information report, prepared according to a fixed scenario. To start with the latter, the exact order of these reports differed according to district. In some cases, there was a specialised information collator; in others, there was a rotation system where each week a different instructor was charged with the duty of preparing the report. But the major characteristics were the same in all districts.

As the organisation of the party was based on economic units, and was originally closely connected with the planning system, in the earlier period these reports must have contained a huge amount of statistical data. However, our respondents told us that this was a mistake. Proper information reports should not contain statistical data, but should be concerned with the general mood of the population. This view was expressed by a political worker who was the information collator in her district:

> [The secretary or the information collator of the local organisation] comes in or rings me up and tells me briefly what events last week stirred people up, and what types of opinion were formed about these events. ... They ask you how you feel or what your opinion is about this or that.
>
> (I.K.)

Thus, the information report was a 'mood report'. Instructors should not gather dry, paper-tasting data, they must get acquainted with reality itself in its movements, in its changes. They must get beyond mere phenomena, they must open the way toward the real opinions and mood of people. They must uncover the depth of their thoughts or feelings. An information report must include personal experiences, the actual presence of the instructor:

> Yes, so what has he heard – that it was good, people were happy about this, unhappy about that. ... I say information can be nothing but the street and actual conversation. In practice, it is a mood report about what bothers people and what makes them glad.
>
> (G.E., secretary)

Instructors had to be present everywhere, had to keep an eye on everything. Theirs was not a nine-to-five job; the working day was not over even when they had completed their duties within the PC, nor even after returning home from meetings of local organisations that might last until 8 or 9 p.m. Anything could be included in the notion of 'the street and actual conversation'. The instructors were obliged to report anything that they observed anywhere if, from any perspective, it might be considered – at least potentially – political.

I am convinced that it must be from the corridors

But the instructors were not simply external observers. If they had been just 'spies' keeping an eye on everything, their personal knowledge would have been restricted to the events they themselves witnessed. Moreover, according to the well-known Heisenberg principle, most of these experiences would have given a distorted picture, influenced by the 'observer'. They would have remained passive, unable to make in-depth investigations. They needed personal, face-to-face contacts, friends who would help them reach into places and provide them with 'real' information on events they had not experienced:

> The decisive factor is always personal connections.
>
> (T.N.)

> A lot depends on the building up of personal connections. I think it decides a number of things. As obtaining information, real information, is very difficult in general.
>
> (P.G.)

The job of the instructors was well complemented by local activists who had access to areas beyond the reach of the instructor, who could provide detailed, individualised information on the whole of the area. At the time of our study it was thought that the importance of this group could increase, as it was an explicit political intention to move the target of political work from the workplace to the local population:

> Therefore it would be important in the local areas to line up more and more party members from the firms; individuals who know the people over there and who are well known, preferably those who are accepted. It is at least as big a test, working in residential areas, as working at a firm. Because in residential areas they know their neighbours better – at least in the suburban part – they know who beats his wife, who gets drunk every evening, who is keeping his garden in order. Only those people whose way of life is exemplary can act convincingly in political matters.
>
> (D.F., secretary)

Instructors had to appropriate the activists' and local party leaders' detailed knowledge and transmit the important elements to the district leadership. Thus, it is not surprising that political workers almost unanimously considered verbal, personal information to be much more valuable and important than written reports received through official channels:

Primary information, that can only be gained through personal experiences. .... If I have to prepare the information report, I must sincerely admit that much more of our own experiences will be included than what was already written down in the reports.

(M.B.)

A free conversation after a local party meeting, that is much more valuable. One can get much better information than otherwise.

(D.F., secretary)

There are the information collators at local party organisations who must gather the information from the corridors; I am convinced that it must be from the corridors.

(G.E., secretary)

The emphasis on such informal 'corridor talks' is especially surprising in an organisation where the overwhelming part of the time is spent on formal, official meetings or gatherings, on preparing formal reports or other official papers. Let's stop here for a minute and think about the meaning of these 'corridor talks'. These were conversations held by participants of official meetings during the breaks or after the end of the official agenda. What was the rationality behind all this? At first sight, they simply provided an occasion after the much hated official pro-gramme for some real talking. For an external observer, the number of meetings an instructor had to sit through during a regular week was simply unbelievable. Most of their afternoons, sometimes even their mornings, were spent in different meetings. The following quote indicates their extent and also the attitude of political workers: 'In the last year I was willing to participate in only two, at most three, meetings per week' (H.4). This raises a question concerning the reason behind these meetings. The recourse to this method seemed to be persistent:

Q: We have often encountered the statement that the large number of meetings almost blocks actual work.
A: There hasn't been any change in this respect. I am convinced that this is one of our methods of work where we are not able to make any improvement.

(M.B.)

And why not? If we refuse to accept the all-too-easy explanation that official work is just a result of bureaucratisation, then we are left with the hypothesis that the time-consuming custom of meetings does have a functional role of its own. This hypothesis can be supported from two different angles. First, meetings fill the time, keep the staff occupied, do not allow them space, time and the chance to let their minds stray, to be engaged in something else. Meetings can be considered simple and efficient methods of brainwashing, the inculcation into the participants of a mechanical activity and a hierarchical framework in which their freedom of movement is limited; in which even the slightest moves must be made in front of others; in which the order of seats and speeches is determined by protocol; in which hierarchy penetrates the whole time until everybody takes it for granted; in which the constant sound of speeches prevents even mental escape. Regular official meetings are perfect ways of stupefying minds and antagonising colleagues, as there is always resentment against those who attempt to escape these mental tortures and succeed. Meetings largely cover the functions that are, according to Michel Foucault, characteristic of modern prison and the 'carceral network': they subject people to hierarchical observation and limit their movements, thus helping the internalisation of control (Foucault 1979a). The only difference is also telling: while the norms of the prison are isolation and silence in order to direct the individual's attention toward himself, meetings precisely prevent this possibility. Meetings select or rather create a particular type of personality. Not everybody is suited to bear this regular torture.

The second latent function of meetings is related to the fact that it is exactly the common experience of the insupportability of official meetings that opens up participants. Here lies the real meaning of 'corridor talks'. Everybody knows that nothing important is said at official meetings; there protocol and a rosy picture of reality reign. The unlucky victims only wait for a chance to escape and go to the corridor where they may finally have a good chat. That's where the instructors come into the picture when, during these chats, they collect the information they need from the tired members. As if the play was staged, only for the real show to begin after the curtain falls.

All this is, of course, pure speculation. Maybe meetings do not possess any specific hidden function, and are just left-overs from the past. But this statement seems to be somewhat naïve. It can hardly be argued that such a number of meetings ever filled a necessary function. They never realised their manifest function; why is this practice so lasting? No technique of power is ever dysfunctional, but often fulfils a function different from what was claimed.

Thus, in getting information, the 'subjective component', or personal relations played a crucial role. But once an item of information had been collected, the personal role of the instructor was finished: 'They do not want a personal opinion. [The role of the instructor is only] to summarise and to transmit' (I.K.).

This is a completely ambivalent situation

The ideas, thoughts, opinions of the instructor were therefore irrelevant. It was a recurrent topic in our interviews and questionnaires that political workers felt nobody was interested in their views. This statement is surprising for at least two reasons: first, because instructors did possess a great deal of independence in their field work; second, instructors' work made very specific demands on its practitioners:

> I think that only those people who are very sensitive to problems and willing to listen to people should join the apparatus today. Those who pay attention to what is told them, and are also able to summarise and mediate. And they must have a personality, . . . must be attractive.
>
> (J.A.)

How does one explain this ambivalence? Did the work of instructors require independence, or did it keep its performers in personal dependence? Did it require a genuine personality or complete impersonality? The way out of these dilemmas leads not through dialectics, but through the realisation that the wrong question was being posed. The job required both; but in different dimensions. This fact was even realised by one of our interviewees himself:

> Q: How do you perceive it – does an instructor possess
>   independence inside the apparatus? And if he/she does, then to
>   what extent? Where does it appear?
> A: This is a completely ambivalent situation. I think that, on the
>   one hand, his hands are tied too much. Here inside the
>   committee, in the writing of the reports and memos. . . .
>   Outside, in the majority of cases I perceive it as being left alone.
>   There, concerning political work, I am completely on my own.
>
> (G.C.)

But there is more to be seen here than a simple separation of 'dependent' and 'independent' roles. The position of instructors required a peculiar change of face on their part. It was not simply that, in one situation, they had to be independent, while in others they did not. In this form, this statement holds true for most jobs, even existential situations. The grotesque character of this job came from the fact that it required independence and personality exactly where these characteristics were only a means to an end; and, quite 'logically', it denied personal opinion and independence exactly where they should have had their most legitimate place in the realm of public activity: in matters of thinking.

The personality and character of instructors were important because of the help they gave in collecting inside information concerning different areas, information inaccessible otherwise through official channels. Instructors had independence concerning the way they represented the party. Their personality was important in convincing others that they were the 'party', and to 'open up' people. It was not by chance that, when asked about personal characteristics that made them particularly suited to a political career, several respondents mentioned the ability to gain confidence:

> The ability to gain the personal confidence of people.
>
> (T.11)

> I can get the confidence of people.
>
> (L.5)

Here we must emphasise that this trap, where friendship and personal relations were used for spying on people about their day-to-day activities, was closed, as it were, behind the back of the agents, the instructors themselves. It may seem incredibly naïve, but it was made possible by the fact that the personal tone and opinion disappeared in the preparation of the final report. Thus, the instructor perhaps did not become aware that personal information was used in an improper way, as the information passed on became anonymous.

This may explain why personal elements were not encouraged, or were even explicitly prohibited, in information reports. But we still have to account for the other aspect mentioned above: the importance of the instructor's personality and the neglect of personal interpretation. This can be understood by referring to the fact that independent judgement and the ability to observe others were only used as a means of doing the job. The instructor had to be able to 'open up' people, to 'see deeply', to grasp the motives of people behind their behaviour. This process was discussed in detail by one of our interviewees:

> One gets acquainted with a large variety of people. First, with the local leaderships, the secretaries. One must know them personally, and also the motives for their becoming members, for taking on party duties. Then I attempted to extend this beyond the secretaries, to other members of the local leadership. To be acquainted with them, to recognise their motives, whether they have ideas concerning the work of their organisation. For some were not even aware of what they engaged upon, it just happened to them. There were cases like that.
>
> (L.G.)

The personality of the instructor counts only because it gives more than mere opinions heard or experienced. It may provide access to the motives of the individuals covered in the information report. There is a need for 'qualified information', and not for the opinion of a thinking person; the ability to perceive others' thoughts, and not thoughts themselves. This ability was also mentioned in the questionnaires: 'I know to some extent the inner moving forces of individuals or groups' (T.7.).

THE MECHANISM OF INFORMATION DISTORTION

These results convinced us that it would be a mistake to explain the structure and the working of the party apparatus by referring to a general trend of 'bureaucratisation'. In formal, bureaucratic organis-ations, personal relations are almost always dysfunctional, as they are incompatible with formal, rational rules. Such an organisation may accept, with a benevolent nod, such obstacles to efficiency as signs of an inherent human fallibility. But the idea of grounding the whole organisation on a network of personal relations is inconceivable in this framework. However, instructors relied on exactly such personal connections in collecting 'real' information. Their whole attitude can be characterised by a distrust of and disgust with all sorts of paperwork, all elements of a formal bureaucracy: 'I consider the most important thing to do – and profess that it must be followed – is to talk. From paper – that information smells of paper' (T.N.). This statement would have no meaning for a true bureaucrat. Thus, we cannot judge this whole mechanism and its breakdowns from the perspective of 'bureaucracy' or 'bureaucratisation'. Instead of offering *a priori* a more 'objective' method of evaluation, let's follow the ways of information distortion, according to the logic peculiar to the process.

Only in a limited circle

The fact that the party apparatus collected information mostly through personal relations could be explained only by assuming an alien, hostile environment, where the only possible road lies through personally trusting few people. But this method carries in itself the possibility of distortion on its own.

First, the time and resources of instructors were limited. One instructor could establish personal relations with only a limited number of people. The collection of information is a tiresome business, it has high 'fixed costs'. Real information cannot be collected in the way politicians skip through a factory, making some small talk with 'simple people'. It takes a lot of time to build up connections, to 'gain confidence'. The potential sources of real information are therefore restricted to a small sample:

> The apparatus moves only in a small circle. Even those that attempt to collect information from a wide area. . . . In a given company an instructor can establish connections with 5–8–10 people at most, even over a number of years. This in itself provides a considerable filtering. . . . The members of this circle are motivated by the same interests and work by the same methods as the apparatus itself. . . . Views and ideas that exist within society but fall outside the political system are as a matter of course excluded from our horizon. They have no impact on decisions made here.
>
> (T.C.)

> The fact is that only the information you look after is yours; if you acquire that information, then you'll be informed. More or less. Your own connections, your own acquaintances mostly define whom you can address if you need something. . . . So [information] is, after all, linked to you personally.
>
> (A.T.)

> Well, as for information from below, that depends on how [the instructor] fulfils his role. How much time does he spend outside, what is his personal relation with the party secretary of a given organisation? He doesn't really go down to levels below that. Thus, he knows the party secretary or the leadership there, and, say, the top level of the state administration. But he rarely goes any further.
>
> (J.A.)

The above quotations also show that there was something more than personal availability involved here: the number and character of the possible sources of information were limited in advance by the mechanism. Sometimes it did not even occur to political workers that they were relying upon a very narrow range of opinions:

> It was based on a very inclusive opinion poll. For example, in the first stage the committee asked the opinion of 105 people. . . . Now these people, they are the elected members of the district bodies, then the leaders, those who play an important part in the political life of the district, like the deputy heads of the district council, the managers of larger firms, the heads of major cooperatives, party secretaries, from

all these circles, well, from most circles, like teachers, leading teachers, so as to have opinions from all strata.

(B.C., secretary)

Our interviewee was not bothered that those listed could not claim to represent the population of the district as, for example, manual workers were completely missing, which is at least surprising in the case of the 'party of the working class'. What then was the purpose of this enormous apparatus for the collection of information?

The first part of the answer is fairly obvious. Even if the over-whelming majority of the data collected was worthless, there would still be some bits and pieces that would make the trouble worth while. The second part takes us beyond the issue of information. It may well be that the main target of the regular machinery of information collection was not information itself, but the inculcation of a feeling in the population that all their steps were being followed, that they were 'being taken care of'. One of our interviewees, on the basis of a concrete case, stated this as the explicit goal of the activity of district PCs:

One of our problems is that here, in our district, a large number of small businesses have been opened recently; and not only here, but in the whole country. And they are without any sort of political direction. Now I'm not talking about direct control, but knowing about the organisations, their problems, how they think about certain things. If we claim that small businesses must be supported, then we should know something about their way of thinking, their interests. We should make them feel that they are being taken care of.

(D.F., secretary)

This example also shows how district PCs attempted to extend their supervision over everything that emerged outside their scope. It did not even occur to our respondent that this 'caring' involved a very specific technique of power and that the targets of this intervention might not have desired this sort of 'attention'.

Significant half-words are left out

But let's return to the steps of the mechanism of information distortion. The next problem may have occurred within the district PCs. Let's review what happened within with the information collected:

Some one to two hundred items [of information] arrive here and they must be summarised somehow. This is the job of the apparatchik who happens to be charged with the task ... or there is a little 'summarising brigade' that does it according to its own taste; leaves this out or includes that. . . . Thus it may happen even – I must add – with the best will that some emphases, half-words, but significant half-words, are left out, until, at the eighteenth stage it arrives at the point where a nationwide decision would be necessary.

(G.E., secretary)

There is nothing peculiar about the fact that some information is distorted when it is compressed. But it is more interesting that this whole process mixed together the information gained through personal contact and thus enveloped in anonymity those opinions or suggestions that were deliberately signed. All 'bottom up' information had to go through the apparatus. This is one of the reasons why the activity of the instructor was so crucial: 'Since I transmit information in all directions . . . I am thus the first filter that can distort the information' (M.B.). All items of information, all personal opinions, were cut up, reshaped, put into other words, summed up. In this way, they lost all their personal character within the apparatus as soon as they entered this impersonal, dry procedure. Therefore it was impossible for a sender ever to receive a personal answer to his or her question. After a time, this made even the most energetic activist cut down on his enthusiasm. Hence the recurrent problem of 'motivating' members, of making them believe that what they say did matter:

The main thing is to do the spoken political work in everyday talks well, and to maintain the belief – on the one hand in party members, on the other not only in them – that yes, it really is worth while for everybody to speak his mind, because it will be summed up somewhere, and it will be taken into account.

(D.F., secretary)

For the time being, we are very happy if somebody puts in a word in a council or district meeting; no matter what he says, just that he says something.

(B.C., secretary)

This helps us to understand another recurrent topic, that the local party organisations do not want to use their independence. The point here is not that 'earlier' independence was not even supported by the apparatus. But what was the point of striving for independence if one knew that, even if opinions were expressed, they would only be swallowed up by an all-encompassing information machine and the sender would never know anything about the fate of his question? The only certain thing was that, at the end of the year, it would all be wasted:

Well, whatever was said in the local meeting, the speeches, whatever was included in the minutes of the meetings, that goes into a file, and at the end of the year, we'll send it to the disposal unit and that's it. Whatever you consider to be interesting, you may retain; but you have already collected that at the meeting, haven't you? . . . It is very rare that an information report sums up what has really happened at the meeting. In any case, it is such a compressed summary that it really doesn't even reflect what has happened there.

(A.T.)

Another problem was caused by the fact that even information gained by instructors may not have reached a higher level; it could have been stranded within the apparatus.

They prefer to hear what they themselves think

Any personal elements (demands, questions or opinions) contained in information reports were cut out as, for the higher organs, only averages, trends, masses of observations were interesting. The only exceptions were anonymous denunciations. An individual problem aroused the interest of a district PC only if direct responsibility or culpability could be linked to it.

But it did not mean that there were no expectations 'from above' concerning the reports. The district leadership had definite views about the situation, the opinion and mood in the area. It refused to hear anything else, was not even interested in differing opinions. The leadership wished to hear the 'whole truth'; that's why they sent out a flock of instructors who mobilised all their ability to convince and all their personal contacts to discover 'reality'. But leaders were only interested in the 'truth' in so far as it was identical with their own views:

Q: In all, to what extent does the leadership expect information from the instructors?

A: They do expect it, but they prefer to hear what they themselves think and believe on the issues. They really don't like it if other opinions get voiced.

(G.D.)

Four years ago, when we made our [sociological] survey, we often got . . . 'we are not interested in what they think, but how we judge the situation'.

(A.L.)

In regular information reports double talk developed. Leaders preferred to hear what they expected, and, even if members had given a detailed account of their worries, this would have reached the decision-makers only via a number of stages, if ever. Why bother, then, with the presentation of truth at all? Thus, by the nature of the mechanism, monthly information reports painted a distorted, rosy picture of reality and were not taken seriously by the instructors themselves:

> I only use the information reports to check up on their memory, to see whether the topics that were covered during the month in our different meetings have been included. And it is also useful to have a look at the courage of the leaders of an organisation, to see whether they dare to put everything down as it happened, in real life. This written information report, due to its form, and especially because of its clumsiness, does not possess much validity.
>
> (M.B.)

The rosy shades of information reports sometimes really prevented the leadership from getting access to certain information, as the mechanism worked in this way even if, by chance, leaders preferred the truth:

> I have an interesting story about it. Comrade X [he was a member of the Politburo at that time] was out here last year on a visit.... That was the time of the new regulations concerning pensions; there was a big public debate about it, and we reported and indicated that here and there it had been met with great hostility. And comrade X asked, 'Why have I not heard about this?' We said we didn't know as we had put it down in our information report. The comrade from the Budapest PC was here too. Well then? 'We also put it down.' Now here is the beauty, that the formal channels [have limited value.]
>
> (G.E., secretary)

The instructor could only believe in what he himself experienced, or what was reported by reliable sources, but it was not at all certain that these experiences would reach those responsible for making decisions. Here the question of regular information reports was linked with that of the indication of individual problems. If the problem of distortion was ever present even in the general information reports, it was all the more so for specific problems. The principle is clear: the instructors must immediately report all troubles experienced in their area. They have no right either to hide any information, or to take operative decisions about any questions, except for methodological–administrative ones. They have to report everything, and then wait for the superiors to take charge.

The practice was different. The situation was fairly similar to the requirements of a formal disciplinary educational system: the demands could not be met, as they were incompatible with the normal business of day-to-day life. But the basic point was not to meet requirements – everybody knows that it would be impossible – but to create a permanent feeling of guilt in the governed in order to make their control easier.

It is a nuisance if something is not in order

The PC evaluated the instructors' work according to its own logic. Since the instructors' job was to prevent conflicts that represented a waste of resources and slackening of work discipline, any trouble indicated that the instructors had failed to perform their duties:

> It is a nuisance if something is not in order. You are employed to keep order, so why are you disturbing the leadership with troubles you have in your area? ... It paints a picture of you as one who 'cannot keep order in his area'.
>
> (J.A.)

> It has often happened that 'something is fishy about you, if this is the case'; this can work against you.
>
> (G.E., secretary)

The whole issue can be summed up by the following remarks:

> Q: May I say that, as the leadership is restrictive as regards information downwards, the apparatus keeps back information from the leadership?
>
> A: Yes, but this is not a fault of apparatus members. It is not that the apparatus hides information. But there is a principle at work here: they 'cut off the head of the messenger who brings bad news'. So it is in one's own interest not to bring any bad news about the area. As – and this is the catch 22 – it is me, the reporter of bad news, who is personally responsible for everything going on in the area under my instruction. ... So in this situation it is very unlikely that the apparatus would present correct information.
>
> (G.D.)

The whole mechanism for information collection is moving in a bizarre circle. In the background here, as elsewhere, is the picture of the internal enemy, the 'alien inside' who is present everywhere. There is a need for the collection of specific information, provided by tested comrades, which can be trusted. If 'they', the 'aliens', the 'non-members' talk of problems, that's a lie, a conspiracy, sabotage. But even in the case of instructors there are two problems concerning the transmission of accurate inform- ation. First, their primary job is to maintain order; any trouble reported is a living proof that they have failed to perform their duties. Second, the shadow of bad news can fall upon the messenger and eventually may discredit him. The mechanism simply does not tolerate bad news, cannot accept a statement that anything anywhere is seriously out of order. It neglects the problem, denies its existence, up to the point where, after a time, even appearances cannot be kept up:

> So it is absolutely ridiculous. We sit here day after day, and in factory Y the situation is getting ready for a strike. They will be perfectly right if they strike. We have debated and discussed for two weeks among my colleagues whether, perhaps, we should think about what will happen if the Ministry or whoever won't make the decision. We should think about whom to talk to, what to say, in what direction to convince the workers to move, etc. Or should we encourage them to strike, because, perhaps after all, that may be the best way to force somebody to make the decision. We are told that this must not be decided at the district level, but we should prepare the political solution and help those outside. Now we are waiting until there is a really huge scandal, and then everybody will run up and down.
>
> (J.A.)

But things have not yet arrived at that point – at least, not as of September 1988: 'Our situation is not bad enough yet, so these self-constraints may work' (J.A.). And when it became much worse than it could ever have been imagined by the instructors, the reaction of the party, as we all know now, proved to be quite surprising.

In all this, there is more involved than the question of information. We have seen an example of the shifting upward of decisions, which is helped by the fact that there is no obligation to make decisions. The unpleasant may be transferred 'above'.

THE DOWNWARD TRANSFER OF INFORMATION

Up to this point, we have only dealt with a one-way, upward flow of inform- ation, the central task of instructors. But they also passed information downward. These items of information were of a different order. They were not related to the actual situation of the area, were not responses to problems signalled from below. Such an information flow was simply missing from the mechanism; the instructor had no interest in that at all: 'This example illustrates that information passed to the top was up to date. This was in our best interest. It is not true as regards the other direction' (M.B.).

Only for the ear of party members

The downward flow of information was not concerned with the daily life of the area. On the contrary, with a time lag, it covered everything that had happened 'elsewhere'. This information can be divided into two groups. The first is a substitute for the missing horizontal ties. In its ideal typical way the mechanism assumes that there are no horizontal information streams within the population outside formal channels. Among the latter, the party plays a special role. It provides the validation for all sorts of information. It is the only legitimate information source. Any other message is suspect and may be alien propaganda. Trust, duty and privilege are inseparably mixed together:

> And the meaning of an instructor's work is also given by – and here we have a scarcity – the provision to party organisations of special instructions and information that are only for the ear of party members, that only address members. Or at least it is better that they should know first.

> (A.T.)

These items of information may refer to simple work experiences, as connections between firms are also provided by the instructor, or to distant events of the district, the city or the country. As long as other sources of information are closed or limited, the need for such information is tremendous. The break-up of existing horizontal ties that was realised in Hungary following the Western model of atomisation but surpassing it in its zeal, together with control over the remaining sources, created a pathological, exaggerated, ever increasing demand for all sorts of information and gossip. On the one hand, all meetings became public demonstrations of procrastination, good only for eliminating the will to participate in public activities and to divert attention. On the other, the only interesting point of meetings became the unhealthy practice of gossiping, where listeners looked upon the 'well- informed man' who appreciated his audience enough to give them a few hints. This ugly and disgusting social scene became so common in our time that it pervaded every element of common activity. Lately it involved not only official meetings, but unofficial workplace get-togethers, parties or even the meetings of friends. In an ever growing circle, the sole topics of discussion were complaints about the 'mood of the public' ('negative information report'), and the latest political gossip (the 'elimination of information shortage'). Needless to say, the same can be said about the atmosphere and style of discussions within the new organisations.

All this was only reinforced by the other type of 'information from above', that which gave clues about the state of struggles within the leadership, the mood of top leaders, the direction of possible changes. As the overwhelming majority of the population did not have even a remote chance of participating in these decisions, they clung to any item of information that may have helped them at least to have a peek behind the curtains, to form their strategies for the future. The most natural, deepest personal concerns were thus mingled with or abused by an anonymous political process promoting irresponsibility.

This peculiar stream of information played a particular role in the activity of both district PCs and instructors. For the former, it was an essential method of keeping the key men of the area firmly under its grip. One of our interviews shed a light on this process through a concrete example, the case of small businesses: 'They need information that they cannot get in any other way, for instance, about political plans concerning the next period – to get something in advance' (D.F., secretary).

It is also a moral obligation, as we always ask

Instructors proceeded in a similar way. Here, as elsewhere, they were in a tightly closed trap. Without any concrete outside help, they had to get information from the economic units and public institutions. The only way to perform their job lay through personal connections, where friendship and the transfer of information, interest and sympathy were inseparably mingled together. No matter what the actual situation was in an individual case – sincere friendship and honest conviction or the cynical pursuit of self- or vested interest – the result was the same: the instructor had to trade information for information. In order to be able to accomplish the task of the upward transfer of information, they had to possess valuable information of their own. Thus we have to qualify the statement quoted earlier that instructors had no interest in the downward information stream: in this (and only this) sense, they did have a basic interest in passing information downward:

Q: How does [the downward transfer of information] work?
A: Haphazardly. We really should be up to date on information concerning changes in economic regulations. Simply because it is also a moral obligation, as we are always asking the firms for information, from directors or party organisations, whatever. Tell us your opinion about this, make a statement about that, leave this or that; and we are unable to reciprocate with

anything. It would be a very good recompense if we possessed information. If we learned about changes even before the ordinance was issued, not at the last minute, we could warn our chosen firms: 'Hey man, pay attention to this, because – '.

(G.C.)

For this, instructors needed to be provided with information. But they complained that it was not at all assured. The information flow was also limited within the apparatus. A couple of years ago, it was already easier to get access to restricted information at a firm than within the apparatus:

> If you are able to obtain whatever you are allowed to have access to, then you will be informed. But it is 90 per cent up to you.
> Q: The mechanism, that –?
> A: Look, the mechanism itself – it seems to me as if we are trying to impede this. For example, I could read a limited circulation paper more easily when I was working as a manager at a firm than here as a political worker. So I need more time and effort to look after these information sources, though any economic manager may order and read these, as, after all, they are not that secret. When I asked for something here, they asked whether they were allowed to let me have it. . . . 'O. K., you can have it, but bring it back immediately, or read it inside.'
>
> (A.T.)

Even 'inside' the house, the same bargaining process was at work as 'outside'; perhaps secretaries gave more information to instructors they favoured? One thing seems certain: it was a recurrent topic in our interviews that personal relations with the direct boss, the secretary, had a major impact on the instructor's access to information. Where this connection was strained, apparatus members felt that the leadership did not support them in their work, that they did not get information badly needed in order to perform their job.

We lag behind events

This problem concerning information scarcity was lately much aggravated from the perspective of the instructors by the openness of the media. Their daily work became almost unmanageable by reason of the fact that people were simply receiving more or less up-to-date information from newspapers. Previously, it was sufficient for the instructors to let out slowly, drop by drop, bits of information acquired.

Now it could happen that members were better informed than the instructors themselves. The commonplace sentence about the party's 'lagging behind' events probably also referred to this phenomenon:

> Now we lag behind events, as people already have the information. Earlier the problem was that we didn't know the facts, not in time. Now we get information, but we have nothing to say. Public opinion has already been influenced by the media.
>
> (P.G.)

The above sentences also indicate that, given the claim about the omniscience of the party, the instructors, representatives of the 'party', could not afford not to know about anything. Earlier, each element of printed information became sacred as access was only permitted under supervision, and the number of printed information sources was limited. Now, the requirement that instructors should read and know everything became an impossible one to meet. This situation has again close equivalents in the formal education system where the earlier myth of the omniscience of teachers, the very base of their authority, became untenable.

With an open media a key bastion of the bargaining process so necessary for the exercise of power by instructors, the monopoly of information, was destroyed.

Our study suggests the following ideal-typical model for the circulation of information within the apparatus:

1 The breakdown or closing of all information streams. All information becomes secret, closed, unattainable. Nobody should possess information about anything, the role of the press is not to print facts, but to motivate. At the same time, all available information should be collected and directed toward the local PCs.
2 The PCs gather and evaluate all information and slowly recirculate some bits and pieces. This happens according to a precise scenario, where the downward information stream must be abundantly countered in each step by information that may prove valuable 'above', at the top. Through monopolising information, the party creates an artificial scarcity that makes possible a peculiar system of compensations and rewards, where information functions as a 'general equivalent', replacing money.
3 The basic result of all this is a pathological hunger for information. The secrecy, the censorship and omissions fail to achieve the desired results. Quite the contrary, they only multiply interest in secret,

hidden pieces of information. For centuries, all sorts of censorship aimed at the elimination of texts and acts that were deemed dangerous and evil; and over the same period the consequence was the emergence of a popular view that, if something is hidden and forbidden, it must be true or at least interesting. This does not mean that censorship has, in the final count, no significant or lasting effect. At the moment individuals voluntarily follow the opposite strategy, they become caught in a trap. They will consider the searching out, accumulation and transmission of information as a crucial part of existence; conversation will be transformed into 'information gossiping' (i.e. gossiping about aliens as opposed to the traditional forms of gossiping about acquaintances). Perhaps in this way an unconscious power strategy attains its end for it leads to the victory of a peculiar and specifically intellectual world-view: a society where communication as the exchange of information and judgements becomes the ideal form of common human activity.

4 With the break-up of the information monopoly, with the openness of communication systems, grit fell into the machinery. The information-bargaining process has broken down as people often obtain information before the instructor himself. But all this may have come too late: the pathological thirst for information has already taken root in the population; it has become a part of our existence, penetrated and impregnated us, and even today successfully distances us from our own lives, prevents us from living it, turns all our efforts and activities not toward creative, imaginative, thoughtful public activity, but toward the mere satisfaction of this information fever.

THE INFORMATION SOCIETY IN EAST AND WEST: A COMPARISON

Such an extensive use of information collection and processing in the daily management of social and economic activities may well lead one to conjure up the image of an 'information society' with respect to bolshevik-type party-states, but all this seems to lie light years away from the 'information society' based on recent revolutionary changes in communication and information technology. The local party committees, as we were surprised to learn, used hardly any of these modern tools that were widely available in the period of our research in Hungary. At that time, party committees still exercised considerable control over local schools and companies. Yet, the latter were often well equipped with computers and video-recorders, some acquired with the help of the local party committee, but within the party there was a dearth of modern technology. In one committee, we were told that they had just received a computer and would use it to get information from randomly chosen individuals in a given factory. In another building, we found a single video-recorder in a large room, used sometimes to project propaganda films.

There are other important differences in the treatment of information in the two areas. In the 'information society', information is treated as a commodity, integrated into the laws of the marketplace. In party-states, instead of becoming a commodity like others, information became the general standard of value. In the 'information society', the emphasis is on the general and easy availability of information.[3] In communist systems, it was the scarcity of information that served a positive function.

Nevertheless, this paper argues that there are considerable similarities between the world the party apparatus was trying to establish and what proponents of the 'information society' are so keen on heralding and promoting. In order to explain this stance, let's first have a look at the literature on the 'information society'.

The idea of an 'information society', together with the related concept of an 'information economy' and concerns about the role of information technology and the transition to a 'service economy', appeared around the end of the 1970s (Porat 1977, Martin 1978, Masuda 1981, Gershuny and Miles 1983). It replaced the idea of the 'post-industrial society' that was popular in the early seventies.[4] There was an immediate burgeoning of conferences and publications about this new fad (Bjørn-Andersen *et al.* 1982 and Sweeney 1982). And the interest seems not to have died out even today; as recently as 1988 at least three different books were published under the identical title of *The Information Society* (Martin 1988, Lyon 1988 and Katz 1988). Most of these books and articles heralded a new revolution, comparable only to the agricultural and industrial revolutions of the past, and stressed that recent developments in information and communication technology could bring about the realisation of the ancient dream of affluence and peace for all mankind.

However, almost since the start, a whole range of sceptical views appeared, taking issue with some of the claims of the new panacea. Some argued that new technologies would make a centralised and bureaucratic control of individuals possible, destroying privacy, thus leading to a realisation of Orwell's nightmare (Rose 1983 and Wicklein 1981). Others called attention to the fact that the benefits of new technologies would not be spread evenly to all strata of the population, but would reinforce social differences, and might lead to the erosion of the middle classes (Mosco and Wasko 1988, and Schiller 1981). In a radical form, sceptics claimed that the whole development of information and communication technologies was promoted by the military establishment or large corporations; behind the smoke of the bright future, we may discern the establishment of a new regime of exploitation (Webster and Robins 1986, and Schiller 1983). Still others called for a humanist critique of technology, by drawing a line between the good and bad uses of the new techniques (Lyon 1988). To sum up, one may say that the standard arguments voiced against industrial society, capitalism and the state were reproduced, only to be directed this time against the 'information society'.

One may well wonder whether these objections pay due respect to the specific characteristics of the would-be 'information society'. Is it an intellectually acceptable approach to say that the 'information society' is just a new trick to hide the power of capital? Can we be satisfied with raising the spectre of all-powerful centralised power, and trusting the 'free market' to eliminate this threat? Can we rely upon the redeployment of a humanist critique, when the most uncompromising observers of our world (Machiavelli, Marx, Nietzsche, Freud) have asserted for centuries that this approach is powerless against and misleading concerning the basic dangers of the modern world? We would argue that a combination of the results obtained by our empirical investigation and the use of the tools developed by Michel Foucault may provide a novel perspective.

This would not be the first attempt to use the works of Foucault for an analysis of power in the age of information. Marike Finlay and Marc Poster both attempted to do so in the past (Poster 1984 and Finlay, 1987a, 1987b). However, the approach in this book is different from and critical of theirs. Marc Poster proposes the concept 'mode of information' as a substitute for the Marxian 'mode of production'. But this analysis merely represents an attempt to brush up the standard Marxist discourse, to make a few rather cosmetic changes, instead of using the tools developed by Foucault for the establishment of new thinking about the problems to be faced in the 'information society'. The same thing can be said of the work of Finlay, who uses Bentham's 'Panopticon', as rediscovered by Foucault, as the model of power exercised with the help of information technology. Here we are left with the impression of reading an at once very radical Marxist and liberal critique, when the major goal of Foucault was to get beyond the insights provided by these perspectives into the relation between power, daily existence and subjectivity in modern society.

The objection of most critical approaches to the idea of the 'information society' is that it will eventually fail to deliver its promises. This is clearly voiced by David Lyon, who states that 'the kinds of vision conjured up by the information society phrase are often too good to be true' (Lyon 1988: vii). We would argue the opposite. The worst elements of this complex of ideas are not that they will not be realised, but that they are so close to becoming reality. The problem is not that they are so far from our cherished utopias and humanist beliefs, but that they represent a fulfilment of these very dreams on a frightening scale. The only possible way of critical thinking is to tackle this question head on. Instead of reactivating the old critical discourses against the new project of the 'information society', the latter should be used to raise objections concerning the very validity of these at once critical and programmatic discourses.

Let's start our analysis with two standard elements of the accounts. On the one hand, in the 'information society', the whole society or the whole world will supposedly be wired up, linked together, to form a whole. All gaps and dark spots will be erased, the world will become transparent.[5] Information and communication will be the glue that holds the whole society together.[6] In the writings of Marshall McLuhan, who is called an important precursor of the 'information society' (see J.L. Salvaggio 1983: 1), the 'global village' is defined, an idea that the alienation and the loss of immediacy that accompanied industrial societies will be eliminated in post-industrial society, where all the conveniences of frequent contacts and small communities would be available to everyone, on a large scale. On the other hand, there are firm statements that easily accessible information will help to increase choices and possibilities, would help to realise one's self. Thus, according to Sweeney, 'Information enables an individual, a community or an organisation to solve its own problems, reach its own solutions, decide for itself' (Sweeney 1982: v). And according to Martin, 'information is that which adds to our awareness or understanding of some topic, problem or event', and later that 'information is an ingredient common to all areas of human endeavour, be they day-to-day affairs of business or matters of life and death' (Martin 1988: 1, 15).

However, the idea that a joint realisation and perfect fitting of the above goals is possible involves serious misunderstandings. Perfect aware- ness, consciousness and self-realisation in a completely wired up society may involve the realisation of a dream, and have a lot in common with the politico-economic project of modern society. But, according to another meaning of modernity, it represents an ignorant betrayal of the very possibilities that can be counted among the most important aspects of modernity.

Modernity as an attitude is based on a dilemma (see Foucault 1984a, 1986b, 1988c). It assigns a high value to free thought leading to free action. The meaning of thought here is different from consciousness and goal-oriented rationality. It is interpreted as the ability to overcome previous beliefs and prejudices, and to withstand the existential consequences of these changes as well, going beyond swapping one set of ideologies and guiding principles for another. Thought in this sense is not only oriented toward objects (in the sense of problem solving), but also toward the subject, questioning assumptions, prejudices and fixed beliefs. It involves constant work upon ourselves, with only one *a priori* fixed conviction: there is no final, given aim for the process of thinking, there can never be the attainment of a 'final' truth, where there would no longer be a need for questioning oriented toward the subject of knowledge, where thinking can finally be laid to rest.

This attitude of modernity is not restricted to thinking in the abstract sense, but involves changes in the 'real' as well. Changes in thinking and behaviour are interrelated, not only from the perspective of the 'philo-sopher', but also for ordinary men. Freedom of thought as the basic value of modernity is correlated with belief in the freedom of action and behaviour; a freedom that does not equate to irresponsibility, but which points well beyond the freedom of choice available in the market-place; a freedom which always leaves open the possibility of 'exit' from one's given frame of existence, once this becomes intolerable. This is the meaning of freedom that is so relevant in Eastern Europe, where one of the most crucial elements of the past regime was the denial of this freedom, whether it meant the freedom to change a field of study, a work-place, or a country of residence. The fact that the Berlin Wall was brought down by an invasion of 'dissidents', and that the issue of access to foreign countries was such a crucial issue for the people there, should not be dismis-sed as mere consumer tourism – though, in a different sense, the party did implant consumerism in the social body, by the same strategy of closure.

No matter how basic this correlative freedom of thinking, acting and behaving is for us in modern society, it does involve a serious loss: the loss of community, immediacy, repeated patterns of existence that gave consistency and stability to 'traditional' societies, but that are also basic for any meaningful human existence. The possibility of freedom as exit implies the possibility of alienation. They are facets of the same coin; they cannot be separated, just as power and knowledge are also linked together. The balancing of the two is a task everybody has to do for himself or herself.

Now projects such as the 'information society', the 'global village', 'post-industrial society' and the like are dangerous because they deny the very existence of the above dilemma. They imply that, by the miracle of technology, we can have both: freedom, individuality and self-realisation on the one hand, and immediacy and intimacy of community on the other. And it is exactly at this point that the dreams of bolsheviks in the early twentieth century and of technocrats in the late twentieth century are dangerously close, not only in their common messianistic beliefs in a utopian society, and in the arrogance of their assertions concerning the 'transformation' of society and conditions of existence of others, but also in the very assumptions concerning 'utopia': the emphasis laid on linking all members of society, the value placed upon complete transparency, the concerns with the 'glue' and 'cement' of society, and, most important of all, their assertion about the joint realisation of individuality and community.[7]

Hence it is that critical perspectives along the lines of Marxist analysis or Orwellian negative utopia are misleading, because they present a partial view. They take existing or possible abuses and restrict the problems presented by the 'information society' to these issues, or claim that it is these questions that lie at the heart of the problem. And it is at this point that the perspective acquired from Eastern Europe, together with the empirical analysis of information management in the bolshevik-type party-state, may provide some insights. Diabolic though the whole mechanism looks, it should not be mistaken for an illustration of an Orwellian world, a complement to an all-powerful secret police. The party did not simply collect information on potential political enemies, and was not just trying to intimidate the population. The whole ritual had very precise positive functions. First, the goal was to distort the perspective of each and every individual. It involved a systematic effort to turn attention away from the concerns of daily life, issues that were close to and important for people, to make them accept that they could have no control over these issues, and to encourage in them curiosity about distant and otherwise irrelevant, meaningless events, over which they could have no influence anyway. Thus, we have a systematic attempt here to make the distant seem close and the close distant.

Second, the party created the image of being present everywhere, of knowing about everything; it attempted to create a belief in the population that nothing they did could escape the grip of the party. In one sense, this can well be termed a totalitarian project. But, in another, this question goes beyond repression. First, this ever present supervision did represent a very real 'linking' of society. In its ideal-typical form, in this system it was the political instructors who personally linked society together, and it was the information they collected and disseminated that made this connection possible. Thus, the function of information in the party-state was the exact twin of the function of money in a free-market society in this deeper sense as well. Second, the psychological consequences of being under supervision do not pass away quickly. The feeling of being supervised impresses this linking on the mind of individuals.

Finally, the most important of these lasting impacts may concern the relation of the individual toward himself or herself. Being supervised means, on the one hand, an attempt to persuade one to behave according to certain expectations. One may accept these requirements, or may fight against them. In this case, there is a continuous internal struggle, an attempt to preserve the self, an increased awareness and consciousness concerning all elements of behaviour; a conviction that one must always behave perfectly and without reproach – if not according to the requirements of the norm, then against them. Supervision thus raises the level of consciousness well beyond the limit of what can be judged healthy; closes the individual into himself, leaves no space for relaxation, permits no attitude or behaviour to remain unchecked. There is no need to evoke the works of Nietzsche, Freud or Lacan to perceive that such a heightened level of awareness is unhealthy, as it purges all active instincts, all innovative energies from the individual. Once one adapts all one's behaviour to a fixed set of rules, be it given by or set up against the prescriptions of a religion, a party or a philosophical school, one loses all ability to do something new. Instead of becoming the puppet of the party, one becomes the puppet of one's own past convictions. Thus, when all actions are governed by conscious thinking, one lacks the most important element of thought: the ability to confront one's own acts critically, and therefore to change. A perfectly conscious man can no longer stand outside himself, and view his own acts critically. He becomes a prisoner of his own mind.

Thus, the function and the lasting effects of information management by bolshevik-type party states go well beyond the attempt to infiltrate the population and intimidate political opponents. Ultimately, they involve the construction of different forms of individuality: on the one hand, according to the nature of the project, the construction of *Homo sovieticus*, an individual who has an instinct to realise immediately what is expected of him, but who is living in a constant state of fear that he might have done something wrong; and, on the other hand, the construction of *Homo anti-sovieticus*, who will act in every possible way against these expectations, but whose behaviour is nevertheless thoroughly conditioned by the same concerns, and who finally becomes completely closed into himself, being unable to change. Being confronted with a threatening and unacceptable power for such a long time, he has lost the ability to conceive of the fact that he may not be right over some questions.

These types of attitudes, no matter how different they are, share something: they are both particularly well suited for the 'information society' project, the idea of a completely wired society, where everybody is emitting and receiving signals, and governs his or her behaviour and dreams according to these impulses, fully in line with the rules of the market. However, this is only part of the picture; the structuralist view, if one likes. It must be complemented with a phenomenological perspective. The members of the future 'information society' would not merely be the puppets of external signals; that approach would not lead us beyond Orwell. But they would construct their very consciousness in line with the rules of the game. The signals mentioned extend to awareness of one's own personal drives and desires, innermost thoughts and dreams that would all be used to construct the 'total personality'. The 'wired society', then, would provide everybody with the opportunity to pick out those instances from the stock of available possibilities that would best fulfil all possible 'needs', with the understanding that the individual obviously has to contribute to the increase of the available stock of possibilities by contributing his or her resources to the satisfaction of the dreams and needs of others. The nightmare-dream of the 'information society' cannot be attacked from the humanist perspective of phenomenology. In the language of Foucault, objectifying and subjectifying techniques of power form a coherent whole.

In a number of points, the bolshevik utopia of transforming man and society, the technocratic dreams about the 'global village' and the 'information society', and the neo-liberal belief that the free market can be used to govern all aspects of human and social behaviour, including education, local government, even law and family life, are dangerously close in a number of areas, building upon each other rather than being opposites.

7 The specificities of the instructor's work

The obligations were defined in such a way that nobody could be innocent.
(Géza Ottlik, *School at the Border*, 1959)

The job of the instructor was, on the one hand, to embody the 'party', to represent personally the party line at the local level; on the other hand, to be the nexus for the collection and circulation of information. The instructor thus occupied a position of considerable power. But the way this power was exercised required of the instructors very special qualities, both in terms of personal characteristics and existential situation. These were instrumental in fulfilling their work. But, as we will see, these characteristics also had a key role, although in different ways, in bringing about the final demise.

SPECIFIC PROPERTIES

The power exercised by instructors had two quite different targets, reflecting a manichean image of a world divided into 'good' and 'evil', 'us' and 'them'. The instructors certainly exercised power in a traditional sense, using constraint and violence against 'them', the 'others', the 'enemies' – but even here their task had a broader dimension. Their power was not just the power of the conqueror nor was it based primarily on an inner coherence or the integrity given by group consciousness. It claimed nothing less than to represent the universal cause of civilisation and 'truth'; the true cause. Thus, from the outset, an intimate collusion was established between power, truth and ethics.

This link cannot be explained by a simple reference to ideology or cynicism.[1] No power may be exercised without risks and resistances. A type of power based solely on repression and violence reigns as if astride a volcano, expending all its energies on preserving its domination and avoiding any eruptions. However, any power that strives for legitimacy, whether honestly or cynically, also falls into a trap. It may well be true that the most beautiful idea becomes a tool for ideological manipulation once it gains ascendancy. But even the most cynical power lays its own trap, prepares for the moment when its promises will have to be accounted for. To study the rationality behind the concrete exercise of power is necessarily to disregard whether the original intentions were honourable or manipulative.

The basic task of the instructor was to connect the party leadership and members. The fulfilment of this task entailed the exercise of power, but this power in turn would only work efficiently and be accepted as legitimate if it somehow represented 'truth' or 'justice' for that circle, both among the members and the 'others', that accepts the truth of power, and is convinced of its necessity. The issue of the truthfulness of power is a trap itself. It leads to the claim that the 'truth' of power can be evaluated, whether positively or negatively; it stimulates the need for identification of a 'benevolent' power. The power exercised by the party was definitely more than the mere use or abuse of authority and position. It laid a claim to its own necessity and legitimacy from a universalistic perspective and required the unquestioning adherence of a considerable number of people.

I believed in the ideas of the party

The 'truth' of the party appears at different levels, and each of these is a possible source of conflict. The first level concerns the truth of the idea itself: without a widely shared belief, this type of power cannot be exercised. If this belief is shaken, disappears, or does not even exist, then we can only talk about power wielded by repressive bodies (modern police, secret police, the army), and in this case the arguments of the article are not relevant. But for everyday life in most Central-Eastern European societies, we could not speak of a police-state in this sense; even if such bodies did play a role there, they mostly lurked in the background.

The second level involves the inner conviction of the political workers. Here the question is whether they are convinced of the truth of the doctrine, and able to convince other party members of these convictions. Otherwise, they won't be able to do their job – at least not efficiently – and will have to revert to more direct methods. The third level concerns the interpretation of the 'ideals' appropriate to the current situation. It is the task of the central leadership to decide which path to follow, to make the resolutions that the instructors must represent. To accomplish this dual role of representing the concrete party line and embodying the 'party' as such, the instructors must also believe in the truth of the concrete line. It is not enough to believe in an abstract ideal; this faith must encompass the ability of the leadership to realise ideas, to choose the correct direction. We may say that faith in the idea is the general precondition for the fulfilment of the job, while the party line is the concrete precondition. And here, as we have already seen, conflicts are not only possible, but unavoidable; moreover, it is exactly the 'best' instructors, the most faithful, who find it most difficult to reconcile ideas with the concrete party line. But let's return to the first level, and review in their terms the possible sources of conflicts in the 1988 situation.

When talking about 'faith', we have to repeat the distinction made earlier between 'us' and 'them', since this faith has relevance only for the former group, but here it does play a key, functional role. In our questionnaires, we found several signs of the importance of faith for a number of political workers. One occasion for the expression of such views was given by the question addressing the motives for joining the party and the apparatus. Although we did not list it in the questionnaire, a number of our respondents cited faith as a main motive:

Because I believed in the ideas of the party.

(O.4)

1 Belief in social development; 2 Personal development; 3 Activity, service.

(L.2)

Because I sincerely believed in its goals.

(D.4)

I am an unconditional believer in this social order, and I felt that because of my knowledge and my work in the movement, I must take part as a party member in the public life of society.

(T.11)

In these examples, the ideas appear at a rather abstract level. But for a number of political workers, there was much more at stake: faith in the 'party' was a central element in their whole upbringing, and thus became a way of life, a form of existence:

I had a very strong emotional motivation . . . that I exist in the literal sense of the word, that I could study, that I could even take part in the political life in this country, is due to the party; there was here a very strong personal tie; if you like, it was based on interest as well. I knew very well, and my parents also told me that if this party hadn't gained power you would never have gone to university, we would not be where we are now, you owe everything to this party, ergo it is yours.

This was one of the reasons. Apart from everything else, it was the basic [reason for joining].

(H.O., secretary)

My parents taught me that everything that happens in the party is unusual, is different, tests you, is something to be followed.

(F.8)

I felt that the party was the only organisation that could elevate the whole society. My origins, my family background, also determined this step. At that time, I felt it natural that my place was there.

(M.3)

In my family from the time of my great-grandfather everybody participated in the workers' movement. Party membership seemed somehow natural for me.

(S.3)

Parental influence (mother's side): 'You have no right not to be there!' Meaning: you have to fight there for the 'better life'.

(A.10)

Now it has turned out that nothing was like it was said to be

Although we have no reason nor even the right to doubt the sincerity of these statements, this same picture can be illuminated from a different angle, using the answers given to another question which concerned the biggest problems faced by the party today. The ideological crisis and loss of faith were among the most frequently mentioned problems (about a quarter of the respondents cited these in an open item). But for our purpose it may be even more relevant that this crisis was not restricted to the level of ideology. For the instructors, faith in the ideas, as we have seen, was not just an abstract theme, but a very basic existential problem. The crisis of faith meant a personal crisis for a number of people; it questioned their work on behalf of the apparatus, even the meaning of their whole lives: consider the following responses to a question concerning the biggest personal problems faced by the party workers:

The kind of perception of the work we have done up till now – what we have carried out in good faith and honesty – that we now encounter in public opinion.

(U.5)

What I believe in and work for in my modest way is now almost universally questioned!

(E.6)

That I myself am beginning to lose certainty.

(R.5)

The loss of certainty, the question of how to move on, to live from one day to another, how to teach my children – a general crisis of values.

(B.18)

We had a strong faith and now it has turned out that nothing was like it was said to be.

(P.4)

One can add to this the observation that in Hungary there are still few signs of a serious questioning, based on rational argument, of the basis of this whole system of ideas, and of the belief in the inevitability of progress. There are only quests for the 'best' way to achieve 'true' development.

The crisis of faith leads to a general feeling of uncertainty, and this has an especially strong impact on the instructors. With this problem, we arrive at the second level of our analysis, the question of the personal conviction of the instructors. Once the values thought to be stable are in turmoil, instructors are no longer able to fulfil their tasks. The loss of inner certainty makes the performance of their job almost impossible:

As long as I experience uncertainty, it is very difficult to govern others.

(B.E.)

[Instructors] cannot provide acceptable answers to either party members or non-members. They are uncertain about the future. They don't see the purpose of their work.

(M.5)

There is a shortage of answers to a number of questions. Life is becoming harder.

(C.7)

How could we help the secretary in his work? There is a considerable degree of uncertainty about what to do and even whether anything can be done in this situation. To instil faith again into the party members.

(E.3)

This also has implications for the other side, that of the governed. The result of this crisis of faith is that the instructor is unable to influence the local party cells, and can no longer have recourse to a strategy that avoided answers to concrete problems by offering an image of a better future: 'Socialism as a theory fails the test of practice. We can only confront the present problems with an image of the future' (O.8). This strategy also fails because even the image of the future was in a bad shape at the end of the 1980s:

> Today we can't give answers to a number of questions, either because we don't have any, or because we are afraid of saying certain things. In recent years we have not been able to offer any hopeful image of the future.
>
> (M.4)

Here we must emphasise that the problem raised is not identical with the general doubt expressed concerning the sincerity of belief of party workers. As we have already stated, it was not possible for instructors to carry out their tasks without an inner conviction. It must also be remembered that the instructors worked in a highly specific environment, very different from that of other party functionaries such as local party secretaries or leaders. The latter connected members and non-members, and thus exercised direct power over non-members. In this relation, the question of conviction does not play an important role; emphasis is on the position of power. However, instructors hardly ever met non-members; even among members, they were primarily in contact with the local leadership. In order to govern them, mere acts and words of external power were insufficient. The language used, the behaviour, the gestures had to be different.

Only a small step is needed to move from the level of the crisis of ideas to that of the 'crisis of confidence'. But this small step can easily lead to the questioning of the whole party line:

> The party has lost confidence because it is not able to realise its programmes. Today it is not even able to offer straightforward direction. Today chaos reigns in every area.
>
> (C.3)

> I agree with the statement [concerning the loss of confidence], and we are helpless when confronted with the statement that it was the party that brought the country to this pass. We promised and failed to deliver; why would there be any trust?
>
> (G.2)

> My experiences are similar, an ever growing number of people are becoming uncertain, or even turning away from the party.
>
> (B.5)

It is not confidence in the party that is diminishing, but trust in the higher, central bodies. The population suffers the consequences of missed or mistaken decisions. This fact cannot be ignored.

(A.6)

I may have to confront the decisions of power

The third level of problems is generated by the conflict between inner conviction and the official party line. The work creates particular stress when instructors must represent a line which goes against their better convictions. This tension is particularly great if this is not related to an isolated case, but concerns the whole line, or the leadership itself. Even if we assume that previously this type of conflict had been rare, at the time of our study it had become rather common:

> While serving the community, I may have to face decisions by political and state power that I do not understand or cannot accept.
>
> (N.5)

> Within the apparatus, I think the leaders in our district are growing a little old. They are above 50, and the members of the apparatus are much younger – 15–20 years younger – and here new thinking is confronted with the old.
>
> (P.G.)

The main task of the instructors was to link members and leaders. We have seen above that the preservation of this connection and the representation of the given party line made special demands on them that were hard to meet if confidence in the leadership was lost. But this job also required a special disposition in other relations, when the emphasis was shifted toward the members.

I love to deal with the people's problems

The specificity of the power of the instructors lies in the fact that it is exercised directly, through interpersonal relations, as a help, a service. A considerable redefinition of the limits of politics was necessary to enable these activities to be included among the tasks carried out by 'political' workers of a 'political' party. The need for personal contact with people on a daily basis, on the other hand, demanded special characteristics on the part of the party's representatives that could not have been included among those required for the pursuit of a political career in any other era.

An item on our questionnaire asked precisely about characteristics respondents thought to be most important for their job. Of the seven possibilities listed, 92 per cent chose the one which stipulated 'keeping continuous contact with the masses'.

Answers to another, open item were even more illuminating. Here we asked what personal characteristics respondents thought they possessed which made them particularly well suited to politics.[2] The following are just a few examples:

> I can make personal connections easily in all areas. I love to deal with people's problems.
>
> (P.6)
>
> The ability to deal with people in a patient and understanding manner; the will to help.
>
> (G.5)
>
> The need to deal with people.
>
> (F.3)
>
> I planned this job as a temporary service. I felt I could easily make contacts with people; I have empathy.
>
> (K.5)
>
> A sense of accomplishment derived from work done for the community; continuous regeneration. The respect and love of people.
>
> (S.5)
>
> Perhaps because I love people I live for them.
>
> (Z.4)

Personal contact with and care for people, the will to help them, love and service, a life sacrificed on their behalf – if we look into the past, we will hardly meet these characteristics in the description of a Greek statesman or lawmaker, a Roman senator or conqueror, a European king or diplomat, a Democrat or Republican representative. There is only one analogy in history, and that is Christianity, with its strivings toward the moralisation and humanisation of relations of power.

We would like to emphasise that it is irrelevant here whether the actual work done always corresponded to this ideal or not. The answer is most certainly not; nor was it even possible. The really intriguing point is that this ideal concerning political work could have been promulgated at all, since it not only goes against the concept of politics as matters concerning the entire social body, but it also precludes the possibility of democracy, if by this we mean the expression of one's own opinions and interests, responsible thinking and action. The main problem is not that the instructors conceived of the governed as subjects, but that they imagined the targets of their intervention as helpless, isolated individuals in need of care and support, who, without their attention, would disintegrate or simply cease to exist.

The head of the firm didn't behave like a partner

A central and especially conflict-ridden area for political workers concerned their contacts with the directors of firms or public institutions. In our interviews, when questioned about problems which proved to be particularly difficult or insoluble, the instructors again and again gave examples of battles waged against these directors. We shall present three such examples in detail. The first two conflicts revolved around a personnel change at the top; in the first case, the attempt to remove the director was successful, in the second, it was not. The third case was of a conflict between the director and the local party secretary that made its way to the instructor.

In recounting the first case, though repeatedly asked to be specific, our respondent used a hypothetical language in describing concrete events. Thus, the instructor got acquainted with the problem when:

> The leadership of the local party organisation or the secretary tells what has happened, what the problems encountered have been, the problems that hinder work or make the atmosphere at the workplace bad; or it may even happen that the life of the whole firm is crippled.
>
> (I.K.)

Of course, the trouble does not emerge suddenly; and a good instructor perceives well in advance the smallest signs of these problems, and attempts to help, to prevent the eruption. In order to do so, he tries to give advice. But why would this task be best performed by a political worker? The recurrent answer seems to be obvious:

> The instructor sits down with a manager of the firm, or the leaders of the party cell, whoever is willing to take part, and does some talking. He/she sheds light on those things that they don't see or can't perceive clearly. It is precisely through the eyes of an outsider that it is easier to clarify these issues.
>
> (I.K.)

The instructors do not take part in these matters as experts; they do not have any licence to pretend to do so. Their expertise refers only to technical matters of party organisation and activity, and the internal affairs of a given firm do not belong here. Nor are their actions justified by their specific knowledge of the given situation, the inside picture of the whole case. Quite the contrary, their help is solely justified by their 'clear, unbiased' sight which is grounded not in their specific knowledge but in their outsider position, in the ability to see things from an external perspective.

Instructors, then, try to relieve the tensions, prevent a situation where 'something cracks, and the whole thing gets outside the scope of the given firm or institution' (I.K.). The basic goal is to prevent the eruption of any open conflicts, the emergence of a 'case'. The good instructor is the one whose work is not even heard about 'inside', whose area is free of problems.

But it may happen that the confrontation cannot be avoided: 'And there are cases when the situation gets to a point where it is obvious that a change is necessary. As in this one' (I.K.).

In the second case, the conflict emerged between the director of a firm and the local party leadership when the former failed to meet the expectations of the latter:

> The party organisation at the firm worked to become accepted as a partner for economic management, to be provided with information about the firm's economic situation – and not just for the sake of the party, but for the workers in general there .... The head of the firm did not behave like a partner. He employed fairly authoritarian methods, and still does. He expressed his willingness to offer information, but he retained the right to make decisions.
>
> (L.G.)

Discussions followed, first at a meeting of the local leadership, then at a local party meeting ('the director was a party member, so there was no problem in this sense'). But these failed to achieve any satisfactory outcome. The next painful step had to be taken: the instructor reported the case to his district secretary. The secretary 'made an inquiry to the supervisory bodies', i.e. telephoned the director of the parent firm, in the presence of the instructor himself. (This should be seen, by the way, as a special favour; it could only have happened at a relatively small, non-hierarchical PC.) This conversation also proved unsuccessful. The instructor then presented the case to the executive committee of the district PC. A big discussion ensued, with everyone presenting his or her opinion. Finally, 'the body ... told the leader of the firm that a firm cannot be manned by such methods. He summoned the director to provide the necessary information immediately' (L.G.). With this, the case was closed for the instructor. The director retained his job. A curious epilogue: it was, in fact, the party secretary that left the firm during the next series of lay-offs – though apparently of his own will.

In the third case, the source of difficulty was a personal conflict between the director and the party secretary of a firm:

> The party secretary comes in and tells me, look, this has happened. He discredited me, humiliated me, pushed me into the ground. What is the situation now? Who is where? Who supports whom? Who stands behind me? Is the district PC behind me, or not? What do you suggest? What should I do? Where should I go? How can I deal with the director?
>
> (A.T.)

Since the problem here manifested itself at the personal level, the instructor chose to deal with it by a similar method. It is well worth quoting his proposed procedure at length, even though, again, the concrete case was presented in a generalised language:

> I'll talk with the director myself. One possibility is that I look him up for some other reasons. I search for the common denominator where I can start. And during the conversation, I mention this case to him, asking what caused the conflict with the secretary. I will become familiar with his way of thinking, and then I can give concrete advice to the secretary. Once I have become acquainted with his thinking in this question, I can open a discussion with him as to whether he has some wrong views. I can clarify the issue. Or, perhaps, he can clarify it to me. It is not certain that –
>
> (A.T.)

The strategy used by the instructor to probe the thinking of the director is quite remarkable. His goal is perfect clarity; and for this, he must explore the depths of the soul, in order to know its moving forces. He employs a conscious, detailed strategy in order to open up the opponent. This behaviour is possible only if the starting point is one of maximal distance and distrust which assumes a complete separation made between 'us' and 'them'.

It is not surprising in itself that the personality of the director or changes concerning the leadership of firms or institutions represent such important questions for an instructor. Everyone who is in contact with a given firm must pay attention to the person at the helm. But why this fixation concerning the director? Why the special connotations? What explains the special prudence and strategy the instructors deploy when dealing with directors? According to one: 'They are the key, "the North Pole, the mystery, the alienness". The directors' (A.T.).

For an explanation, we must refer back to the dual position of instructors, the complete independence 'outside' the party committee and their complete dependence 'inside' the house. 'Outside', no matter whom the instructor was dealing with, he represented the 'party', and thus enjoyed a higher status. If he felt the need to intervene in respect of a 'political problem', he was perfectly free to do so. But directors represented a special problem, especially because in the last few years, there has been a definite shift of emphasis in favour of a certain 'independence' for directors: 'Four years ago the director would go out to greet a 28-year-old kid at the gates' (A.L.). 'If I went there, the director "saluted" me' (G.D.). However, in the last period, the most important weapon of the instructors, the Damocles sword of personal dependency, had become useless:

> Generally they consider you as their equals. They don't treat you as the district PC – or rather very much so, but not that much . . . . They are much more independent, so one has to engage in much harder debates in order to achieve even small results.
>
> (A.T.)

Of course, this independence did have its limits, and the directors knew it only too well. Even if they did not belong to the 'sphere of competence' list of the instructor, that of the district PC still included them. This was handled by the district secretaries. And it is here that the circle was closed. The instructors didn't like to take cases to the secretaries as it indicated that they had not been able to find a local solution. Thus the directors had to be approached very carefully, a solution had to be found before a problem reached a higher level. This was a difficult busi- ness, requiring cunning strategies; or, to put it differently, anything went – even spying on the directors.

This case also indicates why the preservation of the influence and authority of district PCs had become so problematic:

> Q: What means does the party have?
> A: A carrot and a stick, though it mostly relies on the stick. It has no carrots. It might feed individuals with them; but not organisations or collectives. And even individuals only to the extent of 'well, I'll support you, if – '
>
> (G.C.)

The real strength of the party had resided not in institutions or structures, but in keeping individuals in a state of personal dependence. And if, in the past, the grip had been maintained on individuals, so now the loosening, the cutting of ties also proceeded from individuals, from a massive body of individuals, one by one. Slowly, the web was dissolving, the ties were undone, and without any conscious central strategy or master plan, but of their own accord:

Even three years ago, if I picked up the phone and said where I was speaking from, I could very quickly arrange things. Not personal matters, but those that belonged to my job. Now it is very hard to do this by phone; you have to flatter the person, and then perhaps something will be done. But now it is a bad thing to say that the order comes 'from the district PC'. Older people still take it as an authority, but the rest do not.

(P.G.)

SPECIFIC EXISTENTIAL POSITION

In the section above we discussed in detail the personal characteristics instructors considered to be important to perform their job, a position yielding almost unlimited, if only local, power. These were located inside the individual, in his relation toward himself and the others. However, in order to accomplish his tasks, the instructor had to possess some other, external characteristics as well. His work started with an initial gap, a difference between the 'inside' and the 'outside', the 'us' and 'them'; a distance between the members of the apparatus and the ordinary citizens. The instructor was not only different inside, but had also to be kept separate from the population at large. It was only in this way that he could perform the job of continuous supervision and control, mobilisation and stimulation. The instructor could not simply be a man in the street; he had to be existentially independent of the troubles of ordinary citizens.

Lenin got the idea – it is well known – that party workers should have an existential independence; they had to be spared from regular work so that they could devote themselves fully to their task. But this requirement may have helped to realise another goal as well. The party workers, like the wage-labourers of Marx, became free in two senses: not only from their own daily regular work, but also from the concerns and troubles of others. And this second independence in their case became a functional requirement for the performance of their job.

A correct understanding of this existential independence is especially important in the present situation. When an ever growing number of scandals became not only well known, but were openly discussed, these quite naturally became connected in public opinion with the apparatus itself, which exercised an uncontrolled power anyway. This view is well complemented by the memories of the 1950s and 1960s, when members of the apparatus enjoyed a number of special favours (higher salary, privileged access to holiday resorts, shopping, eating, etc.). The conclusion is easy to draw: the above favours are the signs of a purposeful privilegising and abuse of power; the resurrection of the privileges of the old ruling classes. This argument is well known from the work of Djilas (1957).

But this chain of ideas is mistaken at an important point; it takes the consequence for the cause. It is true, on the one hand, that according to a strange, unwritten rule, the party was obliged to take care of those who had become members of its apparatus. For example, it gave a fairly high salary to those who studied at the political academy, and, at least in principle, provided them with a job. There are people who transformed all this into personal dependence. One of our respondents joined the apparatus for the following reason: 'To serve the interests of those people who sent me with their confidence to a political career at my early age' (C.1). But for the majority it became obvious after some time that this contract represented a two-way obligation. If they once accepted its terms, they would find it difficult to alter the direction, and might not ever be in a position to influence the concrete steps of their future career:

Q: And did you think about it, or did you immediately accept the offer [to join the apparatus]?

A: I did some thinking, but there was only one choice. Or, more exactly, that was it, there wasn't any choice.

Q: What other possibilities would you have preferred?

A: Well, I tell you again, if one agrees to go to a school like that, then one has already made the decision – I must emphasise that I would have preferred the correspondence course, but the leadership decided on a regular, day-time basis. After school, three possibilities are given: one is a job in the apparatus, another is party work at a factory or a firm, the third is in an economic field. But this latter one is highly unlikely.

(K.S.)

Furthermore, the conclusion is correct as long as it states that it is immoral to accept extra or luxury goods; but it is a mistake to think that the above-mentioned special favours were necessarily incompatible with the puritan official morality of the party. The majority of the favours received by the members of the apparatus were, in their purpose and effect, not unattainable luxury goods, but were used to save them from the regular troubles of day-to-day existence. They separated, defended and protected, provided a special safety network, but within these boundaries did not give any extras, according to the inner logic of the party. The acquisition of these extras was the business of individuals, and this can be justly considered as immoral and non-functional, even according to the inner logic. Of course, the opportunity for such actions was given by the isolated position and uncontrolled power exercised by the members of the apparatus. But here our goal was not to deny the existence of corruption and abuses of power; we only wanted to point to the difference between the functional role of certain special favours, and mere abuses.

The second comment is related to the present situation. In the case of Hungary, we can probably talk about the result of a longer process. The fact is that this web has been torn down step by step; at the end of 1988, it had all but disappeared. This fact and the dangerous consequences for the party can be illustrated by the following quotation:

> If a party member is not better and more reliable, if he doesn't possess the right information, then he is in no respect different from average citizens. He may even be considered as being at a disadvantage.
>
> (A.9)

One of the most obvious signs of the disappearance of the privileged situation concerned salaries. It may be hard to believe – we were surprised as well – but it was simply not true that in Hungary apparatus members earned a lot in 1988. It was a recurrent topic during our conversations that, for the money a district party committee could offer, it was not able to acquire the kind of qualified personnel it needed. The PCs were looking for 35–40-year-old professionals with a degree in economics, law or engineering, who were able to collect and select adequate information, and who would be accepted as partners by the businesses themselves. The fixed salary they had been given, even a few years before, was somewhat higher than the wages received at a firm, and thus provided some compensation for the extra earnings lost (second jobs, profit sharing, etc.). The members of the apparatus were not allowed to take on any extra jobs. It was probably a remnant of the old contract: the party would take care of its recruits, but expected complete subordination and service. It was the obligation of the party worker to serve the party full time, or regenerate oneself for service (thus the special right of vacation), and not spend time rushing after extra money. But at the time of our research, even the monthly salary was smaller within the apparatus than at a firm for a person with the proper qualifications. One faced a considerable, 3,000–4,000 forints a month, loss in salary (20–30 per cent) if one decided for some reason to join the apparatus. The very logic described above seemed to have turned on its head: at the time of our research, it was not the party that provided security of livelihood for its servants, but several of our respondents stated that only those persons entered the apparatus who could afford it financially.

In our questionnaire, we included several items concerning the financial position of political workers. For example, 'higher salary' was mentioned among the options given as reasons for entering the apparatus. Only 15 per cent of the respondents chose this item: those who had entered the apparatus much earlier, or had left a low-paying job (administrative or teaching positions). Of course, one may say that the rest were not telling the truth. But this fails to explain why at the next item, concerning possible negative points assessed when joining the apparatus, 17 per cent of all the respondents and 23 per cent of those who mentioned a reason at all said that they had suffered a financial loss. Also, at another question, when asked about the biggest problems they faced today, 40 per cent in all mentioned some financial problems, or a plain decrease in living standards. One must add that the admission of such problems went at least as much against expectations as the consideration of a higher salary at the point of entry. One of our interviewees who had talked a lot about the problems of living that apparatus members had to face in the 1980s stated that respondents would not be willing to talk about these issues:

> For example, the questionnaire fails to discuss the topic of whether the individual feels himself secure socially; that is, whether he perceives his financial situation as good.
> Q: Well, there was a comparable question concerning the problems such individuals must face today.
> A: That's true, but they won't talk about it. Anybody with any self-respect will not begin to tell you that, damn it, what a trouble it is to buy thousand-forint shoes for the kid.
>
> (J.A.)

In spite of all this, our respondents did talk or write about their material problems. The majority only put down a few words ('the decline of living standards', 'material problems'); but some offered more extended comments, and it is well worth quoting some of them in full:

> Problems of existence due to the relatively low pay.
>
> (O.3)

> Material problems, daily worries. Beginning with housing, through the everyday difficulties of shopping up to the changes in the prices.
>
> (M.9)

> The guarantee of our living standards, the elimination of 'gifts'.
>
> (M.11)

> Unfortunately they are mostly material, though it is not the most important thing.
>
> (E.4)

Our material situation, of which there are legends circulating in the country.

(K.3)

Our material possibilities are limited. The preservation of the standard of living is the overriding goal. First of all, that of our own. The questions of the country are pushed to the back due to the necessity of solving our own problems.

(J.2)

Low and declining living standards.

(J.5)

To survive in the short run so that our long-term objectives won't become endangered.

(J.8)

Here you don't have any extras. The only thing is that perhaps somebody calls you up to say that something is on sale in the supermarket, and then you go there to fetch a suit or something. But I may go there and stumble into it, so I am basically in the same position as the population at large. There is no advantage in anything, and they will add the bonus to the November salary, and it will be worth half its value [due to tax retainments]. There is a favour that those having a car receive 1,040 forints per month; but that is easily spent on gas. And those who use mass transportation receive ninety forints per month for their card. Well, that's all. Here you can't earn any extras. You can't join an economic venture, can't participate in any-thing – the only exception being teaching. But as mass [political] education is declining, that is also becoming very difficult. So they 'above' should not always take the ascetic line. It always comes from above, due to their 'infinite wisdom', that we should willingly renounce everything.

(P.G.)

Let there be no misunderstanding. We are not trying to assert that the living conditions of apparatus members were worse than the average. As can be seen from the examples given above, a number of the complaints were related to the loss of earlier privileges. But it is clear from the general picture that the special material position of the apparatus was long gone in 1988 in Hungary. In terms of living conditions, they had slid back to the level of ordinary citizens. Moreover, they were now faced with hostile public opinion and adverse conditions – here it is enough to recall the prohibition against taking on extra jobs. But this whole question cannot be reduced to the mere issue of money and privileges. We stated earlier that the distancing of apparatus members from the lot of ordinary citizens, their exemption from daily problems, had served a function: it had permitted them to step beyond the minute questions of existence, to look further than the 'mere' social-democratic fight for higher salaries and wages and thus to represent the 'true' interests of progress and development and to mobilise the governed for the attainment of these distant goals. The 'fighter' was not supposed to lose his vigilance and toughness, to take up solidarity and a common cause with those he should supervise and mobilise:

> In a certain way, one must be tough. As they are always ready to complain that this is not possible, that wouldn't work, and that again won't work either. And it may easily happen that the instructor begins to cry with them. That well, yes, it's true, this won't work, and so on. But, after all, his goal is to try somehow to stimulate, to urge, to mobilise; to say that, well, it's really difficult, but after all, it could still be done.
>
> (J.A.)

Once this distance was lost, the very possibility and meaning of the instructor's work were questioned. The horror of all armies had arrived: fraternisation. In our study, we found several signs that this was in fact happening:

> In daily life we are subject to the very same effects (for example, we have to spend more and more when shopping at the grocery stores) as any other citizen. It is hard to overcome this and proclaim a distant political goal.
>
> (C.4)

> When facing everyday problems of bread, to perform on the political stage and answer the often cruelly realistic questions of 'individuals who are similar to me'.
>
> (S.1)

> [Apparatus members] directly feel the difficulties of the present situation. Most of these are related to living standards. It was often said to me: 'You judge as you live'.
>
> (P.6)

> You are not that great a leader, so they won't think it over ten times before they tell you something. Still, you are not one among them whom they can be at one with. Well, in the last period, this happened

more often. They expressed solidarity – the leadership of the primary
organisations and the local secretaries. Even the members, though
less often. But this solidarity, this is increasing.

(A.T.)

Instructors complaining about the leadership, accepting the demands
and criticisms of the members, and declaring themselves unable to give
a proper answer were signs in 1988 of a communist party that was on the
brink of disintegration. Moreover, the apparatus itself was beginning to
voice the same things as ordinary people, instead of convincing them of
the falseness of their opinions: 'We were even accused that it is the apparatus that stimulates the loss of confidence in the party. And that the
apparatus passes its own doubts on to the local organisations' (J.A.). The
very construction and organisation of the apparatus, established by its
inner logic, was simply not suited for the voicing and channelling of similar complaints. Thus it was not accidental that a number of party workers
were so willing to express openly their views to somebody who was prepared
to pay attention and listen to them. Contrary to our expectations, we had
no problems about willingness to answer our questions:

I think it was a good idea at last to ask the apparatus these questions.
I don't know whether the apparatus was asked about anything until
now. I am just talking about the political workers now, not the
secretaries. But I think it is the apparatus that confronts reality – in
the party organisations of the firms and the residential areas as well.
I wasn't the only one who said in local meetings, when answering
problems raised by members about the party, that I would be glad if
I could 'sit on to the other side'. Because for this [line], or against
these objections, I had no arguments. And it is exactly because of
these things that I say that it was good to ask apparatus members
about the party, the state and their own life. Because I think the
apparatus struggles in daily life with the same problems as ordinary
citizens, only it meets these problems much more frequently.

(P.G.)

The performance of the instructor's job required specific qualities, kept
party workers in constant tension inside and outside as well. At the time
of our study, the sources of tension were increasing, with no
compensating gains. The earlier special favours were either eliminated
or had lost their value. At the same time, the demand for highly qualified
members was increasing. The only way out was to rely on 'faith' to an
ever larger degree. But in the inner work style of the party, there were
hardly any changes. It remained strongly hierarchical, based on a

principle of authority and obedience, where political workers were kept in a subservient, almost humiliating position. It was very difficult to harmonise this role with inner conviction and faith in the case of better qualified apparatus members.

In one of our questions we asked respondents whether they would like their children to follow in their steps. Given such a question, under normal circumstances one would hardly expect negative answers, as that would reflect a basic dissatisfaction with one's job, almost amounting to a crisis of identity. Still, in our case, a considerable proportion, 39 per cent of the respondents, plainly stated that they would not like it to happen. If the different non-answers (no children; did not think about it; would not influence, etc.) were excluded, this went up to 55 per cent, while the yes answers only amounted to 44 per cent.

Some of the reasons given here may be used to support and summarise the argument of this section:

> I would not like it. The meaning of one's work is to accomplish what one is capable of doing. If one is surrounded by constraints in one's work and feels that in a number of aspects one is isolated, that only makes the efficient accomplishment of the tasks impossible.
>
> (H.3)

> I would not like it, as I think that in any political or social situation, with special professional knowledge in hand, his livelihood is much more assured, he is not in a situation of dependence, and it is his own work that determines his achievements.
>
> (P.3)

> No. . . . I got frustrated with the often meaningless fights. There are too many selfish, opportunist 'bootlickers' in the leading bodies who consider the party movement only as a vehicle for their own advancement.
>
> (N.5)

> No. I would like to save them from a lot of disappointments.
>
> (O.2)

> I would not like it. He would not be able to go through what I had to.
>
> (A.5)

> No, because I know about the difficulties, the insecurity of this position, and I don't know whether my child, raised in a different historical and social environment, would be able to face all this with true human equanimity.
>
> (R.1)

The above statements represent only the tip of the iceberg, but in themselves can support our conclusions. At the same time, they raise two additional problems. The first concerns what happened when people left the apparatus, the further professional career and life which, for a long time, were considered the crowning of and the major recompense for service performed in the apparatus. And the second refers to the evaluation, the usefulness of the job that the instructor did. Let's start with this second topic.

SPECIFIC KNOWLEDGE

In our study, we often encountered the statement that political workers felt no sense of accomplishment, didn't see the point of their work, felt that their professional knowledge was decreasing. Others, on the contrary, emphasised quick, measurable results and the acquisition of experience as the major assets of their job. How can we explain this duality? What is the type of knowledge required for and provided by this job? Or, to put it the other way round, how and what did an instructor have to prepare for in order to meet the requirements of the position?

I must get a full picture

Instructors first of all had to collect information, to provide the district leadership with all sorts of knowledge. But they were not supposed to provide individual items of information; they were expected to compose and present a global view of the areas or businesses under their command. They had to mobilise all available resources for the acquirement of such a global picture:

> The only thing expected of me was that, in quotation marks, 'I must get a full picture'. I must know what happens in the local cells, what type of work they are engaged upon, what personnel or organisational troubles are encountered there, in connection with the economic problems of the given unit.
>
> (L.G.)

The instructor had to mobilise all his available resources for the acquisition of such a global picture:

Q: In order to get this global picture, what are your methods? What means are at your disposal?

A: I can only tell that I chose the method of building up personal contacts . . . of course, in such a way that they also get acquainted with me. So it was not that one-sided. I also tried to

open up myself. I tried to make it plain, especially during the
first period, why I would behave in that way.

(L.G.)

This was made possible by the fact that instructors had access to all sorts
of different information. In this way, always in the background, acting as
if in no man's land, they slowly built up for themselves the 'complete,
global' picture of the areas under their instruction. For them, the world
was truly a stage, and the citizens merely players, pawns in their game.

I have experienced a lot

On the other side of the process of information gathering, instructors
accumulated a vast quantity of factual knowledge, learned and
experienced a lot. This learning process was openly acknowledged; it
belonged to the arsenal with which district PCs attempted to lure
individuals to become their members. Forty per cent of all respondents
indicated that they joined the apparatus in order to increase their
professional knowledge. It was by far the most important reason given.
But here we can observe a slight difference of emphasis. The official
evaluation put it on learning, while instructors preferred to talk about
experience: 'If somebody is leaving the apparatus, he is expected to say:
"Thanks for letting me work here, and I learned a lot." I would say that
I have experienced a lot. And this obviously includes learning as well'
(A.L.). The difference here, we would argue, is not just a matter of
stylistics, but another proof of the strange and recurrent duality
accompanying the career of instructors, another dimension of the inter-
play between formal and informal connections, expectations and reality.
The emphasis on 'learning' underlines the importance of the cumulative
acquisition of an already existing stock of knowledge under guidance
and supervision. It can be used to justify the strongly hierarchical
relations between the secretaries (the 'teachers') and the political
workers (the 'pupils'), the complete lack of democratic rights within the
house. Instructors within the house are considered as not yet grown up,
as persons who are not yet aware of what they should and should not do
and know. They need continuous supervision and correction. Thus things
like the humiliating re- and rewriting of internal reports can happen:

Here I am kept at an infantile state – not just me, everybody, I don't
have any personal injuries – where I am even told how to write a
composite sentence or where to put the commas. This goes up to that
level.

(G.D.)

Q: About the revisions [of reports], in more detail?
A: My record was, I think, eleven.

(A.L.)

One of the most curious aspects of the job of instructors was the combination of extreme independence and dependence. Frequently, they had to act in complete independence and isolation. They often perceived it as being abandoned. On the other hand, they felt that they were kept in an infantile state. This duality can be explained by a separation between 'outside' and 'inside' tasks. The difference between the two roles could not be greater. 'Outside', at the local cells, the independence was complete, as the instructor was personally responsible for anything. 'Inside', his hands were tied up at every step. 'Outside' the instructor gained experience, and was 'tested', in a very special sense, no doubt, where the measure of success was the ability to convince and mobilise, where the targets of activity were human beings themselves. An achievement-orientated person may not have been happy with these types of accomplishments. 'Inside' the party worker learned, under the close supervision of the secretary.

Here you are not employed as an economist

Learning, the acquisition of knowledge, was one of the most important results of the job done by the instructors. But the type of information gathered in this job was very specific and could be put only to a fairly limited use. No matter how hard a local PC tried to acquire highly qualified workers, their position did not require wide professional knowledge, and, despite all promises, would not help to increase proficiency. Quite the contrary, the professional expertise of the instructors became obsolete after the five or six years they spent inside:

Q: When you entered here, what were your first impressions? Was your job based on your professional knowledge?
A: Not at all. I discovered this very soon. Even today I get remarks such as 'Here you are not employed as an economist; you should deal with the political aspects of economic matters'.

(G.C.)

This raises problems at the point when someone tries to find a job after leaving the apparatus:

Q: How do you perceive the question of retirement?
A: I only have a hypothesis. Up till now, there was some sort of orientation. Now I see a problem here. I may not be correct.

But look, a professional comes here. He may become stronger here in some respects, but not necessarily related to his specific expertise. Thus, a teacher here won't become a better teacher. Here he will become – I have to use this word – a teacher with a 'broader perspective'.

(A.L.)

If somebody in the rotation system leaves a political career – and the majority of colleagues does not stay here for good – well, where to go now? This will be a problem. You know, the firms are closing ranks, they have the right to make independent decisions. They will say: 'Who wants to become one of our top executives? When did he last work in the profession? But that was five years ago. And what advantages can he offer? That he knows the district first secretary?' There are people who still consider it as an advantage, but really it does not mean anything anymore.

(A.L.)

These quotes point not only to the obsolescence of professional knowledge, but also to a complaint often voiced by party workers about their neglect by the district leadership. This point will be taken up in detail in the next section.

Necessary for an executive job

Even if political instructors didn't gain special professional knowledge while performing their job, according to some this may have been compensated for by the gain in leadership and managerial skills:

I told myself that it would be such a test, such a responsible position that if others thought I would be able to do it, then I should try it. [The job done before] was not at a level where I would have seen the work of a number of firms. Here, I could see large factories, schools, research centres. I saw more and different problems, and made quite different personal contacts.

(J.A.)

Q: What is the function of this transitory situation [at the apparatus] for a member? What does it mean in terms of a professional career?

A: The acquisition of knowledge. And an enormous amount. I am convinced that one can gain a lot of experience here that is not available in any other way. . . . Here you can gain knowledge concerning organisation and leadership that would not be

possible otherwise. Here you get such a broad view of the
internal activity of the different firms that would not be possible if
you just worked at one firm. . . . Here you may experience very
different things, related both to the firms and the higher
organs. You may collect a lot of information in this way.

(J.L.)

The majority [of former party workers] will obtain a higher position,
but I think it is perfectly natural. Four or five years spent at a district
party committee open up one's horizons considerably, and one will
gain a lot of information, experience and knowledge that are
necessary for an executive job. On the other hand, he will be a little
distanced from practical work, but in an executive job exact
professional knowledge is less important than in the case of an
employee.

(D.F., secretary)

The same thing was said in an untaped conversation where a district
secretary also mentioned that the major asset of political workers
leaving the apparatus was their experience with managerial tasks.

But what exactly were these experiences? In this latter conversation,
we were told that instructors got used to dealing with government
leaders in high positions. They wouldn't be shy in front of a minister as
they would already have been in contact with him in their previous jobs.
They had already been close to decision-making, and so had become
used to the atmosphere. These remarks were made concerning the fact
that in the second half of the 1980s, with the increased independence of
the firms, they were increasingly reluctant to accept 'parachutists' from
the party, in spite of the allegedly superior qualities of candidates from
the apparatus. Thus, according to this district secretary, firms made
irrational decisions, against their own interest. But was this assumption
correct? Did political workers really possess qualities of leadership that
would compensate for their fading professional expertise?

If we look at the matter closely, we can perceive that the leadership
opportunities provided by the instructor's job were fairly limited. One
was the acquisition of a 'global view'. But what was the substance of this?
Some information concerning all or most firms of a given district, but
only in a certain way and not in much depth. This would not have been
very helpful in actually running a single one of those firms individually.
The instructor only followed the events, the actions made, and evaluated
the decisions. As an outside observer, he was left in a passive state, even
if he did have knowledge about what was going on. And, in the case of
special situations, he had to wait for the judgement of his superiors. If,

due to a particular breakdown, he was forced into the position of making a decision, it had to be hasty, badly prepared and related solely to his position and not his knowledge.

The instructor's job implanted special patterns in its performers: on the one hand, the desire to see everything, to know about everything, the search for a very passive type of knowledge; on the other, even the most scrupulous accomplishment of these tasks would not help one to become familiar with making decisions, but would 'teach' one the postponement or transfer of decisions, the sidestepping of responsibility and overhastiness in making decisions.

Today, one rather has to forget

To this, we must add that the value of practical experiences gained was rapidly deteriorating in the last years. First, a large part of the 'knowledge' gained meant personal acquaintances which did not in themselves make one more able to perform a concrete job. Second, the majority of the information included in the 'global picture' reflected peculiar, personal or idiosyncratic characteristics of the given firms. This information could not be converted for use in other firms; and if the instructor returned to one of the firms examined, that would only result in unfair advantages, classified as industrial espionage. Third, even the rest of the knowledge was quickly losing its validity. Even in the opinion of the district leadership, the earlier 'truths' caused more harm than good in the last period. 'Where is truth today?' – a district secretary asked the question in a conversation that was not recorded, and added that now they needed young people in the apparatus not only because they could not afford to pay for older, more experienced cadres, but also because 'today, one has to forget rather than learn', and because the younger generation was 'not contaminated with certain demagogic views'. A similar opinion was voiced by another district secretary in the questionnaire, where he stated that one of his biggest problems was that 'the creed that permeated even through our nervous cells causes a lot of sleepless nights now'.

SPECIFIC CAREER

Here we'll discuss three questions, one by one: first, the official mechanism of 'retirement'; second, how members of the apparatus perceived their chances; and finally, the special problems caused by the fact that at the time of our study the function, the activity and the status of apparatus members, who were prepared for a quite different career, were already being strongly questioned. As one of our respondents put it: 'What will be the role and place of a person in the future who spent most of his life in this framework?' (K.2)

You are no longer able to direct your own life

According to the traditional scenario, joining the apparatus involved a two-sided contract. On the one side, one renounced the right to control the further direction of one's own life, and a great part of one's independence in general. As a compensation, the party promised to take care of one afterward. This care, as we discussed earlier, did not necessarily mean luxury provisions, but complete security and exemption from the troubles of day-to-day existence. The contract was preceded by a conscious cadre policy in the districts, where selected individuals were entered on the 'cadre development list', or were put in the 'cadre bank' or the 'cadre reserves plan' of the area. From time to time, district secretaries had a chat with them, asked about their future intentions and how they would react to the possibility of working in the apparatus. An important intermediate step here was participation in party education, especially the full-time completion of the political academy course. The next excerpt shows these steps, and also points out the fact that future members were quite conscious of the stakes involved:

> When I went to the political academy, I committed myself to go where they put me. When you begin such a course – on a full-time basis, I emphasise – then you commit yourself, accept that you are no longer able to direct your own life. And this was the job they offered me.
>
> (K.S.)

In this mechanism, solving the problem of retirement from service belonged to the district PC; the individual did not even have a right to initiate this. After the time for which the given instructor had engaged himself was over – meaning five to eight years in general – the PC planned the 'cadre exchange'. It looked up a candidate from the 'cadre development list' who possessed the same qualifications as the person who was leaving and was thus suited to perform the same job. In this case, the PC also provided an acceptable position for the retired member, usually a middle-level executive position at a firm or public institution, a few steps higher than the one occupied by him at the time of entry.

It came at a good moment

As we have seen, engagement in party work was always the result of a free decision. The fighters/servicemen of the party made a free contract, though it was true that the moment of the offer was carefully prepared. Throughout at least the 1980s, the party had considerable difficulties in procuring the necessary members. The PCs regularly followed the careers of those who were included in the 'cadre development list', and waited for the best moment: the firm where the 'patient' was working being on the brink of bankruptcy; some problems emerging at the workplace; living or housing problems due to marriage or the birth of a child. Then the PC made its offer, usually giving only a very short deadline: a week or sometimes only twenty-four hours:

> At that time, it was not possible to get a teaching job (1969!). I worked as an administrator at an office. In the town they were searching for a political worker. Nobody accepted it, I was asked by 'phone.
>
> (F.9)

> I had some problems at my workplace, so I wanted a change (I spent twenty years at the same place!). And the leaders of the PC also learned about this.
>
> (A.3)

> In February 1985 I got fed up with the hopeless prospect of a teaching career. I 'made myself free'. After a number of offers the district first secretary asked me in a letter.
>
> (H.4)

> In the school where I was teaching the favourable prospect I had been promised was changed. I was promised that I could take my first and second graders continuously up to the eighth grade as their head-teacher. Instead, in an emergency situation, I was required to teach first-graders again in the new school year. At the first approach, I said no, because of the prospects I had. When I was called again in the new situation, half a year on, I accepted it.
>
> (A.18)

> Those were chaotic times. At the firm, the prospects were changing rapidly. . . . And it was at that point that the request came as to whether I would come here. Now they were looking for a concrete and definite answer. . . . They had not offered any special favours. No question about that. As a matter of fact – depending on whose perspective you accept – it came at a good moment. I had become fed

up with my former job. Not because of the money, but the chaos. I wanted a place where I would know half a year in advance that this was my table, here was where I would be, this was my boss, this was what I would be doing.

(G.C.)

Where the situation of the would-be members was secure, a lot depended on the ability to 'convince':

One day the party secretary of the firm asked me to go to the district PC, where they wanted to talk with me as a young party member. Right at the beginning of the conversation it turned out that the reason was quite different. I did not want a change as I liked my job in the foreign trade section quite a lot. Finally, after a long conversation, they convinced me that I would have a chance to do useful and interesting work here.

(A.16)

The first secretary called me in and told about his plans concerning me. I had a week to think it over. During this period, two members of the district EC came to talk with me. The situation was such and they all talked to me in such a way that it was not possible to refuse the 'offer'.

(C.4)

In order to give an indication of what such a 'situation' would look like, here is another example:

Q: What was mentioned at that conversation?
A: I forgot almost everything. Even the situation itself, that was a joke. One visits a district secretary with shaking knees. One approaches such a conversation with a lot of fears.

(G.C.)

At some district PCs this procedure was still at work at the time of our research; 'care' was being taken of retiring members. In the majority of cases, the situation was rather chaotic. But, before discussing present changes, let's summarise the basic characteristics of the official model:

1 In the way the 'care' is carried out, the individual is a mere object of concerns rooted in the inner logic of an official apparatus, where there is not even the slightest intention of hiding this chess-game played with people. Quite the contrary, the repulsiveness of this game is not even realised. This attitude becomes internalised, and members start to speak of themselves, to give an example, as parts of the 'cadre reserve bank'. The way a district PC deals with its actual and potential

members is not much different from the method of the army. It is highly revealing that the terminology used – 'recruitment' and 'retirement' – is that of the army.

2 However, as opposed to the conscripted army, the willing consent of the individual is required here. This is gained either when entering the political academy, on a full-time basis, or when joining the apparatus.

3 Although this was not mentioned directly in our interviews, the above discussion perhaps can clarify a point related to the situation of elderly, former members of the apparatus, or party activists. Public opinion knew only about the high salaries of former leaders and the various corruption scandals, and remembered the privileged situation of the apparatus. Into this picture the problems of existence of the present apparatus, or the low pensions of former members, simply did not fit. However, the two issues are not at all contradictory. The party does care about its employees, but only as long as they are in service.[3]

For former apparatus members, the earlier special favours could not be carried over, as these hardly gave them goods that could be accumulated. The official dwelling, the vacation opportunities or shopping rights could not be saved or transferred; sometimes they were even discontinued at the point of leaving service or the active labour force. All 'extras' had to be acquired through illegal individual enterprise, which not all of them were ready or willing to undertake. Finally, it is obvious that at the moment when traditions are de-valued, their knowledge is unlikely to receive any respect.

All of them found a place for themselves

At the time of our survey, in the majority of the district PCs the old system was no longer working. The prohibition concerning the individual search for a job had been lifted. In a number of cases, the PCs were quite happy that they no longer had to worry about the difficult task of finding a position for their former members. The district PCs 'liberated' their members in more or less the same way as the government, faced with the debt, 'liberated' the social and cultural spheres. There were places where the district leadership was still involved in the process:

If I want to get out, and not as part of the planned changes, then I look for a job for myself, I announce it to my direct boss, who will talk about it with the first secretary. Then the first secretary will also say something, and I will get a chance to leave the apparatus.

(M.B.)

At other places, free exit was not an option, but the sole possibility, as the district PC was no longer able or willing to get a place for its former members:

> Those who left, all of them found a place for themselves, because the offers of the district PC would have represented a step backwards. Now you shouldn't think that everybody here wants to become a director of a factory, or the personnel manager of a cadre 'cemetery'. No, but there is a small step from here. You may become a local party secretary. But I am already 44 years old, and I would rather avoid this step when they want to think about me [about leaving]. If I go for it now, they may elect me by force or sympathy. If I work properly – let's assume that I get elected – I'll do the job for ten years. Then I will be 54 years old. At the age of 54, I would be out of everything. What should I do then? I don't know what's going to happen to me. They will say 'Well, this one has already been in the movement, let's make him an adviser or a personnel manager, or something like that.' So it is very difficult to get out from here.
>
> (P.G.)

In most cases political workers felt that, should they have to look for a position for themselves, they could only build upon what they had accumulated during their job at the PC. But the specific knowledge gained was not very convertible outside, in the 'real world'; moreover, during the five to eight years spent here, their professional knowledge had become obsolete. Without the support of the PC, without direct 'phone calls, it was not easy with this background to find employment. Thus, as they themselves came to realise, apart from the personal connections, the liabilities of the job carried out at the district PCs were greater than the assets.

Men without a future

This was stated plainly by one of our interviewees who claimed that district PCs no longer considered it to be their task to help the further career of former political workers. The lack of provision and care, the dim prospects for the future, were a recurrent topic in our interviews:

> The greatest problem is not that people spend five to ten years of their lives here, acquire a different type of knowledge, and will use it somehow later in their lives. But that there is no guarantee as to what will happen with them in the next period. They are losing their professional knowledge, deteriorating intellectually. Now the

questionnaire fails to ask whether the party cares about its own apparatus. In my opinion, they only take from you.

(J.A.)

There are no guarantees at all that you may return [to your former place]. And then, nobody will take care of you. I have a colleague who has spent ten to fifteen years here, and has not completed any courses.

(J.A.)

And for a number of people, the future, the possibility of a way out, is not even visible:

This is what I can't see even today, how you can get out of here.

(G.C.)

Q: What are your plans for your own future?
A: I have no plans. . . . At the moment, I am a man without a future. . .
Q: So you must cope with what you have here?
A: I must cope with it, accept what is given and try to exist within this setting.

(G.D.)

All this can be interpreted and has relevance at two different levels. Concerning the actual situation in the apparatus, it reinforces the assessment that, far from being a group enjoying comfort and privileges, apparatus members were themselves in a trap, and in an uncomfortable one. They were treated as pawns in the cadre game, lured into the organisation when it was deemed necessary, kept in a subordinate, humiliating position 'inside' the house, prevented from having a say in the planning of their future, and finally discarded when their service was no longer deemed necessary. A person who had enough 'faith' to do all this happily and without a reproach may have felt satisfied. Another who was smart and ruthless enough to push through on his own may have made a career using his position and connections. But many of the members were increasingly feeling defenceless, as much at the mercy of their superiors as the whole population was in the official sphere.

And here we reached the second level. We would argue that the model described here is not restricted to the apparatus itself. It was the whole of official society that was working according to the same principle in each and every segment of public or economic life under 'existing socialism'. It was in this sense that the party imposed its own model, its internal mechanism, on the population at large, and not in the sense of the ideological and police terror implied by a general theory of totalitarianism. And it was this model that was so repugnant and repulsive that all attempts at an impartial, objective, scientific description, all theories of limited pluralism and interest groups, sound so alien from the reality all of us having lived there had to accept. It was a system built upon lies about the way it was set up and about its history, and upon some promises about a better future. It was on this basis that it attempted to infantilise the whole population, by treating them as children who are promised gifts and special favours if they behave properly, but strict punishment if they stray only to frustrate all such expectations at the end.

At the end, the emptiness of all promises could not be concealed. Under this pressure, in a situation of general crisis, the system finally disintegrated. But it left behind an enormous burden in terms of built-in expectations, forms of behaviour and frames of mind as regards the treatment and handling of people. It disseminated techniques of behaviour that will be with us for a long time to come. The positions are still there for initiating movements, saying 'what the population really needs', playing chess with people at their mercy, all with the greatest self-confidence and self-esteem as, after all, they are in no way communist. The new rulers are repeating the mental processes of the communists after 1945 who were not fascists and therefore thought that they were free to do anything. The enormous difference, needless to say, is that now the population does have the means to deselect the élite. But the problem is that, if general elections can replace one élite with another, they cannot eliminate certain patterns and techniques of behaviour. And, even more sadly, the greatest threat is often represented by people who are the keenest on educating and civilising the population, as it is they who take the lead in the techniques referred to above the most strongly and without a second thought.

Forced into a siding

All this was, of course, related to the general uncertainty concerning the role of the party and the position of political workers. The district PCs, it seems, had no time to waste on individual cases. And those individuals who could not 'make a step' felt they had no perspective; their future was closed:

> Today there is no possibility of an honest retirement. My child should be engaged in public activity, but shouldn't become a 'professional revolutionary'.

(R.5)

The return [to civil jobs] is almost impossible, one is forced into a siding, and this is more or less demoralising.

(F.9)

This uncertainty was especially problematic in an organisation built on complete care, which compensated its employees for their loss of freedom of movement and opinion precisely by the promise of complete security and a fixed career, and where, consequently, even the germs of a democratic work-style were non-existent. Instructors in the past had no chance of expressing their differing opinions:

Q: What are your chances of promoting a change here?
A: None whatsoever. Any idea of reform coming from an apparatchik, without prior support from above, carries no weight.

(G.D.)

This career is over

The feeling of uncertainty, even at the time of our survey, was not restricted to the issue of retirement, but was related to the very survival of this type of job itself. Political instructors didn't know who would be needed in the future by the 'party', and who would be considered superfluous. Realisations of a personal dead-end were thus coupled – perhaps not independently – with perceptions of the imminent demise of the whole organisation. Their personal relegation to a siding became connected with that of the whole organisation; and both of them with the enforced loss of direction of the whole country. To complete our overview, let's give here a few accounts by the instructors themselves:

This is wrong from the very start. As it is not at all clear today what the political task of a district PC as a body is ... and what kind of apparatus is required for this task.... There was everything here; I don't know how much material has been prepared about the revival, and there were no results, and I don't know, but it does not make any sense. Thus, first it should be decided whether there is a need for the traditional, instructor job, or not. As, if the local party organisations are to work independently, according to the resolutions of the central committee, then let's not make resolution after resolution, and the umpteenth directive about how to execute the resolution, and send out an apparatus to supervise how it is done. They can't even decide or supervise it in reality, as they can't take part in ordinary regular work, and don't know what is really going on.

(J.A.)

It is certain that some skills cannot be converted to the new process. Hence the basic insecurity. They don't want to slip through the mesh, though at least two-thirds of the apparatus and of the whole leading body must be changed, and a lot of people feel that this is inevitable.

(T.13)

The re-thinking of the status of independent political workers and their role [must be done]; the performance of meaningful, useful activity – and considered such by others too.

(D.4)

Fifteen to twenty years from now I think there will be no careers like this.

(Z.7)

This career I have been engaged in till now is over. One must think about the meaning of a political career in the future.

(T.13)

8 A governmental technology resurrected by the party: the early modern 'police'

For this is what the science of police is all about: a great labour of form-ation of the social body, or rather a labour whose principal result is what we call society or the social body and what the eighteenth century called the good order of population. The following image might be used here: one could imagine the field of intervention of police regulations as the vacant lots in a city, the formless provinces of a vast kingdom, a sort of 'no man's land' which extends wherever the feudal world's traditi-onal customs, established competences and clear relations of authority, subordination, protection and alliance cease to hold sway. Within the formless 'monster' (as the thinkers of police call the Holy Roman Empire) there are, indeed, islands of order and transparency; not every-thing in the ancient society of orders and estates requires regulating; but does not whatever escapes it stand in need of intervention?

(Pasquino 1978: 47)

When discussing the activity of political workers, we often encountered the statement that their activity did not really involve an exercise of power. We have also shown that the activities of apparatus members were hidden not only from the public, but also from the eyes of party members – even the members of the local party leadership or the elected bodies. Thus, it was not surprising that the widely varying types of prejudices were widespread. There were some people whose assessment was identical with official expectations. One of our interviewees described the reaction of his environment when he had joined the apparatus in the following terms: 'Some of my friends looked at me with some admiration that, well, he is the lucky one who has been chosen' (G.C.). But, at least in the recent period, even according to the assessment of party workers, it was definitely a small minority. We encountered far more often the complaint that public assessment of work done inside the apparatus was very negative:

> [The kind of] perception of the work we have done up till now – what
> we have carried out in good faith and honesty – that we now
> encounter in public opinion.
>
> (U.5)

> The feeling of hatred against the workers of the apparatus, both on
> the part of individuals and different bodies. 'If from the party, then
> suspect.' The lack of respect (moral, first of all, but also material).
>
> (B.19)

> The negative assessment of our work; supposed privileges.
>
> (O.6)

It is not surprising that, according to some, this evaluation was fomented
from behind the scenes. The old image of the 'alien', the 'enemy' is
always at hand: 'Public opinion ... is often stirred up artificially' (K.5).
But, to our big surprise, according to some members, these views may
have been promoted from quite unexpected sources:

> For me as a person it is a problem that some present this relatively
> youthful apparatus as the cause of all problems. It is especially hurtful
> when one hears it from people who spent 25 years at central-party
> headquarters or in other responsible positions in the state or the
> party.
>
> (K.3)

The above comments may raise the suspicion that in a sense – to use a
metaphor widespread at that time in Hungary – the apparatus may have
been counted among the excess baggage thrown out by the leadership to
the 'wolves'. This may all the more easily have been the case as, of all
participants, the apparatus had the least chance of expressing its opinion
publicly. The leadership could always find its own ways, and its members
could look for external forums like the mass media. For them, party
discipline was less a question of existence.

With all this, we do not intend to do anything more than call attention
to the fact that in the leadership–membership–apparatus triangle quite
specific games were played; games that should not be reduced to the
simplistic statement that the apparatus was the 'evil force' lying between
the leaders and the masses, both longing for reforms; the 'evil force' that
for a long time prevented the reunion of the wise leaders and the loyal
subjects. In this form, this statement was really nothing but an ideology
serving to mask the stakes in actual power struggles. We should rather
think of the actual functions played and strategies used by the apparatus
and the discourse concerning its role as two separate entities.[1]

The exact clarification of what these stakes were made difficult by the concealment of the exercise of power actually performed by the party, as instructors denied that their daily activity of service and helping had involved an exercise of power. Even in the part of instructor work concerned with putting forward the resolutions of higher party organs, there was a tendency to hide these activities behind the general concept of service; behind the representation of the 'cause' of progress or development:

> My work as an instructor can be conceived of as a type of service. Now if one uses that word, and especially one who is working in the party apparatus, then people think something is fishy here. What type of service can be provided by a ruling organisation? But it is also a condition of my work that an instructor must help the activities of the local party organisations. . . . I mean that he must help the work of the party organisations by serving the cause.
>
> (F.G.)

But if the activity means service on the agent's own account, then the millennial struggle of Christianity and moral philosophy for the pacification of power loses its grip. Thus, concerning the activity and thinking of political instructors, we arrived at the same point as earlier, concerning the general activities of the district PCs and the definitions given to politics. The most important political goal of Christianity was to convince the holders of power to conceive of its exercise as a duty or service to be performed and not as a right or privilege given to them. This approach becomes powerless at the level of programmes employing a type of power whose explicit purpose is to help and provide service. The most it can do is to point out the deviation from this ideal, the gap between 'theory' and 'practice', and reaffirm the original project. In our study, we made an attempt to discern the dangers inherent in the specific exercise of power conceived of as help or service, and not just in its abuses.

Activities done in the name of the 'public' in order to promote the 'common good', embodied in service and help, involve a double game with the public interest. One side is the continuous abuse of power by vested-interest groups. The other side is the question at the level of principles, the reinforcement of the belief in the 'true' public interest, in 'true' development or progress. The belief in the objectivity of development gives a right in principle to the application of power in concrete practices. Once we accept the existence of 'development paths' already laid down, this licence to power cannot be erased, as the obligation to pursue the road to progress gives an absolution and provides legitimacy to those who act in its name. We encounter in a this-worldly guise the classical dilemma of salvation: a goal pointing beyond immediate actions and people, thus justifying the 'proper' interventions. The only solution seems to lie through the denial of the very idea of the inherent objectivity of progress or development.

But while the requirements of salvation, with the exception of the Inquisition, were not sanctioned by the force of repressive organis-ations, in our days the dogma of social development and progress did provide a link between the repressive organisations of the state and the secularised version of salvation. In a way, the history of the medieval period can be written as a struggle between the temporal and spiritual power. Similarly, modernity in a sense may be conceived of as the coalescence and the merging of these two aspects.

With this, a new space was opened up, a new possibility was given for the exercise of power. The title of the Hungarian version of our study, 'In No Man's Land', referred to this fact, following the words used by Pasquale Pasquino, for the reality and the programmes of a quite different period.[2] This term seemed to us to be particularly illuminating in describing the field that served as both a unifying horizon and a basis of intervention for the activities of political instructors. And we were not the first ones to use this term to describe the Hungary of the 1970s and 1980s. Elemer Hankiss also used this term earlier, in a quite different, but complementary, sense. He described with it the unclear situation of the second society that emerged on the fringes of the activity of the party and the state. There, as opposed to the situation described by Pasquino, the 'no man's land' was not a reality that was given and had to be tackled, rather it was a piece of reality that was formed, directly and indirectly, by an activity that was useless and harmful.

The differences between the reality of early modernity and the Hungary of the 1980s were, of course, not restricted to this point. Still, it seemed to us worth while to investigate whether the affinities between the two types of 'no man's lands' were more than just plays with words.

TWO TRADITIONS OF POLITICS

First, we have to stay with words, and return, in a different context, to a question already discussed in Chapter 4 concerning the etymology of the word 'politics'. It is well known that the word 'politics' is derived from the Greek word *polis*, the city-state. What is less well known is that this word had two important Greek derivatives that gave rise to two distinct traditions in the history of political thought. The first is a simple concept with a straightforward descent: *politike*, meaning the art of government.

The second word, *politeia*, however, was a complicated concept even in classical Greek thought, and had a quite peculiar career in early modern times. For Aristotle, this word stood for the good form of the rule of the many, 'democracy' standing for the bad form; for the constitution as such – where this meaning was different from the modern sense of constitution, being less of a legal type; for a mixed form of government, the mixture of democracy and aristocracy, which Aristotle sometimes considered to be the best form; for the manner of distribution of offices; and, finally, for the whole way of life of citizens.[3] In the latter sense, politeia was often referred to as the 'soul' of the city.[4] This concept was revived in the fourteenth and especially the early sixteenth centuries, in the French translation of 'policie' or 'police', carrying at first most of the same connotations as the original Greek (Guenée 1987 and Seyssel 1515).

During the sixteenth and eighteenth centuries, the terms 'politique' or 'politick', and 'police' or 'pollicy' were often used indiscriminately. Nevertheless, the distinction in their meanings became more and more pronounced. The use of the word 'politics' was gradually restricted to external relations, to the 'high' sphere of international power politics, while the derivatives of *politeia* were rather applied for internal affairs. Even within the latter, there were a number of different developments. On the one hand, the traditional Greek connotations represented an important part of the republican tradition, from Machiavelli through Harrington and Ferguson up to Rousseau. In some cases, the derivatives of *politeia* were explicitly used; in other cases, the Latin equivalent of the term, civil society, was employed, with somewhat different connotations, but in a very similar sense. On the other hand, especially in France and in Germany, there was a significant shift in the meaning of 'police', where in the seventeenth century the word took up a more concrete, institutional meaning, and was increasingly applied to the description of a particular governmental technology and apparatus, still in a sense very different from the modern police forces. For the Greeks, *politeia* meant the soul of the city, referring to an 'etheric' phenomenon. During the early modern period in Europe, the concept became materialised. The late seventeenth century police lieutenants of Paris were conceived of as men who 'move or stop at will an immense and turbulent multitude, being the always active and almost unknown soul of this large body' (Fontenelle 1766: v.6, p. 125). The two meanings, the republican and the instrumental one, were by the way not separated completely. Such leading figures of the eighteenth-century Enlightenment as Beaumarchais, Diderot, Rousseau and Voltaire were in close friendship with the contemporary police lieutenants.[5]

There was also a marked difference between the continental and the English derivatives of *politeia*. In England, the instrumentalisation of the term occurred not in connection with the deployment of a police apparatus, but with a different connection between the centre and the social body, embodied in the word 'policy', related to indirect, impersonal, negative and legal influencing, as opposed to the continental 'police' that meant a more direct and positive control over human beings, standing – purposefully, and not by abuse – outside the constraints of law. It is not accidental that there is no equivalent of 'policy' in French; it is translated today by the word 'politique'. The different paths of the derivatives of *politeia* in French and English embody in a nutshell the different paths of early modern development on the Continent and in the island, and also provide some perhaps perplexing implications concerning the continuities and discontinuities between 'police'-ing and 'policymaking'.

It is these connections between concepts and realities, between repressive institutions and high ideals, that were so peculiar about the landscape of politics during the so-called period of 'absolutism', and that are also so distractingly similar to certain characteristics of politics and its daily impact in the so-called 'totalitarian' countries.

ABSOLUTISM AND TOTALITARIANISM

The idea of drawing a comparison between some elements of absolutism and totalitarianism is not new. The writings of Max Weber on militarisation, bureaucratisation, and centralisation seemed to offer a particularly good starting point for such comparisons with the state and party machineries of post-war Eastern European states. But it was also generally accepted that, as the reality of living under absolutism was so different from the reality of twentieth-century totalitarianism, it is misleading to push this analogy too far.

However, some recent works on 'absolutism' seem to open up new perspectives for the basis of these comparisons.[6] Up till now, attention in the literature has been reserved for the centre of power, though in the same period important changes have occurred in the social body as well, where the practices of power starting from above mixed with those coming from below; where the expectations of top-level power were partly built into everyday behaviour, and were based partly on existing techniques and customs. The study of absolutism cannot be restricted to the centre or its apparatus; one must investigate the exact linkages to the day-to-day activities of the population, the successes and failures here, the exact methods employed.

It is from this perspective that we return to the question of whether it is relevant and meaningful to compare absolutist and totalitarian regimes. We follow here the German historian, Gerhard Oestreich, who took issue with Karl Mannheim about the meaning of such comparisons. Without denying the differences, he warned against playing down the extent to which 'absolutism' did entail a significant, in-depth transformation of society:

> The absolute state cannot be held to have exercised a total supervision of public and personal life.... And yet, in another way, private life *was* invaded, and opinion manipulated. The attitudes and the conduct of even the simple subject were shaped, controlled and regulated by the process of disciplining.... This process of disciplining produced a more or less violent change in the structure of society at all levels.
>
> (Oestreich 1982: 259–60).

And later, he refers to social disciplining as a process neglected by Weber, but nevertheless having a crucial impact on shaping the modern state and society, underlying the global processes of rationalisation, centralisation and bureaucratisation discussed by Weber (Oestreich 1982: 271).

THE 'POLICE'

In this approach, the 'police' becomes particularly interesting for us. This institution or apparatus, embedding a specific technology, was charged with very different and broader tasks in the seventeenth and eighteenth centuries than in later periods (Small 1909, Chapman 1970, Bayley 1975, Pasquino 1978, Foucault 1981, Oestreich 1982, Tribe 1988, Axtmann 1990). The target of its activities, neglected in earlier studies, was the population itself; or, according to the terminology of Foucault, we may say that the population itself, as we conceive of it today, was to a large extent constituted by its activities, and by similar technologies. This neglect may be explained by the separation of the social sciences in later periods, and the subsequent, if anachronistic, transposition of this situation to an earlier period. If we study only the economic, political or social aspects of absolutism, then the 'police' becomes lost from our focus, though its activities were concerned with all the above areas; with their integration, harmonisation and differentiation.

A crucial aspect of the development of 'police' were certain regulations centring around the public life of some German towns around the beginning of the sixteenth century (Oestreich 1982: 155–65).

Some examples are the ordering of fairs, the regulation of prices, the measures to be taken in the case of fire, floods or epidemics. These regulations had earlier precedents, but around the crisis of the feudal ages they became widespread and more intensive, spreading to ever larger aspects of everyday life. At the period the police did not mean an institution or an apparatus, but an ensemble of regulations and the organs created for their enforcement. At the same time, during the crisis of medieval cities, it was also charged with the specific, positive duties of assuring the public good and the cohesion of the community. The strange dream (or nightmare) of the existence and well-being of the community supported by force was thus born.

The real growth in police technologies was caused by the connection of this institution to the idea of the 'reason of state', developed in Italy (Meinecke 1957, Church 1972, Dyson 1980, Foucault 1981). The police became the branch of the absolutist state with the task of assuring the main goal of these states: the growth of the forces of the state, together with the health, well-being and satisfaction of the population at large. At this point, it may be well worth listing the topics covered in the chapter headings of the famous book by De La Mare summarising the police regulations of the whole period: religion; customs; health; [the necessities of life]; highways; keeping the peace; sciences and liberal arts; commerce; manufactured goods and mechanical arts; servants, domestics and nurses; the poor (De La Mare 1705–38).

The rationality behind a similar list escapes us today, and even the compilers of these regulations were often not aware of the underlying rationality. Duchesne, who gave a summary of De La Mare's work and an outline of the chapters that De La Mare was not able to complete, himself was not able to provide an explanation for these activities' spreading to all conceivable areas. As a justification, he could evoke only that the 'police has for its object the general interest', and added that 'the objects which it embraces are in some sense infinite'.[7]

Within the absolutist states, connected to the doctrine of the reason of state, the specific task of the 'police' became the acquisition of information necessary for rational government and the enforcement of the central measures, thus helping in the proper realisation of the activities necessary for the growth of the forces of the state. The police was destined to become, besides the military, the justice and the finance departments, the fourth branch of state. Its area of competence included everything related to the common activities of individuals, their health, wealth and happiness. Thus, from this aspect, the police even spread to the other three areas as well. The police almost became a state within a state, whose primary target, according to the utopias about the 'well-policed states' of the period, was 'communication', 'society' and 'man' (Foucault 1981, Raeff 1983). It was charged with directing the activities of the subjects toward the common areas of individual and public interest: the growth of the forces of the state and the increase of individual wealth and health.

It is from this perspective that the attention of police became directed to the economic sphere. In the earlier police ordinances, the field of economic actions was only one of the areas to be regulated; in some cases it was missing, and aspects of economic life were regulated separately. Then, economic questions began to be given a more and more pronounced role in the activities of police and the textbooks of mercantilism or *Polizeiwissenschaft* (the science of police). With an inversion accomplished in the eighteenth century, the police became a field within the science of economics (as opposed to the previous, reverse situation, when economic issues were part of police matters); finally, with the publication of Adam Smith's major work, the police fell once and for all outside the field of economics (Meuret 1988).

The goal of the police was not restricted to the formulation of the space where the co-harmonisation of state and individual concerns became possible; it was extended to the moulding of individuals as well; to the enforcement of forms of behaviour compatible with the target; to the development of the forces of production and, its most important element, 'man' himself. The end-project of this process was taken for granted by liberalism; and certain techniques of normalisation were only reinforced by the latter. This was the task to be faced by the so-called 'less developed countries'; and it was the project [rediscovered] by the ideology of bolshevism as the *telos* (the purpose) of history.

This project needed agents. They were the commissaires, lieutenants, prefects or intendants of police and their subordinates. Their tasks, according to seventeenth-century definitions of the 'ideal police', were the following: the acquisition of knowledge necessary for the rational government of the state, the collection of information, in the form of 'reports' covering all aspects of the day-to-day life of the people; the right of intervention in case of unusual situations, the emergence of 'problems'; help and advice in matters of correct behaviour, conduct of life, concerning matters of health, economic activities and religion, the spread of proper forms, the 'enlightenment' of the population; finally, the mobilisation of the population for the independent performance and enforcement of all these activities, the transformation of spying into confession. In order to realise these goals, the intendants must be present everywhere; they must remain silently in the background, dealing only with isolated individuals. The task of police is the construction and connection of proper individuals; it assumes docile subjects that are isolated and obedient. As Fouché the police minister of Napoleon, said: 'Nature makes the Jacobinists and the Police makes the citizens' (in Buisson 1958: 12).

'POLICE' AND STATE-PARTY: A COMPARISON

These remarks already indicate that there are surprising similarities between the early modern police and the communist-party apparatus, going into the minutest detail. Let's review, then, some of the identical techniques and methods of procedure between the apparatus of the state-party and early modern apparatuses of government. While most of the historical examples will come from practices or treatises concerned particularly with the 'police', some will be from different contemporary sources, to show that the emphasis is not on the label 'police', but on the functions that the early modern police was performing, among other similar apparatuses and techniques.

The level and aim of discussion

One of the curious characteristics of the state-party is its predilection for certain global, wide-ranging categories, used both for mobilising and analytical purposes. One may say that modern Western parties also use similar tricks in the electoral debate – like references to the common good, the nation, welfare, the health of the economy, etc. But the concepts used by bolshevik-type parties are quite different: on the one hand, they are more general, in some sense meta-theoretical, lying 'below' the sphere of these modern concepts; on the other, they are 'creative' of the later concepts, attempting not only to prepare the ground for them, but actually to found them. Such key words are 'ground' or 'pillar', the 'soul' or 'conscience', the 'cement' and the 'order'. One only has to read the writings of Lenin, the resolutions of a party congress, or programmatic accounts on communism to find loads of similar statements: the party is the 'ground' or the 'pillar' under our feet; it is the 'conscience' of our age; it is the 'soul' of the people or the 'cement' of society. And the more mundane preoccupation with 'order', interpreted in the widest possible sense, is the key preoccupation of all central and local party organs. This purpose serves to maintain the status quo and thus existing privileges. There were attempts to explain it purely by motives of personal interest, but we think the logic then would be reversed. The concern with order is a much broader preoccupation than the abuse of power; the former is not just a justification of the latter, but its precondition. In principle, communism represses any innovation, even those that eventually could have proved beneficial to the system or to the holders of power, if it was thought to upset the order.

While such concerns are almost completely absent from the rhetoric of modern politics, or are much underplayed, they were central to the early modern police; and the way they were posed cannot but recall the style and reality of bolshevism. One of the central preoccupations of sixteenth and seventeenth century treatises on politics concerned the order of the world; its current absence, and the measures to re-establish it. The problem on which all this discourse converged – or, rather, what was considered the negative reference point by almost all – was the realisation of Machiavelli: it is not only that the external constraints of religion were lost, but the underlying internal ontological assumption of the medieval world view, the positing of a purposeful God beyond everything that is happening, was lost as well. Fortuna and fate had reasserted their role on the scenes of human society.[8] And on the opposite side to Fortuna, a new reality began to dig its space; something quite different from the old pacifier, religion: it was police (or pollycy, or policie). In the works of Etienne Pasquier, the eminent French historian of the sixteenth century, we find a preoccupation with the question of whether it was Fortuna or 'police' that contributed most to the maintenance of France.[9] The meaning of this new concept was as vague as its spelling. For Pasquier, 'police' was the equivalent of prudent council. But, in different uses, it referred to the modern policy, polity, constitution, political action at the same time, but was different from all as it was related to the actual constitution of all these activities. Markedly, it had nothing to do with anything similar to the modern police, especially because it had nothing to do with law. It referred to all sorts of expedient actions that lay completely outside the old framework of the law.

While in Pasquier the opposition between Fortuna and 'police' appeared on a general, metaphysical level, in other writings of the sixteenth and seventeenth century, the concept of 'police' took on a more mundane meaning, among others, concerning what actually does provide the 'support', the 'ground' of political community. A particularly widespread metaphor concerned the 'columns' or the 'pillars' of society. Let's contrast here two seventeenth-century works by Turquet and by La Mothe.[10] Both mention four such 'pillars', and in each case, these correspond to different branches of the – nascent – state. Three are identical; these are the army, the justice and finances. The fourth is different; and in both cases, this is the most important as it provides the underlying foundation of the whole edifice; it is, if you like, the 'pillar of pillars'. For La Mothe, it is religion; for Turquet, it is the 'police'. The latter is perhaps the first case where the word 'police' is applied in a concrete, institutional sense meaning a technique of government and a body called to administer and execute these tasks. It is an important step on the long road from the Aristotelian concept of *politeia* to the modern police force. And, as we would argue, on a different road, toward the state-party as well. Finally, we should also mention that the concept of the 'pillar' is also often associated in this literature with the bourgeoisie.

The metaphor of the 'soul' is also frequently used in the period. It appeared in the characterisation of the activities of the lieutenants of police of Paris, who were supposedly the 'moving soul' of the multitude of people in the city; or in theoretical treatises according to which the police should help in procuring both the goods of the body and the soul of the population (De La Mare 1705–38, Preface). For obvious reasons, the word 'cement' does not appear in the early modern literature, but there are all the more frequent references to the need for the police to assure the connection, the link, or, to use a contemporary word, the 'communication' between individuals (Turquet 1611: 4–5, Crucé 1623); to establish and maintain social life – society itself. This preoccupation again is not restricted to treatises where the word 'police' appears. The same idea, the establishment of magistrates that establish and maintain organic social life, dominates one of the classic works of the period, the *Politics* of Althusius (1610). Institutions and offices that do not simply represent or govern the political body, but that target the whole social body in all of its living and daily relations; that attempt to ground daily life and create the organism, the community – this was at least as important in the contemporary political literature as the question of political sovereignty that is almost exclusively discussed in modern histories of political thought.

Finally, perhaps the most important common characteristic of the early modern 'police' and the bolshevik-type state-party is the preoccupation with order, the need to establish and maintain order at any price. One can refer both to the burgeoning theoretical discourses of the general question of order in the sixteenth and seventeenth centuries – why does order exist, what is the nature of order, etc. – and to the correlative political literature on how political order can be maintained and assured. Given the civil and religious wars of the sixteenth century and the wars, especially the Thirty Years War, of the seventeenth century, this preoccupation was understandable; but even in the late seventeenth century, it seemed that the predilection survived though it was no longer functional (Miller 1990).

Scope of activities

On the one hand, we have here a preoccupation with the basics of society, in an active, founding sense, both on the part of the early modern 'police' and of the contemporary state-party; on the other, a concern with all sorts of activities, and in minute detail. Our empirical study of the district-level party committees of Budapest demonstrated that, even in 1988, almost any economic or social activity was deemed worthy of the attention of the party, be it the development plan of the district council, the market price of cucumber, the provision of schools with computers, or the seating order in the common refectory of a school and a factory. And it is enough here to glance into the titles of the books in the enormous survey of the police by De La Mare – four volumes published, of over three thousand pages, containing only the first six of the projected twelve books – to show that the early modern police had a similarly all-encompassing scope of activities.

De La Mare's work is a compendium of regulations; and the German *Polizeiordnungen* of the same period are also ordinances, regulations, papers. But there also came into being at the same time an apparatus whose task was to supervise the execution of these resolutions, the relation between ordinances and apparatuses being exactly analogous to the relation between the party resolutions and the apparatus. Resolutions are quasi-legal regulations in the same way as the ordinances were. These latter had the same binding effects as laws had, but they were passed solely by the king, without having recourse to the popular representative bodies. And the apparatus that was called to execute these resolutions was also highly specific.

It is almost an unquestioned commonplace to use the discourse of 'bureaucracy' in the description of the party apparatus. However, in spite of certain similarities, it is a mistake. The discourse of the bureaucracy applied to the early modern period is anachronistic, especially for the description of the 'private service' of the king (as opposed to the civil service of the emerging state 'bureaucracies'). And the most important agents of the police – or similar apparatuses or institutions – were precisely related to the court, and to the king personally. They had a very particular relation to the traditional administrative organs and the population at large. They stood outside the whole formal legal framework. They were special envoys for specific, emergency purposes – for a long time, they had no fixed residence. The requirements of their jobs showed that one cannot talk about bureaucracy in any sense of the term.

Let's take two examples here, comparing early modern techniques to the tasks of the political instructors. The first are the intendants of Colbert. In our study of the party apparatus, we assessed two major out-of-house tasks of apparatus members: the representation of the party, meaning at the same time the representation of the given line, the concrete resolutions, and the more elusive sense of representing the 'party' as a mythical–mystical entity; and the collection and dissemination of information. Here, our analysis centred on the importance of personal elements, direct, face-to-face connections as the precondition for the performance of the multiple, manifest and hidden functions associated with the exchange of information inside the state-party. If one compares these findings to the analysis of the activities of the intendants, the analogies are quite remarkable (King 1972). According to King, the tasks of the intendants can be described by the same two concepts, information collection and representation, and even the methods of their accomplishment are almost identical. Colbert's instructions to them used almost the same language, the same analogies and tricks that party instructors told us about in 1988 – concerning the need to be informed about minute details, and not just broad overall trends; the need to establish friendships and to use these intimate connections for the collection of 'real' information, etc.

The second example is even more surprising, as it comes from a country where the early modern police as an apparatus did not exist at all – England. But the court existed in the same way as in France (one should not forget that, for a long time, the Italian and the French courts represented the desirable model for the English court), and the kings did use special envoys – the members of the Privy Chamber (Starkey 1977). The quasi-mystical manner in which these envoys represented the king had much in common with the way the party was 'represented' by the political instructors, with some obvious differences. Thus, for example, the belief in the mystical powers of the king was shared by the whole population in the sixteenth century, while in twentieth-century Eastern Europe, it was restricted to party members; or, at least, only they were supposed to believe in this mystical substance. The question whether it was met in reality or not belongs to the curious games of 'voluntary compulsion' played in these countries.[11]

Manners and methods of procedure

Besides the type and scope of the activities and the concrete tasks of the apparatus, there are numerous analogies between the early modern police and the state-party concerning the manner of their implementation, the language used, etc. There is the well-known statement that, without the party, there would be complete chaos and anarchy; its equivalent with respect to 'police' can be found in the work of Turquet (1611: 369). There is the recurrent idea in the textbooks of that particularly ugly and boring pseudo-science, the political economy of socialism, of the 'harmonic and proportional' growth of the socialist economy, the exact analogy of which can be found in a number of early modern works (Turquet 1611: 6, 16; Laval 1613: 319). Or, to give a very concrete example, there is the prohibition concerning the industrial activities of agricultural enterprises that was in effect in Hungary up till the end of the 1970s, the elimination of which was considered to be one of the proofs of the benevolence and the astuteness of the system of 'late paternalism'; a restriction that has no meaning whatsoever in the twentieth century, but that can be found word for word in the classic work the *Polizeiwissenschaft*, Justi's *Elements of Police* (Justi 1769: 86). This work, by the way, is a 'beauty' in itself, the closest model to the socialist textbooks on political economy. If we take away the ideological garbage from the latter concerning the working class and the progress of socialism, we may recover all the major positive tenets in Justi's book. This amazing similarity can perhaps explain not what Marx meant by putting Hegel the right way up, but what this actually amounted to, as the ground of Hegel's views on civil society were laid down by the activities contained in and related to the *Polizeiwissenschaft* of Justi. Hegel's famous metaphor of the owl of Minerva gives a very graphic account of how it happened. In this sense, the bolsheviks were only too faithful to the original Marxian scenario.

The same analogy can be observed concerning the way police administrators should behave toward their job. Modern civil servants must be efficient, responsive and responsible, but they do not have to exhibit particular zeal toward their job. Quite the contrary, this would be counter-productive, as it would disturb ordinary daily business. Not so in the case of bolshevik apparatchiks and early modern police officers. Early police treatises are full of enthusiastic claims about serving the public good. According to Duchesne, commissaires should throw themselves with enthusiasm into all sorts of social relations (Duchesne 1767: 8); and even the well-known Italian economist, Verri, exclaims at the beginning of his treatise how much he would like to make some useful contribution to the public good (quoted in Schumpeter 1954: 178).

The zeal which police officers – and party functionaries – were supposed to exhibit not surprisingly led to comparable attitudes being expected on the part of the population at large. First, they had to implant in the population the belief that no matter what problems they had, they could always turn to the police. According to De La Mare, police officers should disseminate in the population the opinion that, if anything happens to individuals, they should immediately feel that the police is there to help.[12] This means that police officers must be constantly available. In our follow-up study of the role of the communist party in Hungarian villages, we found the same concerns, and met with exactly the same sentences. We heard that the door of a village party secretary must be open day and night; that he or she should deal personally with any conceivable problems of the inhabitants, be it the provision of bread or obtaining foreign medication; that he or she must be the first up and the last asleep in a village. This latter statement, incidentally, has a long history – it was first applied to the Roman censors, an institution that was deemed particularly admirable in the early modern period in general. And this leads us to our second point: officers who take such a minute and loving care of the fate of their subjects demand full respect from them. This is a respect which censors did receive in the past – such famous historical figures as Cicero or Cato started their career as censors; and in eighteenth-century France, a high-level police job also meant a good prospect for a future political career. Now, while for modern police officers both this career and the desire for public admiration are obviously out of the question, both eighteenth-century police officers and bolshevik-party secretaries asked for the same respect; and to some extent they did receive from some people something comparable. Concerning the rest, they relied upon something censors did not need and early modern police administrators could not have – the terror of the modern political police. The ideal-typical function of Roman censors is in itself very interesting, both in the early modern and in the bolshevik context, as it represents a curious combination of moral and repressive functions.

Finally, we may mention the self-importance and exuberance emitted by French or Prussian police administrators; their use of contemporary science for purposes of social engineering, and their belief in their own importance and mission, comparable to the arrogance and – in a sense limited in time and space – innocence of their bolshevik counterparts.

The common good as ultimate purpose

It is not easy to reconstruct the reasons behind such activities, as the exercise of power is always hidden behind a thick layer of justification. Nevertheless, the specific rationality of power can be excavated through an analysis of the various components of the activity, as the concrete ways in which power is exercised possess a certain particularity. In the case of the 'police', there is one reason that always comes to the fore, and that is the direct, overriding importance of the promotion of the public good. In modern societies, the service of the public good also lies behind all sorts of public services, state administration, professionals, experts and the economic system as such, both as a programme and as an ideology. But the contribution of all these services to the common good is indirect, ultimate and not immediate; and, most importantly, it is not connected to a single apparatus or institution. Something comparable to the early modern police would be completely devoid of all meaning in a modern framework.

In the early modern period, this was obviously not the case, as a large amount of intellectual effort was spent in defining the scope and reason for the activity of the 'police', and in administering these tasks. And not only was the task of directly serving the public good meaningful, but it was connected to an overall project of forming and transforming all sorts of social relations; it was connected to the transformation of the whole society, or rather the creation of a society as such. As it is increasingly being realised, again and again, by a number of different writers, 'absolutism' was not just a vehicle for the despotism of the king, was not just the pursuit of mercantilist policies in the interest of an army, or mercantilist policies to help and support monopolies; it was a comprehensive project, endowed with its own sense of mission. One could say that, *mutatis mutandum*, especially if one discards the ideological rubbish related to the working class, bolshevism was set on a very similar project of social engineering, with a very similar sense of mission. Most importantly, this gives bolshevism its specificity, setting it apart from earlier Asian despotism, or contemporary Latin-American or South-European authoritarianism, centred on the domination and exploitation of the subjects. In this sense, there are only two precedents for bolshevism – the emergence of the modern state, with its theory of reason of state and its police; and Christianity, with its similar mission to transform reality. This does not make the reality of bolshevism more acceptable; quite the contrary, it makes it more insupportable. The most totalitarian aspects of this system result precisely from its missionary attempts at a positive transformation of society, from this specific civilising zeal. At this point, it is worth while to remember that, besides the police, the other major enemy of the modern discourse of civil society, liberalism and enlightenment was the clergy.

While thus we risk the suggestion that bolshevism meant a repetition of the programme of the secularisation of the missionary transformation of society, first attempted by the early modern states, the reality that surrounded it and that was produced was obviously far from being identical in the two cases. Living under the France of Louis XIV, the Prussia of Frederick the Great or the England of Henry VIII was an experience quite incomparable to the experience of living in bolshevik Russia. Perhaps that is the reason why such historical comparisons were never much in vogue, though time and again there appeared works that drew attention to the significant similarities between 'bolshevism' and 'absolutism'. It is only recent revisions in the concept of absolutism and methodological excursions concerning the epistemological status of the history of thought that made possible a serious analysis of the similarities between early modern Europe and the Eastern European party-states; an analysis that does not require the two ways of life to be identical in order to assess the structural, or rather programmatic, similarities, going well beyond a mere claim of the similarity of all sorts of tyrannies and absolutisms.

The bolshevik state-parties, thus, are not the same things as the early modern polices. They belong to a different period in history, and to a different geographical region. But the programme, the governmental rationality and the corresponding technology of government that are embedded in and can be excavated from the regular, daily activity of the apparatus of the state-party are the same.

Bolshevik-type state-parties rediscovered the early modern 'police' as the hidden essence of history and development and duplicated it in the modern bureaucratic state and political police. These latter provided instruments that increased the power of the 'police' in its missionary zeal to transform society; instruments that provided frightening potential for total control, but that nevertheless belonged to a different rationality, and thus could never be used properly. In this sense, it is interesting to note that, since the 1970s, there has been a widespread feeling that the use of modern information-retrieval techniques might have a horrible impact in the Soviet Union. But this has never happened, simply because in this way the vital personal connection in the process of information collection would have been lost.

PASTORAL POWER

The analogy between the party and the 'police' is only reinforced if we consider a technology that was incorporated in and served as a model for the 'police' itself, the pastoral technology of power. According to Michel Foucault (1981), this technology emerged as a measure to counter the all-encompassing impacts of the early civilisations – to use the terminology of Lewis Mumford, the 'megamachines' (Mumford 1967). The main characteristics of pastoral power were the following:

First, the pastor exercises his power over people, and not over a given territory. Members of the 'flock' are individually subordinated to him. This personal dependency is more important than any formal ties. Second, it is presupposed that, without the pastor, all communal ties would disintegrate and individuals would be disconnected from each other. Left alone, they would not even be able to support themselves. The task of the pastor is to 'take good care' of them, to make them 'happy'. Third, even if care is extended to this-wordly matters, the most important goal is salvation. In order to assure the salvation of each and every member, the pastor must have detailed information about the activities of everyone, as, in the final count, everything will matter. Fourth, this is all the more important for the pastor as he is personally responsible for the salvation of every member of his flock. His salvation is conjoined to that of the flock. Therefore, discipline over the self and continuous supervision over the flock are required. Finally, as the pastor cannot be personally present everywhere, he must implant the need for self-examination and for the constant review of conscience among the members.

All of these sound strangely familiar if we recall a number of points made earlier about the activities and opinions of the instructors. It is our contention that the pastoral technology of power, through the mediation of the police, found its way into the communist parties.

INTELLECTUALS AND THE 'POLICE'

Such a connection is all the more plausible as there are many other affinities between the communist party and the pastoral technology. The similarities between intellectual and priestly functions are well known. It is not accidental that Konrád and Szelényi started their genealogy of the function intellectuals played in Eastern Europe by a discussion of the roles of priests (Konrád and Szelényi 1979). Several aspects of the party – its dogmatism, its emphasis on rituals, its tendencies toward gerontocracy and the proclaimed infallibility of the top leadership, among others – often evoked comparisons between the party and the church. To this, one can add the still not fully comprehensible practice of stage trials, with the public confession of false crimes as their culminating moment. On the other hand, we also documented in our study a relentless intellectualisation of the party apparatus. Intellectuals and priests, the party and the 'police', were all parts of a historical trajectory whose confusing connections still await analysis.

It is a well-known fact that the present social role and importance of intellectuals or professionals is connected to the rise of the modern state. As civil servants, professors, teachers or doctors, professionals are trained and largely employed by institutions that belong to the state. Nevertheless, it is not easy to give a more positive account of what exactly intellectuals are, or what qualifies a job or an activity as an intellectual one. Formal training and expertise are obviously important characteristics, but, on this ground, one would run into difficulties in separating professionals from certain highly skilled workers. Our problem here is not the search for an exact, universal, scientific definition, but, from the perspective of the book, to account for a distinction that obviously exists in modern societies, but where the accepted criterion of expertise does not seem to work.

Confronted with the same problem, Konrád and Szelényi offered the concept of 'cross-contextual knowledge' (1979: 31). According to them, 'intellectuals' should be defined according to their knowledge, but in a special sense. They possess a type of knowledge that is not restricted to the performance of certain given tasks, but that can be carried over to the solution of similar problems under different circumstances, due to the broad range of their expertise. Intellectual knowledge involves familiarity with a global picture, as opposed to the performance of certain specific tasks, without awareness of or interest in their broader implications. We would like to take this definition as a starting point, but give it a somewhat different meaning. We accept that the specificity of cross-contextual knowledge lies in the relationship between the whole and the parts, but would like to argue that when the targets of intellectual activity are human beings themselves – this is true for most professions that are considered to be 'truly' intellectual, like teachers, priests, civil servants, doctors – the functional relevance of cross-contextual knowledge is that it makes the coordination of the whole and the part, or the adjustment of the individuals to the requirements of the whole, possible.

Thus, the specificity of modern intellectual expertise is not restricted to the knowledge of books or ideologies, an awareness of the global picture – the traditional picture of a theologist or a philosopher. The specificity of modernity with respect to intellectuals consists in the fact that they 'descended' to the ground, and were concerned not only with pure questions of speculation, but with the secular adjustment of the whole social body. Instead of searching for eternal order and 'truth', and offering counsel on the way to salvation or the philosophic conduct of life, they were concerned with the concrete realisation of order and the adjustment of behaviour according to the joint requirements of 'true' knowledge and social order. Instead of studying philosophy or theology, modern students study a number of 'disciplines', where the dual meaning of the term itself testifies to the widening range and type of influence exercised by intellectuals in modern societies.[13]

Today, in the Western countries, we find all signs of the disappearance of these traditional intellectual functions and the consequent professionalisation and privatisation of expertise in a narrower sense. Not surprisingly, the neo-liberal attack hardly makes any distinction between the state and the intellectuals as targets. The unity of concern with politics and the whole society on the one hand, and with individual behaviour on the other, is forever broken. Nevertheless, if we are concerned with the functions performed, the continuity is obvious. The proliferation and escalation of counselling services are progressing unchecked, no matter whether in the private or the state sector (Halmos 1978). And if we are concerned not with the 'state' as a mythical entity – whether good or evil – but with the functions performed, the creation of an efficient and governable social body, then the state can be considered as the precondition for the modern combination of market economy and civil society; an entity that has successfully run its course and partly made itself obsolete, partly receded into the background.

In the liberal world view, the adjustment between public and private interests occurs automatically and naturally, due to the market. The only problem is to provide and assure the institutional framework which makes it possible for the market to work. And yet this approach is not able to explain why the specific statements made by Adam Smith could not have been uttered earlier. The liberal response may have gained some sophistication since the early nineteenth century, but is basically identical with what Jean-Baptiste Say said to this question in 1828: it is because, until now, men have been ignorant; but Adam Smith suddenly lit a light in the darkness.[14] What the liberal answer ignores is that the adjustment of public concerns and private interests has a number of preconditions concerning human behaviour and motivation that may be assumed or assumed away today, but that were actually implanted in behaviour through centuries of history. This is the basic argument, among others, of Max Weber concerning the Protestant ethic. And the early modern 'police' was an apparatus and technology concerned specifically with such coordination.

From the perspective of the nineteenth century, this was seen as a liability, a hindrance to and destroyer of economic life. Contemporary 'police' officers certainly did not see themselves in this light. Their major concern was to assure the joint well-being of the state and the population, and for that purpose, to perpetuate free trade. However, they found that, due to a number of factors, it was necessary to pursue an active policy in order to ensure the freedom of trade. It meant the proper 'order' of trade, the elimination of different internal barriers, the supervision of product quality, weights and measures, and the maintenance of 'good faith' in commerce. Even the performers of these functions considered these activities to be only temporary. Justi explicitly stated that this bureaucracy would eliminate itself, once it had successfully performed its task (Schumpeter 1954: 171). The fact that the actual wielders of power clung to their positions explains the actual unfolding of events, but does not alter the disturbing implications of Justi's claim in the functional sense concerning both Western and Eastern Europe.[15]

THE DISSOLUTION OF THE SCIENCE OF POLICE

Let's stay here, with Justi and the final accomplishments of the science of 'police'. We have seen earlier that, throughout the seventeenth and eighteenth centuries, the distinctions between 'politics' and 'police' were often not made clearly, and that this led to confusions concerning the scope of activity of the emerging governmental apparatus, the police. Justi made the first systematic attempt to end this confusion.[16] According to him, politics has a negative meaning, and is concerned solely with the external affairs of the state, concerning its security. The task of 'police', on the other hand, is positive: to assure at the same time the happiness of individuals and the growth of the strength of the state. He tries to mark out a distinct, well-defined sphere of existence for the police, and thus separates 'police' questions from both economic and political ones. The 'police' should not deal with economic and financial questions as such, but it is its task to 'see to what extent it is possible to increase the intakes of the state without harming the public' (Justi 1769: 4). And the 'police' should stay clear of all strictly political affairs; it deals 'only with offences that don't have any impact on the constitution and the maintenance of the state' (Justi 1769: 4). In listing and justifying the activities of this police, Justi is talking about the need to promote the social good, by helping the growth of what we would call the 'productive forces' of a society (Justi 1769: 19); the need to care about the interests of the inhabitants, where 'the police should take the necessary measures so that everything responds to the goals proposed' (Justi 1769: 43); and he is repeatedly using the expression 'the police must pay attention' with respect to the most varied aspects of daily life.

The work of Justi is the summary of two centuries of development; but soon after their publication his main theses were attacked and rendered outdated. On the one hand, it was claimed that Justi's definition of the tasks of 'police' as the whole of internal administration was too broad. His follower, von Sonnenfels, claimed that the tasks of 'police' should be restricted to problems of internal security.[17] In this way, he paved the way toward the modern concept of police as an instrument of crime prevention and law enforcement. An identical transformation happened in the same period in France, fuelled by less theoretical concerns. Napoleon's minister of police, Fouché, reproached the old 'police' for exactly what Justi considered its distinctive feature, its separation from politics (Lévy 1966: 488). Fouché thought that the Revolution could have been avoided if the 'police' had done its proper task and had focused its activity on the internal enemies of the state, instead of being bogged down in endless family debates, the supervision of charity, traffic, the local market, etc. In this way, the limiting of police activity not only went beyond Justi in further narrowing the scope, but received modification: instead of being separated from politics, it became reconnected to it. With Fouché, we have a new concept and reality Justi could not even have conceived of: the political police.

In the light of this discussion, the old discourse about 'police state' can be put into a new perspective. It no longer appears as a pejorative term, but as the real mission of bolshevik-type parties, quite literally according to the very principles of historical materialism. And, more than that, it may help us in the understanding of modern mechanisms of power, by eliminating the wall built up by liberalism, denying the similarity and even homogeneity of some of the techniques applied in modern, liberal states and those of early modern states.

As, in the case of this whole discussion, the emphasis is not just on the apparatus of 'police' (where the analogy is close in the case of bolshevik-type party-states, and non-existent in modern liberal-democratic states), but on the function or role to be performed: the harmonisation of the individual and the public, and the minimalisation of the distance between the two. And this task cannot be restricted to the 'police' or the communist party, but extends to the whole modern institutional network, or civil society itself. One may say that civil society is the field, the sphere of reality that is the result of this process of harmonisation, where the main goal is the creation of a perfectly legitimate social power which will be impossible to oppose rationally.

DESPOTISM AND EFFICIENCY: THE EMERGENCE OF THE DISCOURSE OF CIVIL SOCIETY

In recent discussions concerning civil society, one often encounters the claim either that the struggle between the state and civil society, also stated in the language of the struggle between tyranny and slavery, represents a universal in the history of mankind; or, conversely, that until the end of the eighteenth or the beginning of the nineteenth century, the state and civil society were one, and it was only after that time that the independence of society with respect to the state asserted itself. Neither of these accounts stands up to inspection. We would propose here an examination of the conditions under which the discourse of civil society emerged and re-emerged, as this concept was not used frequently or indiscriminately in the history of the last two hundred years, but is connected to quite specific, and relatively short, periods. Three such instances were the period around the year 1800; the re-emergence of the concept in Western Europe as an answer to the crisis of the 1970s; and the sudden flowering of this discourse in Eastern Europe in the 1980s. The last one has already been discussed in Chapter 1; the first two will be analysed and compared here.

1800: CIVIL SOCIETY AND LIBERALISM VS. THE STATE

The central idea behind the claims made on behalf of civil society, in the most general terms, was the assertion of the rights and interests of the whole of society against something perceived as a tyrannical and despotic power. Now, in this, at a general level there is nothing new: since the birth of political thought in ancient Greece, one of the key questions has been the denunciation of and struggle against tyranny. However, the way the question was posed at this time immediately betrayed that the problem now was different, much more specific. In the past, the discourse against tyranny was couched in the language of the forms of government – the direct opposite of tyranny, the 'bad' form of one-man rule, being the monarchy, the 'good' form. In the late eighteenth century, the denunciation of tyranny was not connected to a reassertion of the monarchy; nor, for that matter, to any of the other possible political forms of government, but was related to a novel, non-political use of the concept of civil society. In other words, it was exactly in this way that the concept of the civil society was reinterpreted in this period, and dissociated from its previous synonym, the political society. We have here a distinctly novel phenomenon, an immanent opposition made between a political and a non-political concept on the same field, and not just as a normative statement of difference from an exterior position – as Christian humanist opposition to war was in the sixteenth century.[18] The discourse of the civil society gave a new form to the old distinction between the opposition of 'us' and 'them', 'us' meaning in this case the totality of society, and not just conceived as the whole political body, but in a more 'total' sense; in a sense where any activity done by any individual was incorporated from the inside and from below into the new, global and total concept of society as a source of resistance.

The peculiar characteristic of this concept of civil society and its irreducibility, even unintelligibility, in the context of traditional political discourse can be made intelligible if we consider what the opponent of this discourse was, what the exact form of 'tyranny' against which it was deployed was, as this concept of tyranny was also redefined, reinterpreted. Tyranny no longer stood for the abuse of one-man rule, the pursuit of the self-interest of the prince as opposed to the pursuit of the common good (defined previously in the form of justice), but the word tyranny was joined to the state. State tyranny and state despotism are for us such common terms that we fail to realise the innovation which the joining of these two words meant two hundred years ago, as, in the context of sixteenth- or seventeenth-century political thought, the term 'state tyranny' would have been completely devoid of meaning. For Hobbes, this phrase would certainly have sounded nonsense – and not because, as the liberal interpretation of Hobbes would have it, Hobbes in his *Leviathan* was an apostle of tyranny. Quite the contrary, Hobbes only summarised the development of the political thought and reality of several centuries that represented a comprehensive project, the early modern attempt to make tyranny impossible. The political society and institution embodied in the early modern state was, among other things, exactly the outcome of this development.

The struggle against tyranny, in the traditional sense of the term, was a problem not of the late eighteenth, but of the fifteenth and sixteenth centuries. At that period, first in Italy and then in the whole of Europe, the traditional, normative constraints on political power broke down. The previous limits on the prince's pursuit of his own self-interest – i.e. tyranny – suddenly became ineffective. In the medieval period, there were several techniques deployed to convince the ruler that it was in his own interest to follow the dictates of justice and the common good. Otherwise, he would be excommunicated; God would turn away from him, and punish by epidemics or natural catastrophes; his subjects would no longer be obedient; neighbouring princes would come and conquer his territories; he would be killed by his own servants, etc.

Whatever we may think of the validity of some of these arguments, they were taken seriously at that period, and some of them were quite plausible, and did happen – or events were interpreted so – time and again. But these links between expediency (personal interest) and public good broke down around the fifteenth century. Contemporary thought is full of attempts to discover new – or revalidate old – methods of control; but Machiavelli's *Prince* exposed the uselessness of all of them. His own attempt, the reassertion of a pagan value, *virtù*, however, also proved unrealistic. All attempts to ennoble the ruler and control his mundane, personal interest failed. The despair that is so audible in some of the best works of the period (More, Guicciardini, Boccalini, Machiavelli himself) reflects this sense of hopelessness.

The solution was found in a way that was as simple as it must have sounded impossible or incredible at that time. If there was no way to restrict the rulers in the pursuit of their self-interest, then they should be bound exactly by this pursuit! The phenomenon that at the same time made possible and embodied this development was the emergence of the modern state.[19] The modern state was the child of a compromise, the assertion of a – possible – identity of interest between the ruler and the ruled; a type of relation, a form of government, that probably never existed anywhere else. It is this that gives uniqueness to Western development. It can be characterised by a norm that made a virtue out of a necessity in a way that would have sounded to Aristotle or Aquinas as utmost folly: stating not only that the ruler should follow his own interest, but also that the interest of the ruler is identical with the interest of the whole of his subjects, because, as the story went, the interest of the ruler consists not in the oppression of his subjects; quite the contrary, in their numbers and well-being, health and wealth. The more subjects the ruler has, the more prosperous are the cities and the countryside, the more taxes a ruler can obtain, the larger will be his army, etc. It was this space, this problematisation, that was the common home of the different rulers of the period – enlightened or not. In this way, from the ashes of the medieval state of justice, the modern administrative state was born. Thus, while it is true that, on the one hand, the birth of the modern state represented the depersonalisation of government, on the other, it did not just mean the emergence of a new bureaucracy; rather it led to the extension of the personal rule and personal officers of the king to the whole of the social body.

The state was deployed as a final answer to tyranny; as a mechanism that eliminated the very possibility of tyranny. In this framework, a tyrant would only work against himself, as by oppressing his population, he would make himself a sure loser in the contemporary world of power politics. In this world, the ruler *by virtue of and not in spite of the pursuit of his self-interest*, perceives himself and acts as a friend and associate of the 'people' against the nobility, and is supported by contemporary intellectuals. Hence the contemporary adulation of the mystery of the state.[20]

All this remained valid only up to a point, until the second half of the eighteenth century. In this period, there was a sudden and quite shocking realisation in contemporary political thought; the painful loss of a taken-for-granted certainty, the value of the state; the feeling that the state itself can be despotic. For most people, there was no great novelty in this realisation. In spite of the explicit and in some ways, by the nature of things, genuine concern for health and wealth, for the majority of the population the growth of the modern state did not represent a beneficial event, neither before nor after this period.[21] They attempted to do all they could to preserve their independence from this new type of power, both in the countryside and in the cities; in the latter, it was more difficult, as city governments were closely integrated with the new organs of state power. But now, the fact that state power is despotic was realised by 'more important' people, much closer to the centres of decision-making: the very administrators of this modern state power. And it was made in a very specific context: that of the inefficiency of the interventions of the state. The first dissonant voices concerning the state that were raised by people of influence and power did not question the project itself: the identification of the interests of the state and of the population, the need for the supervision of all sorts of behaviour by the centre in order to make it conform to the norms of reason and the interests of the state – that was identified by definition with the interests of each and all. Rather, they realised that the methods used were not efficient in attaining the goals. Thus, in the effective attack against the activity of the state from the early decades of the eighteenth century the denunciation of despotism was connected to and supported by claims concerning its inefficiency. In this sense, the underlying discourse of civil society and liberalism was discovered not by Paine or Hegel, but by d'Argenson.[22] In this way, the question of law in terms of human rights could again be posed.

The early modern solution to the problem of the dissolution of the feudal state of justice with the help of the doctrine of the interest of state happened outside the framework of law. It was made possible, on the one hand, by the overriding importance of a new, positive concept of the public good, requiring constant intervention, and not just the maintenance or the restoration of the status quo; on the other, by the fact that the interest of the state made an objective, orderly state of affairs possible, as opposed to the disorder of injustice and tyranny.

Now, even in the sixteenth and seventeenth centuries, the questions of efficiency and tyranny were related to each other, but in a different way than in the eighteenth and nineteenth centuries. Then, the efficiency of the solution was given by the identification of the interest of the political society, the state, with the king's. In this way, the management of society as a project became conceivable, and also possible, as the person of the king, the existence of a single centre as a reference point, provided at once a decision-making model and the possibility of enforcing actions pursued solely out of the expediency of a positive public interest. For the efficient functioning of this model, the old legal framework had to be exceeded or abolished, as any rights or privileges only represented a limit to the efficient functioning of the centre: the 'true representative' of the whole. From this came the model of sovereignty: the coalescence of the legislative and ordinance-making power; the claim that the pleasure of the king has the force of the law – a claim that may be absolutistic, but, in the language of contemporary discourse, not tyrannical. Now, once the locus of interest had become the individual as opposed to the king, the whole question of the relation between legality and efficiency had to be rethought. Earlier, the lawyers were considered to be the major enemies of efficiency and *thus* the state, as any law could only represent a hindrance to the immediate needs of the king, identified with the state or the public: these were considered synonyms, beyond ideology. Now, the locus of interest became the individual; anything hindering that interest was deemed to be not only tyrannical, but as threatening the efficient working of the whole society – rethought in economic terms, outside the political body; thus, there was a return to the importance of legal guarantees in the forms of individual human rights.

The terms of the earlier equation or identity – the common interests or the interests of the state are identical with the interests of each and every individual – remained the same, but the direction of their relationship had changed. Instead of the centre impressing this interest on everybody, it was redefined as the sum of the interests of the members. By this act, the king was finally completely dropped from the picture as the transmitter of this identity of interest. The state, the child of the ruler's attempt to dominate all other social forces, was first diverted by the humanists and administrators who used it to tie up the king in his own interests; and finally the child devoured his father, displaced him. Through the developments of the next two centuries, the state itself, as an impersonal impersonator of the common good, lost more and more ground, due to the increasingly autonomous functioning of society itself. This made possible the contemporary neo-liberal attacks on the state.

In this framework, the rethinking of the defeat of despotism and the victory of civil society, or liberty, or liberalism is particularly relevant for the present situation of Eastern Europe. The victory was not unconditional. Society did not appear unscathed, unchanged after the centuries of 'absolutism'. The interventionist state was defeated for ever; but the new organisation and self-organisation of the civil society occurred in the framework created by the previous investment of state power. One may even risk saying that the early modern state power disappeared once it had accomplished its task; once the social body was made ready for more indirect methods of government; once it was made sufficiently homogeneous and docile; and, conversely, once more efficient methods were found to realise this same purpose. This, again, did *not* mean a cunning victory for the extension of state power, in the same way as the acknowledgement of the prince's right to follow his own self-interest in the pact of the sixteenth and seventeenth centuries did not mean the victory of tyranny in the traditional sense. It meant rather the redefinition of the previous 'contract'. It took into account the developments created by the investment of two centuries of state power and the resistances that it created, and redefined the contract in the following terms: while previously only the prince's pursuit of private interest was deemed compatible and equivalent with the common good, now this was extended to the whole of the population. The agency whose goal previously was to enforce the proper behaviour that was compatible with the common good in the whole population now became charged with the task of singling out only those few whose behaviour, whose interest, was marginal – in the sense of not being compatible with the common good. This agency was the police.

The discourse of the civil society was thus first deployed against an active, interventionist state that did not represent simply the tyranny of a minority, but that exercised power in an attempt to influence the minutest details of daily existence in the name of the very interests of the governed.

1980s: CIVIL SOCIETY VS. NEO-LIBERALISM AND THE STATE

The reappearance of the discourse of the civil society in the West in the last decade happened in a different situation.[23] Though certain elements of the old, interventionist state survived or rather resurfaced in the welfare state, and though certain civil-rights questions concerning the activity of modern government, police or the secret police could have been raised even in advanced liberal democracies, it would be way off the mark to compare these instances to problems of despotism in the early modern states or in bolshevik-type party-states. The concern of the modern Western discourse of civil society and despotism is about a quite different phenomenon: bureaucracy, the increasing rationalisation and bureaucratisation of daily existence. In other words, while the first appearance of the discourse of the civil society happened before Marx, the new deployment is most closely related to a counterdiscourse to Marx, the ideas and concerns of Max Weber. In this, there is a marked difference from the earlier discourse on civil society; a difference that is perhaps emphasised insufficiently in the modern literature. This is partly due to the fact that the discourse of the bureaucracy has gained enormous ascendance and popularity throughout this century, and has been applied, quite indiscriminately, to the early modern period as well.

In one way or another, most writings from the contemporary Western scene collected in the book edited by John Keane are connected with the problem of bureaucracy.[24] This presents us with two questions. First, does a critical discourse directed against bureaucracy provide us with an adequate tool to analyse the specific power relations that are deployed in modern society? Second, what would be the best way of situating the stakes of the current discourse of civil society in Central-Eastern Europe – the early nineteenth- or the late twentieth-century versions?

It would seem obvious that this comparison should be made with the latter one, first, because the realities are much closer to each other; and second, because it is exactly the concept of the bureaucracy and the related struggles against the state that seem to provide a common field for the revivals of the concept of the civil society in both East and West. However, if we grant thought its proper historicity, following Foucault, and once we question the taken-for-granted characteristics of a seemingly universal 'bureaucracy', the similarities in the problems faced by Europe in the early nineteenth century and by Eastern Europe now seem to be surprisingly similar.[25] Many aspects of the contemporary intellectual debates in the East, with their strong, dogmatic liberal overtones, point also in this direction.

With one important difference. In the case of the West, all this represented a novel problem some two hundred years ago. In the case of the contemporary East, it is a strange, forced replay, for, after all, the spread of liberalism was not restricted to the West in the nineteenth century. The current, dogmatic adherence to liberalism in the East is quite understandable, as it is deployed against an indisputable 'police' state. But it also has an element of the absurd in it.

BOLSHEVISM: THE ABSURD MADE INTO DAILY REALITY

The historical excursions of this chapter may help to explain why it is that the discourse of the civil society is revived today in Eastern Europe in its classical, early nineteenth-century form, as one element of the revival of the standard classical liberal pattern. The basic problem is not with the revival of an innocent, outdated liberalism in Eastern Europe, but the deployment of an early modern institution in the twentieth century. In spite of a number of structural similarities in the 1940s of Eastern Europe to early modern Western Europe, the problems were not the same, as, after all, though old methods of social and political control did survive, these became contaminated with modern elements. Centuries of civilising mission were deployed in Austria as well as in Hungary, Czechoslovakia or Poland. The way the new elements were accommodated in the old framework was perhaps not qualitatively, only quantitatively, different from the situation in Western Europe, where it was a fact of life – and also a matter of conscious policy – that the innovations were always enveloped in old clothes. The bolshevik attempt to redeploy these outdated methods was thus unnecessary and doomed from the start. Something was blatantly out of place. A certain type of discourse, a technology of power, was redeployed that was the answer to a different problem – perhaps that's why it was not possible to use the indirect method employed in the seventeenth century of leaving the old framework intact. While this system was so repressive, it was also absurd and grotesque; it behaved always as if something was not in the proper place; it deployed a sophisticated machinery without tolerating any dissent, only to realise later that the problem was not the one for which this machinery had been developed – as if it were the mistake of the patient that it had the wrong illness, not the one for which the treatment had been diagnosed.

Still, two factors made the deployment of this system, the making of a material reality out of a discursive absurdity, possible. The first was the destructive impact of world wars – of the first in Russia, of the second in eastern Central Europe – creating a situation resembling that of the original emergence of the police, the period of religious and civil wars, and then the Thirty Years War; and second, the fact that Eastern European societies were not 'fully modernised'.[26]

The insufficiency of the previous modernisation efforts made the attempt at the 'full' realisation of the potential of modernity and progress possible. This project, aiming at the complete mobilisation of society for the realisation of the common good, did evoke an immediate echo in both a part of the masses and some members of the élite. Still, as it soon became obvious, the concrete project meant a step backward, rather than forward. The modern state represented the depersonalisation of government, while the party personalised it, made it the court of the ruler. It represented an absurd reversal of the Western European process, where personal envoys in the early modern period represented an important strategy used by the princes to establish and complement the modern state apparatus. The same absurdity happens with another crucial target, mobilisation. The goal of the early modern state was to mobilise the whole population for the productive and military goals of the state. This was not particularly successful. The new discourse of liberalism and the civil society around the turn of the nineteenth century claimed to represent and mobilise the whole society against the previous, interventionist and oppressive mobilisation attempts. The result was a new compromise, not a clear victory for any of the protagonists. But perhaps the most lasting and most important aspect of all this was related to the new heights of mobilisation. We have an important stage here in a long process, where the despotism of power leads to ever new and more intensive, more complete, mobilisations of the whole society, the whole personality; with more and more demands on the willing, complete and devoted adherence of the individuals; where the personal will be dissolved in the political, in the quest for a perfect society, without power. The results are, and will be, yet more compromises, with yet more territory gained from potential despotism; with two problems. On the one hand, the complicated nature and occasional irrationality of these new compromises will always prepare the terrain for the redeployment of the liberal (in a neo-liberal or other form) critique of government, thus questioning and annihilating some of the hard-won concessions. On the other hand, to use a metaphor from chemistry, the progressive dilution of personal and interpersonal relations will perhaps be the most lasting and irreversible result of all these changes, as successive struggles require an ever more increasing devotion to yet more new causes, destroying the distance that divides the political and public from the personal and the intimate; and, as one of the consequences, redirecting the uniqueness of human experiences, relations and energies into the circumscribed, limited, 'secured' locus of 'the private'.

While mobilisation in the name of the civil society is thus not an unmixed blessing, the end of the communist system was caused not by this mobilisation, but by a complete demobilisation. One could perhaps say that, as long as it was possible to mobilise the population, the communists always attempted to effectuate a countermobilisation. Once all possibility of such mobilisation and countermobilisation had gone, the system ceased to be able to function.[27] This may explain why the fall of the system was accompanied by very little popular enthusiasm. In Hungary, in Poland or in Slovenia, people clearly expressed their wish for ending the communist party's hold over the government. But while a few decades ago it would have been – and was – met with enormous relief and popular enthusiasm, now the reception was markedly subdued.

According to an English saying, every family has a skeleton in the cupboard. In the case of bolshevism, there was nothing else in the house. The skeleton thus is not just the bureaucratisation of the party; not the fact that the working class is not the true bearer of history, or that the party is not the party of the working class; not even the millions of the victims of the terror, and the incredible details concerning the management of the terror. It is the complete absurdity at the core of the whole project itself.

At a first glance, the party did give an answer that seemed plausible to a number of crucial questions in the troubles of the twentieth century in Eastern Europe; it did perceive certain problems, internal contradictions in the way elements of capitalism and liberalism were accommodated to the existing power hierarchies in the East; moreover, following Saint-Simon and Marx, it did have some perception – from a highly peculiar perspective, though – of the internal problems of a liberal method of government. In this way, it could fancy itself as being a more advanced, post-liberal method of government, when in reality it only took over from Marx what was, even in Saint-Simon, the most obsolete part of the analysis: the resurrection of the old system of welfare 'police' that was originally deployed – one may say, with some simplification – in the name of the creation of a bourgeoisie, but now from the point of view of the proletariat. In an absurd way, it resurrected mechanisms that were used in the seventeenth and eighteenth centuries for the purpose of the 'civilisation' or 'embourgeoisement' of those who were not civilised already in the special sense of the methods applied, for the proletarisation of all social classes – where the project of the 're-bourgeoisement' appears as a radical counterdiscourse to the official doctrine.

9   Conclusion: the success of a failure?

> ... perhaps even freedom is not a proper expression, as more is involved here, an absence of bonds, of heaviness, the freedom of experience, the possibility to take charge of the world; for this, it is not enough that we should neither be under surveillance, nor imprisoned in any way, but we must preserve the innermost structure of our soul unimpaired.
>
> (Péter Esterházy, *Indirect*, 1981)

The study of the communist-party apparatus was full of surprises for us. Both of us had to reassess several times our own preconceptions and prejudices, as our former mental frameworks could not accommodate, let alone explain, what we had actually found. Perhaps it is needless to reiterate that this reassessment did not mean an acceptance of such activities, not even understanding in the Weberian sense. It refers purely to the coming to terms with these activities as facts, and the possibility of analysing their internal rationality and external impact.

THE FUNCTION OF THE PARTY APPARATUS

The shake-up of former certainties had its positive reward. We felt that by studying the apparatus we became acquainted with a segment of reality whose existence and characteristics had escaped us before, but that nevertheless had had a profound impact on the reality of Hungary and Eastern Europe in general. We did not feel that we had found in the apparatus the master key to the hidden mechanisms of the world we had lived in for so long. The very metaphor of a key unlocking the secret is wholly misleading with respect to the communist state-party. The party was not a hidden secret, the unmoved mover, in terms of a conspiracy theory. Quite the contrary, our study showed us that the 'essence' of communism is that there is no essence, no such hidden secret. Power within the system cannot be localised. It is rather the whole system that forms a complicated web, where the strongly asymmetrical power relations dominating the surface are counterpoised with networks of hidden checks and countercurrents. Each and every element in these networks needs the other, would be helpless without its support – the central party organs without the apparatus, the apparatus without the activists, the activists without the members, the whole party without the police and the secret police, and vice versa at each and every point. Yet, need for support is inextricably intertwined with control and supervision. A communist system is like a Strindbergian drama played out at the level of a whole society, where the different parts are not let loose, even after all sentiments have burned out.

The party apparatus plays a specific and crucial role in this whole game. In an important sense, it provides a background on which the whole establishment is founded. Not in the sense of a solid, stable basis, but as a mobile network of personal links. The most important self-proclaimed role of the party is to keep the whole society, the state, the country together. It is the task of the apparatus to accomplish this unending, impossible, positive task.[1] Such an undertaking depends on a curious and unstable combination of inclusion and exclusion, especially given the combative nature of the party and its targets – thus the intimate links between the party, the police and the secret police. Repressive organisations make possible the work of the party, and prevent other links being formed between the subjects. But the party itself is not a repressive organisation, and the classical concepts of tyranny and dictatorship are highly misleading when applied to this peculiar reality.

Rather, instead of centring on the concept of repression, we found that the power exercised by the crucial intermediate link of the whole system, the party apparatus, involved different requirements and consequences. This duplication of society in terms of a mobile network of a selected and devoted few had important corollaries both in terms of personal characteristics and the results of these activities, the 'nature' of the web. Membership within the apparatus and the ability to fulfil the tasks required a personality that was different from any accepted picture of a politician. It involved characteristics that were connected not to the making of decisions and the fulfilling of certain positions of responsibility or privilege, but to the handling of and dealing with people, in all possible sorts of ways.

On the other hand, these activities and the web created by them were spread to all possible aspects of human existence, entrapping their subjects as well as the objects. The mechanisms that were set free by the system mobilised and created complicated networks of responsibility, obligation and fear. It was a system that nobody living there could have completely escaped, where the slightest connection with the system led only to deeper and ever more complex involvements, where the more one fought and acted, the more entangled one became. The testimony of so many former prisoners of Stalinist camps, that it was only inside the prison that they felt themselves free, should perhaps have been taken seriously, and not only concerning the darkest Stalinist periods, but, *mutatis mutandis*, the whole life-span of the system as well.

This book is based on a concrete empirical study, carried out in a given country at a highly specific time. Our aims were also limited, specific. We did not pursue the elusive goal of giving a global picture of communism, not to say socialism, not even restricted to the case of Eastern Europe. We neither wanted to give a comprehensive account of the political and social system of Hungary, nor of the current changes within this system. Our purpose was much more limited. Instead of trying to come to terms with the totality of social and political reality, or the full nature of communism, our work was only concerned with the question of what permitted the functioning of this system at the level of daily existence, how actual government was accomplished there, what some of the factors were that contributed to its internal dissolution, and also with its possible lasting effects, the difference it made in the history of those countries that were affected by it. Still, it is exactly these concerns that may invest our study with a relevance that can go beyond the case of Hungary.

The deployment of the communist-party apparatus followed the same model everywhere in the region. There is no reason to expect that it worked in a different way in any country. The possibility of making comparisons is limited, as, due to the reasons analysed in the Preface and the Introduction, there is very little information available on that topic. Nevertheless, it is possible to compare four different pieces of work with our results. One is the already mentioned book of Fainsod (1958) that provides an analysis of the Smolensk archive, the only data files that were previously available on the daily activities of the communist party. The second is an article by Gill (1987) that gives some research notes on his detailed investigations concerning, among other things, the organisational rules of the communist party; rules that were long considered to be merely ideological distortions and pieces of disinformation, but that he considers to be much more than that (Gill 1988: 1).[2] The third is the classic book by Rigby (1969) on the history and functions of party membership in the Soviet Union. Finally, the fourth is an empirical study on the establishment of communist power in Moscow (Sakwa 1987a). While, of the four, only the first studies the apparatus itself, all are based on extensive empirical research.

In his chapter on party controls at the *oblast* (province) level, Fainsod lists and discusses the different activities carried out by the PC, and states that 'one cannot but be struck by the all-embracing character of their interests' (Fainsod 1958: 66). These activities were related to the collection of information and the enforcement of the often meaningless or damaging resolutions of the centre, creating tensions and needs for improvisations. Nevertheless, '[t]he business of the obkom [oblast party committee] as it found reflexion in the bureau protocols mirrored the life and problems of the oblast' (p. 69). But this 'mirroring' was not just a passive activity. Local life, especially agricultural production, was rather a battlefield, a target of constant positive intervention. A crucial aspect of control was related to cadre policy. But, apart from the security police that provided an independent check, based on grass-roots denunciations from below, 'obkom supervision over the raikoms [party committees of smaller regions] was in no sense limited to appointments. It encompassed every activity in which the raikoms were engaged' (p. 89). Instructions covered such details as how to organise mass listening to radio broadcasts of the sessions of the Congress of Soviets, what percentage of women should be elected to the chair of village cooperatives, or how each collective farmer should begin his work. The final paragraph of the chapter is well worth quoting at length, because, in spite of some obvious differences, it conveys so well some of our own experiences during the interviewing:

> [T]he overall impression, as one reads the obkom records, is not one of sedate and orderly processes of administration. An all-pervading atmosphere of urgency and tension appears to dominate everything that the obkom undertakes. Over and over again, one gets the sense of a group of men operating under tremendous pressure to realise seemingly impossible objectives, and exercising a similar pressure on their subordinates in lower party and governmental organs. Like firemen summoned to a blaze, they rush from situation to situation, dealing as best they can with the emergency which confronts them. They try to be sensitive to the ruling priorities of their superiors, and to communicate that same sensitivity to their inferiors in the raikoms. The rhythm of their life is dictated by deadlines and goals; they are almost violently achievement-oriented. They know that success or failure, even life or death may depend on their ability to satisfy the expectations of their chiefs. And yet, behind the fury and

the urgency, one also catches a sense of almost desperate desire for relaxation and security.

(Fainsod 1958: 92)

Many elements of this paragraph have a familiar ring and find an echo also in other assessments of Eastern Europe and the Soviet Union. The expression 'putting out fire' was an accepted metaphor for the way the whole system worked in Hungary in the 1970s and 1980s. And one of the most surprising statements from the paragraph quoted, the idea that the apparatus was achievement-oriented, was repeated by Glazov (1988: 43).

Gill's (1987) paper was written much later, on the basis of a different, and more comprehensive, material. But the basic points are remarkably similar. He wants to discard the misconception according to which the Soviet communist party, especially in the crucial period of the 1920s and 1930s, was a tightly organised group exercising totalitarian powers. He rather puts the emphasis on dedicated activists placed at all points of society that were 'living links' between the party and the population at large. The party was not so much a bureaucratic organisation attempting to administer everything as a mobilising force attempting to create a break-through. As a conclusion, he states that the purposes of the party did not require a highly organised structure. Rather, '[w]hat was necessary was a party presence at a multitude of points throughout the society, which could provide a framework for the direction of the energy and commitment of enthusiastic activists and for the channelling of more forceful measures' (p. 578).

Though not concerned with the apparatus, many similar points are made in Rigby's (1969) book on communist-party membership. He shows the mobile and ever present character of the communist party as opposed to the simple concepts of 'bureaucracy' and 'bureaucratisation', the extent to which the party succeeded in deploying itself into the society, through the extended arms of the membership. He emphasises that the integrative role of the party extends well beyond mere questions of administration, and therefore the 'leading and guiding role' of the party must be taken seriously as an attempt not just to govern the whole society from the centre – where it may well have always failed – but to transform the whole society, to create new institutions, a 'new man'. He also makes a distinction between potential power geared in the system and its actual use. Finally, to our knowledge, he was the first writer who used the expression 'state-party system', as opposed to the widespread idea of the 'party-state' (Rigby 1969: 2). We would only complement his analysis by stating that the apparatus was not just an organisation aiming to provide bureaucratic supervision to the vast network of membership, but itself embodied the duality of a strict, hierarchically organised bureaucracy and a mobile, personalised network.[3]

Sakwa studied the supposedly most rigid period of bolshevism, war communism. Instead of being a monolithic system, he found that it was rather a peculiar, fundamentally unstable, mixture of utopianism and pragmatism, more flexible than was previously assumed. According to Sakwa, '[t]he legacy of war communism was not a monolithic power system but one riven by internal contradictions, above all between its economic and political aspects' (1987a: 267). The centre of this new system was based on the party which became the kernel of the state after the first few months of the new power. 'The legacy of the civil war and bolshevik practice was that even the most minor of issues had to be referred to the party committees for adjudication, a facet of the "petty tutelage" against which the opposition rallied' (p. 272). It was an organisation with extreme vitality, with constant plans for reforms that nevertheless always remained unsuccessful. In spite of all changes and discussions, the basic characteristics of the system were never altered later. Instead of talking about a later, bureaucratic degeneration, Sakwa concludes that '[a] new type of party had come to power during the October revolution, but during war communism a new system emerged that remains the basis of the new society' (p. 279).

The similarity we found between these results and ours is remarkable, and gives strong support to the implications and validity of our results. The actual daily reality or the international situation of a medium large soviet town in 1936 and of the Hungarian capital in 1988 could not be more different. Nevertheless, the intermediate party committees were working in surprisingly similar ways, performing the same activities and encountering the same problems. While many practices were undoubtedly different, or changing through time, the party apparatus remained untouched in its basics, showing that the basic institution, the 'ground' of a type of society often remains unchanged, even if all other aspects of social and political life change. The life-span of these institutions is coexistent with the socio-political system of which they are the central elements. Such an institution was the monarchy before the French and British revolutions – thus the concern with 'chopping off the head of the king' in both cases; and such an institution may well be the police in the case of modern societies. At least, according to surveys of the police, there is a remarkable consistency in the structure and organisation of police forces throughout the nineteenth and twentieth centuries; a persistence that cannot be found in any other organisations.[4]

This identity was thus not one of reality, but of an institution, of a structure. This illustrates well that our attempt was not to give a 'comprehensive picture' that would include, among other things, the historical, cultural and social background of these countries. These are all no doubt important issues, but would have had an impact in any case, no matter what system was established after the Second World War. Our interest was limited to the specificity of bolshevism, the difference it made and why this specificity deviated from the generally accepted views; a difference that, in our view, is due neither to similarities in history (the internal constraints of each country), the imposition of a specifically Eastern model on the region (the impact of Russia), nor to some general characteristics of 'society' that each political system, or at least each 'industrial society', must face.

It is at that level that our study perhaps can shed new light on some issues of theoretical order concerning the 'nature' of communist systems. Our results questioned the relevance of such widely accepted, taken-for-granted terms as the 'bureaucratic apparatus' and the 'party-state'. And it was in the same direction that we pursued our analysis further, this time along Foucaldian and not simply structuralist lines. Our aim was not just to describe a structural constant, but to reconstruct a specific rationality built into that structure. In this way, connections could have been established between the communist parties and the early modern 'police'.

BUREAUCRACY AND PARTY-STATE

A simple distinction is helpful to specify and delimit the extent of bureaucracy and bureaucratisation within the party apparatus – a distinction that, by the way, was often used and was considered crucial by the apparatus members themselves. This is the difference between 'in-house' and 'out-of-house' activities. In-house activities concern paper-work done inside the building of the party committee – highly bureaucratised, routine, hierarchical activities. An excellent description of this is given by Voslensky (1984). But let's not forget that Voslensky was describing the day of a medium-high level central-committee apparatchik, whose activities, and the options that were available to him, were almost as far away from an ordinary district-level apparatus member as from any other common member of society.

Party workers in the district party committees in Budapest were also doing a lot of paperwork. But for most of them, it was only one part of their job; and they considered it to be the least important part. They very often went outside, out of the house, to the individual businesses, local councils, public institutions to which they acted as instructors. The characteristics of these activities were anything but bureaucratic. They required improvisation, knowledge of the personnel, daily awareness of local conditions and up-to-date information on current problems.

This distinction between in-house and out-of-house activities can help us to redefine the very concept of the apparatus, in a way opposite to the established definition restricting the meaning to the top levels of full-time party workers (either as the central-committee apparatus, or as regional or other local secretaries), but that is not an arbitrary definition, but was commonly made by the apparatus members themselves. According to the terminology used inside the party, the administrative workers of local party committees (typist-secretaries, members of the economic or accounting units) were excluded from the concept of the 'political apparatus'. But, more importantly, when full-time party workers were talking about the 'apparatus', they excluded their immediate bosses, the district party secretaries, as well from the term. On the basis of our results, we can offer a solution for this perplexing usage; a solution that would at once explain some common misunderstandings concerning the party apparatus. 'Real' apparatus members – where the adjective 'real' does not refer to an ideal situation, an external value judgement, but to the functional characteristics of the activities themselves, the actual job done – are the ones who do the out-of-house work. The definition of the 'real' apparatus excludes exactly those two layers, those two functions that in the accepted usage of the term identify the party apparatus – the secretaries and the bureaucracy. The 'real' activity of the apparatus is what is carried out by full-time party workers beyond the paperwork, beyond the bureaucracy, 'on the spot', outside, in real life. What lured and fascinated party workers, what made them join the apparatus and kept them going once inside, was exactly this intoxicating feeling of being able to get close to the 'real thing'. And what frustrated them was that they were still too far from reality: they had too many firms and institutions to instruct, they could not be there enough, there was no time to get acquainted with everything.

The communist party controlled and governed all the major – and often even the minutest – aspects of the daily activities of firms and public institutions. But it wasn't the monolithic rule of a bureaucratic state. All words in the above statements are partial, misleading or even meaningless. The system was governed by a relatively small, mobile apparatus that was personally present in every segment of social reality and kept the machine going. This was the basic moving force of the system, the *sine qua non* of communism. The previous reforms within the system were not just blocked by 'faceless apparatchiks', considering only their personal advantage, and thus destroying all initiatives that were trying to establish something better. The reason for the failure was that any attempts at political or economic reforms immediately threatened the very working principle of the communist party, by making the apparatus superfluous.

The party apparatus was not a bureaucracy, nor was it just a clientelistic network. These two phenomena were rather two possible end-products, crystallisations of different aspects and segments of the apparatus. The apparatus was a strictly hierarchical, tightly controlled quasi-military machine that took upon itself the impossible task of governing the whole country in times of peace. It required heroic efforts and motivation on the part of its regular soldiers, and placed them under tremendous pressure. To cope with the situation, to avoid the ever present possibility of a failure and a crackdown, to obtain a certain degree of security in a system where everything was uncertain, nothing was stable, predictable, of fixed value, several processes were set in motion, on the basis of different individual and group strategies, but in a way that is susceptible to general, theoretical analysis. Bureaucratisation and the formation of clientelistic networks provide two such models.

But the inner logic of the apparatus was different from and hostile to both these practices. As long as the apparatus was in place, it always presented a potential, and often actual, threat to them. On the one hand, it prevented the formation of a proper, rational bureaucracy, because the frequent ad-hoc campaigns and the strong dependence on personal, individual characteristics – most importantly, at the level of the first secretary, but going down to the smallest district instructor – made the crystallisation of a formal organisation impossible. The apparatus as such was a highly bureaucratised organisation. The state agencies controlled by the party also were highly bureaucratic. But the connections between the party and the state, the party and society, were not bureaucratic, could not be bureaucratic, and the strength and the 'nature' of the system lay exactly in these connections. On the other hand, while the formation of personal networks of patron–client relations was a necessary strategy for personal survival and advancement, such networks always came under pressure when there was any change within the given sphere of the party organisation; there was always a threat that the rise of a genuine, faithful apparatchik to high position would destroy the network, throwing everyone back to the former, uncertain situation.

Another major misunderstanding concerning the (former) communist countries is related to the concept and role of the 'state'. One of the most often used categories for characterising these systems, a term that entered common language in the same matter-of-fact way as the bureaucracy, is the idea of the 'party-state'. In this way, communist systems are identified as special, extreme types of the general category of state power. Communist systems are 'party-states' because it is the party that governs the state. But still, the problem is whether we can talk about 'the' state as a fixed entity. Are communist systems just special cases of the general category of 'party government'? Does the communist party simply 'use' the state; or does it create its 'own' state – a state formed in its own likeness? And does it use the state at all? Can it act 'without' the state? Is it useful to mention, to talk about 'state power' when the communist party – i.e. the apparatus – does something?

Let's start with a distinction between the different levels and functions of the state. At the top level, we have the central organs – the ministries, the state secretaries, the planning and other bureaux. This level was widely studied in the past. These investigations, and everyday experience in Eastern Europe, made it clear that all strategic decisions were made inside the politburo. The organs of the state were just the executive organs of the party. This model as a general approach is also valid for the lower echelons of the state hierarchy.

But this is only part of the story. It concerns the state solely as a bureaucratic organisation and as an organ of central government. But the daily supervision in communist countries, the 'hard core' of the meaning of the term 'totalitarianism', implied much more. And it is here that the very concept of the 'state', used in the modern meaning of the term, rapidly loses all relevance.

What is the state at the local level? First, it is the local government; in its communist form, the local council. This was supervised and governed by the party, and used as an agent for the execution of the party's resolutions. Second, the state includes the repressive apparatuses. Leaving aside the army, which played no systematic role in local life, the party had very specific connections with the police and the secret police. The party had no legal control over or even a direct link with these apparatuses. The local party used them indirectly, through the local agent of the government, the council. But there was another important connection between the party and the police, concerning information. As was discussed in Chapter 6, the local party only gathered and processed anonymous information; 'mood reports'. All individual items of information belonging to the regular police forces or to the secret police were taken out of the sphere of activity of the party committee and transferred to those agencies. The party was thus to be dissociated from the material reality of all future actions to be taken.

Looking at the businesses, the economic units, the whole idea of the party-state becomes even more questionable. It is often claimed that the whole communist system was managed as a giant firm. The fact that all property was owned by the state helped to maintain this fiction. But local firms were not just parts of an all-encompassing, monolithic state. They were not directed by the local council, and supervision by higher state agencies was only occasional. The local firms were controlled and supervised rather by the district and other regional party committees. The central characteristic of the former communist systems was not the homogeneity of state ownership, nor the power of the state bureaucracy, but the sphere of activity of the regional party committee.[5]

As this reference to the economic units makes clear, the point here is not just an analytical distinction between the different organs of the state. The problem is with the whole model that reduces the nature of the communist systems to a special case of the general category of the 'state', according to which the local communist party is simply a link between the higher- and the lower-level state authorities – the top level setting up the targets of the plan, and the lower level 'policing' those who fail to meet the targets.[6] In reality, it was often the other way around. The party apparatus was a link between the higher and lower levels of the state. But it had a crucial, specific, independent role in the game. In a sense, starting from the middle, from the function of a link, it was able to change and to define the field of possibilities and thus reality itself at both ends of the connection. It was not accidental that a metaphor that often emerged in our conversations in different contexts was the question of the dog and his tail – is it the dog that wags the tail, or is it the other way around?[7]

In spite of all appearances to the contrary, the activities of the apparatus were not irrational or haphazard. They followed a specific rationality and, from the inside of that rationality, they made sense and were not simply parts of an arbitrary ideology. Also, even if the party was obviously not a 'leading and guiding force' of society, the 'cement' holding it together, and was not able to do and see everything through its apparatus, the apparatus had a crucial role in this type of society; this particular entity was coexistent with the party apparatus. We took the apparatus as an object of serious analysis. It seemed to us right to do so, as the party had had a tremendous impact on the lives of so many people for such a long time. But, on the other hand, none of the claims of the system about itself could have been taken seriously. The whole system was absurd. Within this system, the apparatus may have accomplished rational and even crucial tasks, but the apparatus *was* superfluous.

The analysis of the rationality of a system that is *a priori* claimed to be absurd seems to be a contradiction in terms. Yet, it was exactly through such a serious, systematic examination that we were able to come to terms with both the absurdity and the truly threatening character of the fallen regime.

THE RATIONALITY OF THE PARTY AND ITS ABSURDITY

The attempt to reconstruct the inner rationality of the activity of the members of the party apparatus, to take their utterances seriously and make them objects of analysis as items of thought, did lead to fruitful results. It was possible to distil the discursive programme, the specific governmental rationality and the corresponding technology of government embedded in or resurrected by the bolshevik-type state-parties. This rationality, it turned out, did not really have much to do with the original bolshevik, communist, let alone socialist, ideology. Ideology was also present in these systems, both as a ballast that had to be got rid of, and as a trap set up by unmet promises that eventually returned to haunt them. But it was not a model, nor a genuine moving force.

The actual content of this programme, however, proved to be surprising. A project that was claimed to represent an advance on liberalism, that was claimed to represent the vanguard of modernity, the way to bypass the most developed capitalist countries proved to be nothing more than a long-forgotten governmental programme of the early modern period – the 'traditional' concept of 'reason of state' as the internal increase of the forces of the state. The party (i.e. the apparatus), the 'conscience of our age', turned out to be nothing more than a late-day resurrection, a replica of a central instrument of the project 'raison d'état', the 'police' – again in the old, early modern, and not in the modern meaning. Bolshevism only succeeded in rediscovering techniques that were forgotten – no doubt, in a Freudian manner – so long ago and contaminated with modern meanings so thoroughly that even historians of the period often failed to retrieve their original, functional meaning from beneath the dust of centuries.

The positive discursive programme underlying bolshevism and the birth of the modern state was identical. The realities into which these programmes were inserted and which they transformed in certain ways were, of course, very different. It was this difference that gave the two most important characteristics of bolshevism – its extreme violence and its absurdity.

The first point is well known; there is no need to talk about it at length.[8] Modern-day absolutism had much more powerful techniques at its disposal – both in terms of physical, scientific technology and in terms of the repressive power of the state – than the early modern absolutist state, and had far fewer restraints, due, for example, to the loss of divine law. The second point was also made, especially in works of art. Some of the best works of cinema, theatre or literature dealt precisely with the theme of the tragic absurdity of the system.[9] However, in the social and political sciences, the whole concept of absurdity seems somehow out of place. Scientists prefer 'serious' subjects. They like to treat a political system as an object of study, and cannot handle the idea of 'absurdity'. To start an analysis with the claim that the object is absurd seems to question its very meaning. But in this way they took their subjects too seriously.

The absurdity of bolshevism has two different aspects. It was absurd, as it gave an old solution to a new problem. The problems faced by Russia and later the Eastern European countries were real and serious enough – backwardness, poverty, the consequences of lost wars, etc. – but the solution given was never equal to the situation. A method that emerged in response to the problem of state-building in the early modern period should not have been resurrected in the twentieth century. Moreover, while earlier the bourgeoisie as a social class was a cornerstone – even if not the source – of this project, now it was oriented against this class. Bolshevism used some earlier techniques of 'embourgeoisement' for the proletarianisation of the whole society. But bolshevism was all the more absurd because it did not only resurrect an old mechanism that no doubt was obsolete, but it claimed that it represented the future. Driving a Model-T today on the streets of London would no doubt seem quite difficult. There may be other places where it could come in quite handy. But to claim that it represents the car of the twenty-first century would be the height of absurdity. This raises the problem: what made the establishment of such a system possible?

The study of this question would go well beyond the scope of this book. It would involve a reconstruction of the original problematisation on which the project of the 'reason of state' was grounded, and would also involve a genealogy of the 'police', starting from the Greek concept of *politeia*. Second, it would involve a study of the ways in which the old project and technology could have dissolved into and been reactivated in modern socialist thought and practices. Here, a no doubt crucial position is taken by Saint-Simon.[10] Third, it would require a study of the circumstances surrounding the establishment of these regimes. Concerning the latter, some comments have already been made in the last section of the previous chapter. Concerning the first two, in lieu of such major undertakings, here we can only offer two hints – one on the order of thought and methodology, the second on that of reality, the actual existence experienced by bolsheviks during the period in which the ideology was formulated.

First, no matter how Marx tried to put Hegel on his feet, there were many things they shared. Among others, there was the idea that history is somehow the realisation of 'truth'; that the true laws of human and social existence can be discovered through the study of history. Reading Marx with a Foucaldian eye, such an approach represents only an attempt to raise concrete, accidental historical answers given to specific problematisations to the level of universals. If one looks for solutions and truth in history, one only resurrects the long-forgotten ghosts of the past. Someone looking for the 'real' truth of history should not be surprised if he finds the 'effective' truth.[11] Perhaps Marxism failed to remember the old wisdom that one should look only for things that one wants to find.

Second, to understand the possibility of the absurdity, perhaps we should take seriously another major tenet of Marxism, the idea that existence comes before consciousness; something definitely true of actual human beings. Now, what was the reality of daily existence for bolsheviks? What was their most important concern, their major adversary and constant threat? It was the police. To lead an existence that escapes the police forces, to create an organisation that 'beats' the police on its own ground – that was a tremendous task, a permanent daily struggle.

The original goal of the bolsheviks was to realise the truth of history on the basis of daily existence, starting from material reality and not from ideals and utopias. What they got was the same thing – except that the meaningless, empty universal categories had to be supplemented with something 'truly' real and material. They 'discovered' – i.e. resurrected – the 'historical truth' behind the major aspect of their own daily existence, the police. And the contemporary crisis and the widespread hatred toward the agents of state power, the actual police, formed a background that was enough to enable the bolsheviks to seize power in a society demoralised by poverty and war.

It was a subject of extended discussions whether the bolshevik revolution was necessary or not. For us, it seems hard to make any sense of this debate. First, something that proved to be absurd, both in the order of thought and in daily reality, could not have been necessary. Second, talk about historical necessity in an extremely volatile situation can only be carried out at a level of abstract discourse that has lost all sense of reality. The key question in such situations is whether something is possible, and what will be realised out of the enormous range of possibilities. A small factor, a minuscule event, an accident may well have a profound and lasting impact, establishing for a long time – not to say 'for ever' – the limits and ranges of future possibilities. All that is important in our case is that the bolsheviks had the momentum at a crucial time to make history.

The fate of communist systems is inextricably tied up with this absurdity.[12] In a way, the whole history of bolshevism was nothing but an attempt to conceal that absurdity. On the one hand, it had to close all contacts with the outside world, to eliminate all external points of reference in order to keep itself intact and alive. No information from abroad was permitted, no chance of making comparisons, of imagining that it might be possible to live otherwise. On the other, it had to keep up internal pressure, had to establish its own reality, had to convince others, and, last but not least, itself that it did exist. Terror was necessary to make the unreal, the irrational, the absurd real. Terror did not establish bolshevism, and was not its essence. Quite the contrary, terror was necessary to hide away this 'essence'. It was deployed in order to make people blind to the actual working of the system and to the possibility of a different way of existence. The external and internal measures of control complemented and reinforced each other. Internal pressure could only be maintained if the house – the country – were closed, if the lid were on the sealed pressure-cooker. And, conversely, the external boundaries could only be maintained when internal control was close, nipping in the bud any possibility of an eruption.

All fateful histories come to an end. This is what has happened right now with communism. And, in our view, the end of communism is also deeply bound up with its cosy relationship with the absurd.

THE END OF COMMUNISM

A system that is widely considered as absurd and irrational can only be maintained by massive terror and fear. This feature was not lacking from the history of bolshevism. But this system was more than a simple dictatorship; one could say that its absurdity was more extensive. It also fancied itself as being in the vanguard of history and progress. The basic tension of the system was not between repression and fear, but between fear and faith.

If the history of bolshevism was the struggle to keep the absurdity hidden, then a counterstream of this whole history was related to the loss of 'faith'. It cannot be denied that bolshevism started everywhere with a considerable amount of genuine faith – massive and intensive popular support from an influential and substantial minority. It is also true that the great original impulse was followed by a gradual, continuous decay. The encounter with communism, faith in communism, was a relatively short phenomenon with most people; a short pleasure with a long hangover. No doubt, even if bolshevism was a phenomenon rooted in certain intellectual circles, the intellectuals were the first to reject their former beliefs. But the system did not collapse because of their disillusionment. The basic question here is the critical mass in terms of the loss of faith; the instance when such disillusionments lead to the sheer impossibility and the internal collapse of the system. And here intellectual and sociological analyses and merits are quite separate matters. In his books, Milan Kundera gave an analysis of how he – and his fellows – gained and lost enthusiasm in communism. He gave a satirical description from the inside of what Czeslaw Milosz has written about tragically from the outside. Once Kundera's hero has lost his faith, communism was dead for him – nothing but a rigid, irrational, authoritarian system remained. Many of his contemporaries felt the same way throughout Eastern Europe. Still, the regime remained basically intact; it could function. It only lost this ability when even members of the district party apparatus experienced the same feeling as Kundera did some forty years ago. This was partly a cognitive realisation of a failure; but it was also an event of mass psychology, something comparable to the end of a mass delusion. It was not just a realisation that grave mistakes had been made, but a collective discovery that the whole purpose was wrong, and could not be maintained. Communism as an avant-garde intellectual movement may well have ended much earlier – in Hungary in 1949 or in 1956, elsewhere at the latest in 1968. But communism as a social reality, as an object of sociological or even psychological analysis, ended somewhere around 1988–9. Finally, in October 1989, communism was even finished with as a political reality in Hungary.[13]

Communism dissolved itself when its failure, its absurdity, became obvious even to the crucial sections of the party. A ruling élite or class releases its power only if it is torn from its hand. The party apparatus eliminated itself with a shy, sorrowful, contorted smile, coloured with a feeling of shame.[14]

Communism was absurd because it resurrected an obsolete technology of government that had to go. But this whole process was given another twist by the fact that the technology of early modern 'police' itself was destined to dissolve itself once its mission was accomplished. It was a technology that aimed at setting up forms of behaviour, unleashing forces that would function by themselves once their deployment was successful. Therefore, the failure of bolshevism does not concern simply the disappearance, but the question of the extent to which these forms and modes of behaviour were instilled in society. Instead of talking about success and failure, we should rather analyse the extent to which a failure has succeeded.

THE LEGACY

It is extremely dangerous to talk about the legacy of communism. There is already much discussion on this topic. It has many different forms. It includes general exhortations addressed to the public at large. It includes attempts to excavate former crimes, punish the guilty, stigmatise the exposed members of the former system, especially informers of the secret police, including large-scale schemes for assessing and identifying individuals. The argument is already all too often used in political struggles to denounce the opposite side, pro and contra. It involves mutual witchhunts and blaming politicians, especially in election periods.[15] Claims are made that nothing has been changed, that the same persons remain in top positions everywhere, that individuals everywhere exhibit the same types of behaviour as in the past. Current methods of privatisation are denounced as attempts by the former nomenclatura to save its power, influence and privileges.

Most of these concerns are understandable, and many of the claims do raise very serious and burning issues. Some of the best sociological studies of the region were precisely concerned with the attempts of the former nomenclatura to save its positions for the future.[16] But any study of a legacy is a deeply dubious undertaking. On the one hand, it is a moralistic crusade, operating with a clear dividing line between what is good and what is to be condemned. On the other, it questions and studies present forms of behaviour, but orients all blame toward the past. It represents a curious combination of exhortation and investigation, where evaluative distinctions (good and bad) are intrinsically linked to *a posteriori* factual discriminations (between the past and present). In such an undetermined situation, almost anything goes, anything may be said. Anything one does not like may be attributed to the past, with the only signposts being clear, factual links with the past – party membership, family ties, positions or privileges accrued in the old system. In this way, any ethically meaningful distinction between good and bad in the past is eliminated.

Our goal is to address the issue of legacy only to the extent that this study says something specific. Not that we intend to use it as a pretext to smuggle in or express our opinions concerning any current or general issue, but it does give both a reference point to which present practices can be compared and the extent of the impact of the past – the 'legacy', or, to use the terminology of Foucault, the effects of the programmes on the real – can be assessed, and hints about the orientation of the impact – where this impact should be felt most strongly, and where it requires the most attention – perhaps on the part of every one of us. This study may provide some clues to the question of legacy by reconstructing the way past mechanisms of power worked at the level of daily existence. It is highly significant that the same books proved to be useful in helping this 'exorcism' that tried to do the same thing in the West, not independently of the study of the possibility and legacy of the other totalitarian system of the twentieth century, fascism.[17]

But here we have to face another danger. If the search for the legacy presents problems of knowledge and analysis (how to separate in a present practice or attitude the impact of the past) and a political dilemma (blaming each other for behaving like a communist), it also entails an ethical pitfall. The weeding of the legacy of the past should not lead to pontification and preaching. The creation of a feeling of guilt, of a bad conscience, is a method that is all too handy in such situations. After Nietzsche, we know the disastrous impact such strategies may entail, and also that it is a favourite – and most effective – tool of intellectual power.[18] Among others, a basic problem is that preaching always assumes a one-sided relationship, where the person giving the sermon never questions his/her own acts or behaviour, only blames the audience and raises its sense of guilt. This is a double mistake. First, because the major problem with past discourses about totalitarianism was that they always only addressed the totalitarianism of the other side. They never entailed self-analysis; never led to the doubt which Pierre Hassner was talking about in the starting sentence of his article: 'le totalitarisme, c'est moi' (Hassner 1984: 15). Second, this is especially out of place because – as we will argue – the intellectuals, the supposed subjects of this sermon, were exactly the stratum most affected by totalitarian reality and discourse – in many different ways and senses.

This material may provide some clues as to how to break out of these circles. Former members of the middle-level party apparatus were individuals at least as much entrapped in the whole system as anybody else, being victims and agents at the same time.[19] A non-rhetorical study of the impact of the past must start with the statement that, instead of clear divisions and markings (who was or who was not affected, who can be absolved and excepted, and who is to blame and to be held responsible), one must operate with careful shifts of emphasis. In order to have clear and sharp statements, we have to be very careful with the wording.

It is true that the past system had a severe, often devastating impact on everybody, by destroying values, social connections, forms of behaviour, and also promoting and conditioning other forms, both in a positive and negative sense, through those who conformed to and who resisted these. This means two things. First, if it holds true, then nobody can claim immunity; nobody was free or unimpaired. But, second, to state the obvious, the statement that nobody was unaffected does not mean that everybody was conditioned by the system; that we were – or even are – entrapped for ever. It only means that the scenario favoured by quite a few people – according to which 'we' were and are independent of the system, while 'they' were produced by it, and thus must be led by us and be re-educated, an important undercurrent of the discourse of 'civil society' or talks about the need for the return of the intellectuals to their true mission – is a mistaken and dangerous concept.

All the more so as, even if no stone was left unturned, the effect was not the same on everyone. Certain groups and certain individuals were subjected to this impact much more than the others. In order to identify these groups, it is necessary to recall the type of power exercised under communism. This concept was a combination of a strict protestant work ethic, a catholic sensitivity to the forces of life – the idea that power was related to the source of life and movement, but that it was a dangerous, evil force that must be constantly supervised and regulated – and the resurrection of the Greek concept of power as *arkhé*, as initiative, as opposed to the idea that power is simply rule or position. The consequence was that bolshevism tried to influence and supervise all decisions, all movements, all initiatives; it dreaded anything that was new, spontaneous, uncontrolled. Its major target was to replace an anarchic, uncontrollable, ungovernable society with an orderly and thoroughly disciplined one. It tried at once to destroy and then to replace, stimulate and instigate all activities, 'activity' itself. This explains why the two major targets of bolshevik supervision were the major sources of energy and innovation (at least in modern societies), economic and intellectual life. It controlled these activities, which meant that it repressed all attempts to engage in such activities outside its scope; but at the same time it needed personnel to manage these areas effectively.

This dual attitude, this dual power, presented a dilemma to all those people who were the potential targets of this strategy, all people with initiative, internal power, dynamism and motivation. The choice was diabolical for them, as it involved either suppressing all initiative and activity, killing life in themselves and being satisfied with trifling jobs and activities; or accepting the offer of the party, and joining, first of all, the official system, then the party.[20]

The choice made was a matter of individual decision, where it is extremely difficult to evaluate clearly any of the possibilities chosen in themselves.[21] But the existence of the choice did not depend on individuals. This was something everyone had to face. The modalities or the circumstances of this choice were different in the 1950s from the 1980s. Through the decades, there was an obvious move toward liberalisation. However, it is not at all clear that this move was an unmixed blessing, especially from the perspective of the present. If the softening of the system made life and choices about existence easier, it also blurred the distinction between compromises that had to be accepted and more or less rational choices, the pursuit of an acceptable self-interest.

And it is perhaps at this level that the most lasting and dangerous impact of bolshevism will be with us for the longest. This concerns the 'depth' of personality, the self, its – allegedly universal, but definitely real – need to identify itself with its own activity. Communism not only forced individuals into choices about life where they did not have a decent choice to make, but, using very delicate, probably highly unconscious mechanisms, it made them identify themselves with the results of their own decisions. It forced individuals to choose labels prepared by the system, made them stick them on their own foreheads and finally to behave accordingly. Communism involved a peculiar game of self-stigmatisation.[22]

An example of this curious play with and impact on subjectivity under communism would be the case of self-censorship. The case itself is well known, and does not require a long introduction.[23] In Hungary in recent decades, there was no formal censorship; there was no office that assessed all writings and decided whether something could be published or not. This did not mean that anything was publishable. Censorship operated at a more subtle level, using the editors of a magazine or of a publishing house, whose real opinions were not very different from those of any writers or scholars. Thus, ultimately, censorship resided with the authors themselves.

In this game, the limits between what was and was not publishable were not clear. Each and every written piece published recreated these limits, leaving a scope for testing the limits, pushing them a bit further, opening up possibilities, widening the gap, as long as the framework was not torn apart. Each act of testing the limits legitimised itself by not provoking a response, and became a starting point for fresh provocations of this kind, until the boundaries that had been flexible so far were crossed, some political potentates became angry and repressive measures followed – not very severe ones compared to the terror of the 1950s; intolerably harsh ones, it one employs contemporary Western standards.

Still, the major problem concerning subjectivity did not lie here, in our understanding. None in the past could have avoided this limit-testing game in Hungary. To do so from the start would have been suicidal and meaningless, and there were extremely few cases of explicit rejection of these unwritten rules. The problem was not with the necessity, under the given circumstances, of putting up with compromises. It was with the exact psychological mechanism by which these compromises were made. The problem was rooted in the way writers became identified, also by themselves, with their own product, and the way these mechanisms were deformed under the specific conditions of self-censorship in 'socialist' Hungary.

The problem had three aspects. The first was a concept of writing rooted in the classical version of German philosophy, with its strong pastoral-moralistic overtones. Whatever one writes down should come from one's innermost soul. One should identify completely with each and every word written down. That was the basis, a long-standing, influential historical legacy. The second was the obvious impossibility of fully adhering to this principle during the communist period. The third concerned the actual way writers related to their own work, influenced by the given tradition and by the given circumstances.

They used writing not as a tool for expressing and thinking, but as a way of declaring the full external truth and of opening up the truth inside the self. This was impossible; everybody had to respect the external constraints. Therefore, from the start writing became conditioned by a frustration. But the actual output was not simply the result of external pressure and constraint. Many things could have been written down; it was important that these be identified and analysed. It was still the work of the author, even if in certain ways it was deformed, compromised, unclear. It was one's own child, even if it had certain birth defects. It had to be defended against all types of attack. In the given tradition, it required identification. In this way, the exact nature of the compromises had to be forgotten. Identification, the strongest and most dangerous of emotional commitments, distorted sight, and from the inside. On the one hand, the line between necessary compromises and plain truths was blurred; on the other, an all-pervasive cynicism prevented the accomplishment of work and thinking that, after all, could have been done.

Up till now, we have discussed the peculiar impact of the system according to individual, quasi-psychological categories, motivation and initiative. But the relative importance of these impacts can also be assigned to definite sociological categories. There were two strata that were most affected by communism, in many different, but reinforcing, respects: the intellectuals and the entrepreneurs, both in the broad sense of the terms.

First, they were the ones who were the most clearly and directly repressed. They were persecuted personally and as a given social class. They were forbidden to work according to their own standards, to follow their own course of action. Second, these were the strata that most clearly had to face the choice described above, that was given both as an opportunity and a fate. Here again communism was quite faithful to its principles, in its own peculiar way. Its pronounced goal was to be egalitarian, to open up the possibility of mobility toward the functional upper levels to everybody. And it did so, on the condition one faces the existential choice described above. It tried to establish a 'socialist' meritocracy. But not everyone had to face this choice to the same extent. Those who had some footing in the élite – through family connections, whether in the party or the remains of the intellectual élite – were less forced to make these compromises. The third step, in both chronological and logical sequence, was the mixed blessing of the 'second society'. This opened up the possibility of an activity quite independent of the all-encompassing eyes of the first society, but at the price of an almost complete lack of established standards.[24] In the case of intellectuals, it led to a definite lowering of standards and 'inbreeding'; in the case of entrepreneurs, to illegality, a return to petty profiteering and a reopening of the gap between private and public interests that had been closed, not fully, nor without difficulties, by liberalism and modernity. The two major legacies of communism are the impairing of thinking and of doing proper business.[25] And while it was the second economy and society, the peculiar, muddy, grey and rosy situation, created by the stubborn resistance of the whole population to external pressure and the consequent struggle to work one's own way through, under any circumstances, that have made life in Hungary in the past and the transition process in the present much easier and smoother than in the other countries of the region, it is this same situation that, with its lack of form, with its lack of sharp dividing lines, may impair to some extent the future course of events.

FINAL REMARKS

Communism today in Eastern Europe and the Soviet Union is not just fatally ill. It has gone beyond the stage of clinical death. It cannot be resurrected. Our interviewee proved to be right: the system immediately collapsed as such, once the party apparatus was taken out. The different situations of the former communist countries reflect the extent to which the collapse of the party entails the collapse of the whole society and the economy; something that is closely related to the role the party apparatus played in the past and the extent to which no other links were established in the given society.[26]

The most important characteristics of daily life under communism were a certain type of pressure: a situation and a feeling that everything was controlled and supervised, that somehow in the background everything one does was observed, summarised, taken into account, assessed; that there was no escape from this hidden, background web of connections. Communism ended in daily life when this pressure was dissolved, and when ordinary business started to be dealt with according to its own logic, and not according to the logic the apparatus wanted to impose on the population. The lid was taken off the pressure-cooker and the individualised guidance of our public and often even our private selves – in the fields, among others, of work, traffic, cultural and social activities – was over.

This end was no doubt instigated by external factors – by the increasing inability of these regimes to keep the external world out and at the same time to keep up in a certain way with the rest of the world. This end was also inevitable, as something that is absurdly out of place cannot be maintained for ever. This gives us the meaning and limits of the frequent talks about 'return to normality'. But the exact answer to all these challenges, the moment of the change, depended upon the answer of the communist party itself, at the different levels of the apparatus. There ought to have been intimate connections between the views and feelings of low-level political instructors and major high-level figures of 'reform', such genuine apparatchiks as Gorbachev or Pozsgay – even if allegedly both were hostile to and unsupported by the apparatus.

In the 1980s and even in the 1970s, there was no 'communist dictatorship' in Hungary. The communist system was gradually eroded from many sides, by many factors. But in a way it was still in place, it still had an impact on large segments of daily life. The fact that the apparatus existed could not be ignored by anybody. The end of communism in Hungary was a specific response, an event at the end of a long, gradual process, and was closely related to the dissolution of the apparatus. In spite of all the previous changes, this represented an abrupt break, after which everything could be, and was, redefined.[27]

The fact that communism is dead does not mean a panacea, does not necessary entail a 'transition to democracy'. This theoretical framework, so often used to describe the events in Eastern Europe, is misleading, because – with the possible exception of Poland – it was not simply the end of an authoritarian system. The end of communism may well lead to authoritarianism, though in the more developed countries of the region it would be highly unlikely. It may also lead to a balkanised Americanisation, for which the communist legacy provides a particularly fertile breeding ground. In each country, a vast complex of different problems is pressing: a joint legacy of communism, wars, backwardness, national conflicts and international debts, of which this last could easily be the most devastating. There are many possible future scenarios as consequences of this situation, and, especially in the short term, no responsible programme can be too optimistic. The future may bring ugly aspects, but it will not lead to a return to communism anywhere.

The possibility of bolshevism is closed for ever. The problem now is to minimise the impact it may have on shaping the future.

Notes

PREFACE

1 As this book contains the results of an empirical investigation carried out in Hungary, all specific references will be made about this country only. Nevertheless, many of the remarks have a validity extending well beyond the case of Hungary. The mechanism this books intends to present and analyse, the bolshevik-type party apparatus, has nothing specifically Hungarian about it. A central aim of the analysis is to present this in the purest form, and thus to have a relevance for comparative studies of the region. Nevertheless, in order to avoid both the trouble of having long and tedious qualifications, and the mistake of unwarranted generalisations, we will try to present the Hungarian case and refrain from a general, frequent reference to the general term 'Eastern European countries', except when we are explicitly discussing some general aspects of the systems. In this way, we intend our book to serve as a basis for detailed, future comparisons, something that could only be hindered if we tried to be overtly general and synthetic at each and every page. The ways in which communism ended in the different Eastern European countries are not variations of a general model. On the other hand, we do believe that the concrete case of Hungary gives us many insights into crucial aspects of these revolutionary changes, and occasionally we will point to some similarities. In the past decades, there has been a considerable discussion about the extent to which Hungary could be used as a 'model' case for the other countries of 'existing socialism'. This idea became obsolete well before it lost all meaning, due to the changes. But we would argue that it may be valid in a different sense. Together with Poland, Hungary was the country that in some ways was the first to be 'over' with communism; first in 1956, then, in a different sense, with the economic reform of 1968, and finally at the end of the 1980s. But while Poland always presented a highly exceptional case (historical traditions, the church, uncollectivised agriculture, the strength of Solidarity, etc.), Hungary in many respects was similar to the other countries, except in being swifter in the changes and smarter (or just luckier) in making communism bearable. Therefore, its path may be relevant for comparative reasons.

2 See Gombár (1987), Lengyel (1989) and Hankiss (1990). These are all reviews of the Hungarian literature on social, political and economic problems, and are thus comprehensive assessments in themselves.

3 The book does not aim to be comprehensive, focusing only on this particular element in the transition, and its role in the road leading toward it. For more global and synthetic accounts of the transition, see the writings of László Lengyel and Jadwiga Staniszkis. On the transition in Hungary in English, see also Urbán (1989), Bozóky (1990), Bruszt (1990), Körösényi (1990).
4 This atmosphere is well documented by Fidelius (1987).
5 Here, in making the interviews, she was helped by Márta Havasi, who was an instructor of the local committee, and was writing her dissertation with Mihály Bihari.
6 See Horváth (1988a), and its English version (1988b).

1 INTRODUCTION

1 The distinction between the former *nomenclatura* system and the apparatus is fairly straightforward. The nomenclatura referred to two things. First, it was a list of positions in the state and the economy that were to be filled only by those persons of whom the respective party organs approved. Second, it was used to denominate those individuals who were actually filling these positions. The apparatus, on the other hand, included the full-time party workers of the different party committees who were taking up 'political' and not just administrative positions (financial, clerical). Thus, far from being identical, apparatus and nomenclatura were rather mutually exclusive categories, though many members of the nomenclatura had spent time inside the apparatus. The nomenclatura included the top-level decision makers of the state and the economy who were all to some extent manipulated by the apparatus through the latter's exclusive control of appointments. It was this tension between, and not identity of, apparatus and nomenclatura that was crucial for the maintenance of the whole system. The nomenclatura system was abolished in Hungary by a central committee meeting of 8 May 1989.
2 See, for example, Djilas (1957), Nove (1982), Voslensky (1984), and Lane (1988). On the history of the nomenclatura system, see Rigby (1990: ch.4). For the standard account on the nomenclatura, see Harasymiw (1984).
3 This is the book by Avtorkhanov (1966). Sparse empirical studies of the party apparatus in Hungary include a few articles by Csanádi (1987), (1990a), (1990b), Kolosi and Szabó (1973), and parts of the recently published, earlier studies by Fazekas and Köllő (1990).
4 This may reflect a usage that seemed to have been common among members of the central-committee apparatus. At least, in the interesting memories of Agnes Ságvári giving an insider view on the Hungarian communist party in the 1950s, members of the apparatus of the central committee generally referred to themselves as 'the' apparatus. See, for example, Ságvári (1989: 58).
5 For example, a recent study by Rutland (1990) on the regional aspects of *glasnost* and *perestroika* had to make do with the analysis of regional newspapers, as it was not possible to get access to the apparatus itself.
6 The classic and recently republished book by Fainsod (1958) was often mentioned, but rarely used in the literature. There were even fewer attempts to use the Smolensk archive containing the only sources of information on the

detailed activities of any communist-party apparatus. The only serious attempt was made by A. Getty (1985) who used these data to reassess the Stalinist purges, and created quite a stir. On the debate, see Sakwa (1989a: 55).

7 See Avtorkhanov (1966: 369ff.) and Bauman (1974: 136). In Hungary, Mihály Bihari (1987) was writing about a 'party-centred' political system.

8 See Hassner (1984) on the trajectory of the concept in the West, and Rupnik (1988) for its recent resurrection in the East. Barber (1969) collected together many definitions of totalitarianism.

9 See, for example, Curtis (1969).

10 See especially Arendt (1958) and Neumann (1965).

11 See, for example, Fainsod (1953), Moore (1954), Friedrich and Brzezinski (1956).

12 A study of regional decision-making in the Soviet Union that has a paradigmatic value is Hough (1969). The standard book of the approach is Skilling and Griffiths (1971). For a recent overview, see Solomon (1983).

13 This chapter in no way is intended to present a comprehensive picture of the theoretical field of Soviet and Eastern European studies. The 1980s saw some return to the theories of totalitarianism even in the West, reflecting both the changes in international atmosphere (the Afghanistan effect) and the wide impact of dissident writings (the Gulag effect). Some of this is discussed in Hassner (1984). On the other hand, more empirical studies put the emphasis on the way the communist project was sent off course and deformed by reality, highlighting some traditional, historical influences, concerned less with the specificity of bolshevism which was considered mostly as an ideology which was becoming less and less relevant in any case. There was also a gap between the studies of the élite, the top leadership, and mass political attitudes. See the studies on nomenclatura and clientelism (Rigby and Harasymiw 1983, Harasymiw 1984 and Willerton 1979), and on political culture (Brown and Gray 1977, and Bialer 1989).

14 For comprehensive reviews of political opposition and dissent in Eastern Europe, see Schapiro (1972), Tökés (1979), Curry (1983), Bugajski and Pollack (1987), and Skilling (1989).

15 A study of the background of the opposition is a task that still remains to be done; and something that has become all the more important and indispensable as some former opposition leaders are playing such an important role in the political and intellectual life of post-communist societies. The real importance of such an undertaking should lie not just in a straightforward analysis of the social and political background. An exceptionally fruitful study of this could be conducted along Nietzschean lines. We are particularly thinking here of his category of 'descent', as applied, for example, in his attempts to trace back some of the most important – and questionable – characteristics of classical German philosophy to similar attitudes and perspectives of German protestantism. From this perspective, it should be remarked that the two major sources of opposition in Eastern Europe were those who were disappointed, disillusioned with socialism and the possibility of reforming it; and those who were raised completely outside the framework of the whole system, being always hostile to it. They both present specific problems. The first group, in spite of all attempts to deny the past, did preserve many patterns of thought and methods. These people are

thinking in terms of movements, of mobilising people, of telling them what is truth and what to do, of taking for granted that they have the right and ability to lead others, to assess and classify them. They have an internal conviction that they are the élite, and assume that the 'masses' should follow their lead. It seems to us that many of the past conflicts within the opposition were along these lines (for some indication, see Lipski (1985), though at that period Lipski was understandably not very interested in and was even perplexed by these conflicts). This problem is not just of antiquarian interest, but lies at the heart of many current political developments in Hungary, Poland and even Czechoslovakia. In the case of the second group, the influence of a bolshevik mentality is obviously much less present. The problem here rather is that, due to their life-long opposition to all aspects of communism, the system only appeared to them as a threatening, oppressive external machine, and therefore they failed to notice the specificity of this system. For them, it was just a tyranny, a dictatorship, an authoritarian regime. They always, from the beginning, remained on the outer edge, preserving an external, backs-to-the-wall perspective, seeing everything in black and white, and therefore were often unable to see the extent to which society itself was successfully altered in many indirect ways. Needless to say, they were even less able to notice in themselves any lasting impact – should there be such a thing.

16 See, among others, the works of Michnik (1985), Konrád (1984) and Havel (1985). On this idea, and its relationship to the concept of 'Central Europe', see also Arato (1981), Keane (1988b), Ash (1989) and Rupnik (1989). In Hungary, until the last moment, the 'reformers', especially the so-called 'reform-economists', kept addressing the political élite, without even noticing the ambivalence between the general discourse of 'democratisation' and the everyday activity of presenting different projects to the current élite; the incompatibility of 'reform' and 'democracy'. This problem is discussed by E. Szalai (1990). On the 'reform economists', see Kovács (1990).

17 This attitude may gain importance with the necessary implementation of harsh economic policies in the future. Here we must again emphasise that we are not thinking about explicit blame and revenge. We only want to point out that it is psychologically easier to contribute to the implementation of a harsh economic measure if one is convinced that in the past the population lived an 'easy wandering' consumer life, without taking responsibility for the true situation. In this respect, the election programme of the Civic Forum, emphasising sacrifice, the need to work harder and the importance of limiting consumption on the assumption that the country was previously living off its own future, contrasts strangely with the speech of the prime minister, himself a member of Forum, on the state of the economy, deploring the earlier practice of over-investment, and the lack of concern for the vital needs of the population. See *East European Reporter*, v. 4 (1990), 2: 20–2 and ibid., pp. 8–10.

18 Mihály Vajda can be mentioned as a characteristic representive of this position. See Vajda (1988), and also his debate with Simecka, Brodsky and others, in Schöpflin and Wood (1989), and Századvég (1989).

19 See, for example, Havel (1985: 44), also Benda *et al.* (1988).

20 The colour 'rosy' was often used to describe the communist party of the 1970s and 1980s, to indicate that it was no longer 'red'. The colour 'grey' was

used, for example, by Siklova (1990) in a somewhat similar sense, to indicate a zone between the official sphere and the outspoken dissidents.

21 The term 'discourse' (and its adjective 'discursive') in this book follows the terminology of Michel Foucault, especially as it was expounded in Foucault (1976a, 1976b and 1977c). It can best be defined by the distance it takes with respect to the terms 'theory' and 'ideology'. In both cases, reality and truth exist outside thought and text. The only question is the extent to which they ('theory' or 'ideology') reflect reality correctly. The difference between the two is that in the 'positivist' framework a wrong theory is just a scientific error, while in the case of 'critical theories' there is a reference to explicit or hidden intentions, a distinction between true and false consciousness. With the concept of the 'discourse' Foucault and other contemporary French writers put the emphasis on the independence and specificity of texts, and Foucault also emphasises the extent to which discourse and thought have an independent impact on reality. See also MacDonell (1986) and the recently started periodical *Discourse and Society*, published by Sage.

22 See Zinoviev (1981) and Haraszti (1987).

23 A comprehensive account of the history of mobilisation and demobilisation in Hungary can be found in Hankiss (1990).

24 For dissidents, the positive task of keeping the system together was done solely on the level of ideology, and it was maintained externally by the repressive forces of the state. The dual, at once positive and negative, power of the apparatus failed to appear on their horizon. In this respect, a crucial paragraph from Havel's essay is worth quoting at length:

> The whole power structure ... could not exist at all if there were not a certain 'metaphysical' order binding all its components together, interconnecting them to a uniform method of accountability, supplying the combined operation of all these components with rules of the game, that is, with certain regulations, limitations, and legalities. This metaphysical order is fundamental to, and standard throughout, the entire power structure; it integrates its communication system and makes possible the internal exchange and transfer of information and instructions. It is rather like a collection of traffic signals and directional signs, giving the process shape and structure. This metaphysical order guarantees the inner coherence of the totalitarian power structure. It is the glue holding it together, its binding principle, the instrument of its discipline. Without this glue the structure as a totalitarian structure would vanish; it would disintegrate into individual atoms chaotically colliding with one another in their unregulated particular interests and inclinations. The entire pyramid of totalitarian power, deprived of the element that binds it together, would collapse in upon itself, as it were in a kind of material implosion.

(Havel 1985: 31–2)

We argue that, as the later chapters will show, Havel's description of a metaphysical order almost perfectly fits a very real phenomenon: the activities accomplished by the party apparatus; activities that were hidden from the population, that appeared for them at the level of mental processes – fears, rumours, ideologies – and operated effectively there, but that nevertheless did possess a very real existence. While the apparatus was in place, 'living in truth' was impossible in the sense implied, and the 'power of the powerless' was limited. When and where it was possible to confront the apparatus at that level, the apparatus was rendered useless, and the system was replaced by a mere authoritarian military dictatorship. An example of this can be seen in Poland in the case of the KOR and Solidarity and the surviving influence of the Church that lay behind them. 'KOR' is the acronym for the Workers' Defence Committee, an organisation created by Polish intellectuals to help workers who participated in the events of 1976 and who were subsequently prosecuted by the authorities. It had an important indirect role in the creation of Solidarity (Lipski 1985). See also the Hungarian strategy of the 'second economy' (Kenedi 1982, Manchin 1988, Hankiss 1990, Hann 1990).

25 In his introductory remarks to the fourth volume of *East European Politics and Societies*, Ivo Banac asks the question why the field of Eastern European studies is so marginalised by the Western academic hierarchy if it is such a promising area of intellectual study, and finds the only possible answer to be that 'the scholars of Eastern Europe have failed to capture the intellectual imagination of the larger scholarly community', and that instead of being a sect, they should 'creatively . . . arouse the interest of other scholars' (Banac 1990: 2). See also the almost identical remarks made by Ken Jowitt concerning the paucity of theoretical imagination (Jowitt 1990a: 196).

26 The most influential figures are Philippe Ariès, Norbert Elias, Michel Foucault, Reinhart Koselleck, Lewis Mumford and Gerhard Oestreich.

27 See especially the works of Marcuse and Adorno.

28 It should be mentioned that, concerning the East, events pointing to exactly the opposite direction occurred in the same year in Czechoslovakia.

29 'Project' in this context is close to 'programme' but is less compact and specific. It refers to an inherent directionality of historical changes that are neither random nor accidental, directed by neither conscious wills nor rigid historical laws. It is also close to the discussion of 'discourse' in Foucault (1977c) but refers to general historical trends rather than to the mere internal logic of texts.

30 Ariès, Elias, Foucault or Mumford all became popular around this period.

31 For a cursory survey, see the works by Beik (1985), Coleman and Starkey (1986), Fox and Guy (1986), Starkey (1985), Starkey *et al.* (1987), Parker (1989) and Hsia (1989). For a reconstruction of networks of power in a local community in seventeenth-century France, with some surprising similarities with the recent past of Eastern Europe, see Fontaine (1990).

32 On this Nietzschean concept of 'effective history', see Foucault (1977a).

33 He was conjuring up the spectre of the right-wing militias' activities after the fall of the 1919 bolshevik regime in Hungary. This was a standard tactic of the hardliners of the communist party to justify their need to hold on to their power.

2 MICHEL FOUCAULT AND THE STUDY OF POWER

1 In his last books, he showed less concern with this question. Still, in one of his late interviews, he expressed continued interest in the question of bio-power (Foucault 1984d).

2 For the best works, see Gordon (1980, 1991), Dreyfus and Rabinow (1983), Rajchman (1985) and Deleuze (1988).

3 This is close to the meaning of one of the Greek terms originally used for power, *arkhé*. See Myers (1927).

4 These are called 'two-dimensional theories' by Steven Lukes (1974).

5 This concept that retrospectively he considers to be so crucial for his whole work emerges only in his last writings. See Foucault (1984e, 1986a, 1988a, 1988b, 1988c).

6 About this idea of a question as an answer, see Foucault (1988a: 17).

7 Coming to terms with this specificity was a major preoccupation of Foucault from the start of his work. See, among others, Foucault (1963, 1967, 1973, 1976a, 1976b, 1984c).

8 This topic is discussed in detail in all his analyses on the birth of modern institutions. See Foucault (1961, 1975, 1979a).

9 Concerning Foucault's relationship to Kant in his last period, see Foucault (1984a, 1986b), also Gordon (1986) and Munoz Darde (1990).

10 This starts with his lectures given at the time the first volume of *The History of Sexuality* was published. See Foucault (1980b).

11 See Foucault (1983a: 221). For a particularly clear example of the confounding of the government of the self and the state, see Eliot (1632).

12 See Foucault (1983a), and also Rajchman (1985).

13 See, for example, the account of Bauman: 'The [pre-war] dynasties [...] confined their governing ambitions largely to revenue raising, and were essentially unconcerned with the administration of the daily lives or productive initiatives of their subjects' (Bauman 1989a: 74).

14 In the book, we'll give ample details from the interviews or questionnaires not only to document our analysis, but also to reconstruct the atmosphere of party committees and the situation in general. In interview selections, imaginary initials are given for each individual respondent, and 'secretary' is added if the given person was a district secretary or first secretary. In the case of questionnaires, the capital letter stands for a given district, and the number is the code of the respondent in the sample.

3 THE ACTIVITY OF DISTRICT PARTY COMMITTEES

1 In the following, we will use the abbreviation 'EC' for 'executive committee'. This covers what in the literature is generally called 'bureau'.

2 'Fetishisation' was part of the jargon often used by party people. Here it means the 'courage' to name something directly instead of using double talk.

3 See Polányi (1944), Schumpeter (1954) and Spiegel (1983).

4 Let's not forget that, throughout classical British political economy, the perspective of the writers was not that of existing, living individuals and groups, but that of the 'commonwealth'.

5 This metaphor is the central topic in Plato's *Theaethetus*.

6 In our study, we prefer to keep the awkward term 'sphere of competence' or 'competence list' and not use simply the word 'nomenclatura'. First, because this gives a better translation of the original Hungarian word that was used, and therefore conveys the atmosphere better. Second, the use of the 'Russian' word would take us too easily back to the already described,

matter-of-fact identification of the list with the persons, and the persons with the apparatus. This practice, by the way, was eliminated by the 8 May 1989 resolutions of the central-committee meeting. Though the party only voted itself out of existence on 7 October 1989, the earlier data was at least as important in the process of self-elimination.

7 One could add that, behind the arguments, it is possible to discern signs of an attitude deeper than the need for or the responsibility of the party: the idea that, no matter by what organisation, the firms and institutions must be supervised in detail; they cannot be left on their own. At the time of our study, some of our interviewees had doubts about the competence of the party concerning these matters. But they had no doubts about the necessity of such supervision itself.

8 One instructor made the following remark to the question concerning why he joined the party: 'I did not want to believe that so many people couldn't find a solution to the troubles of life' (T.6).

9 This expression was a standard euphemism for supervision and control.

10 This will not give us exactly the mirror of the previous results, as the middle answers are left out of both analyses.

11 It is not possible to give here an overview of the way the concept of bureaucracy was used in the literature on communist political systems. In general, two objections were made about the common, indiscriminate use of this term. According to some, even if the concept of the rational, formal bureaucracy is inapplicable, the rule of the communist party still involves the rule of a certain type of bureaucracy (see Hirszowicz 1980, and Bihari 1987). However, there are others who stated that, in view of the way the party was working, the very concept of a bureaucracy is misleading. Such claims are voiced by Avtorkhanov (1966), Stewart (1968), Hough (1969) and Unger (1974). This topic will be taken up in the concluding chapters. This can be supported by the excellent review of the ethos of bureaucracy by Belohradsky (1989), which shows how different it was from the ethos of the communist party.

4 WHAT IS 'POLITICS'?

1 One should recall the statement made in the first section about the mission of the party to assure development.

2 Braudel is citing a statement made by Lenin, and widely accepted among Soviet historians, that, left free, every village market would in the end reproduce capitalism (Braudel 1977: 62).

3 See Chapter 3, p 48.

5 THE BACKGROUND AND VALUE SYSTEM OF PARTY WORKERS

1 In the latter case, we omitted housewives.

2 See Hankiss *et al.* (1983). This study provides a general background for a number of lines of investigation in this book.

3 In the Hungarian educational system, there is a marked difference between the more scholarly universities and the other, more technical, institutes of higher education, here translated as 'polytechnic'.

4 Here we should remark that the bottom age limit for becoming a member was 14 years for the KISZ (Hungarian communist youth organisation) and 18 for the party, though exceptions could have been made.

5 This question is taken from Kirkpatrick *et al.* (1974).

6 See Hankiss *et al.* (1983).

7 This question is taken from the 1981 survey of the European Value System Study Group. See Harding and Phillips (1986).

6 THE TASKS OF POLITICAL INSTRUCTORS

1 This item was taken and modified from Kirkpatrick *et al.* (1974).

2 Here we also used a modified item from the same questionnaire.

3 See Masuda (1981: 75). One may wonder whether the treatment of information as private property is really compatible with easy access. Masuda's book, by the way, is an almost perfect example of the modernised version of an early modern 'police' utopia, especially concerning the way he hopes for the integration of the whole society into a system working according to a single logic.

4 See Bell (1973) and Inglehart (1977). The career of Daniel Bell is especially interesting here, as he represents a direct personal connection between the 'post-industrial society' and the 'information society' projects. Moreover, since his earlier book on the end of ideology, he has maintained a consistent view that the natural evolution of contemporary society represents an easy and immediate realisation of the utopian dream of a society where conflicts will disappear.

5 This dream of a perfectly transparent society, by the way, is distractingly close to the similar political dream in eighteenth-century France. See Foucault (1975) Foucault *et al.* (1976) and Meyer (1983).

6 See Fleming (1983). At this point, it would be interesting to ponder upon the other factors that at one time or another were considered to be the 'glues' or the 'cements' of society. To name just a few: religion, morals, love, the police, the communist party, the market. Thus, in a sense, information is supposed to fulfil some of the functions that in other societies were performed by these other agencies! I do not think that it can seriously be proposed that information or communication always had this function. In a tautological sense, the exchange of ideas and facts always provided some links between individuals or groups, but it is a far cry from the proposition about information as a 'glue'.

7 As a concrete example, let's assess the curious relation between pre-modern, modern and 'post-modern' elements in the two approaches. In the case of the communist party, gossiping, a *par excellence* pre-modern attitude, was used by a project of forced modernisation to make people governable from the centre. It attempted a return to the immediacy of communities with the help of a repressive, alienating apparatus. The utopia of the 'global village' has surprising similarities with this view. It uses the most alienating aspects of modern civilisation, the tools of indirect communication, to bolster a claim about the end of alienation, and a return to the immediacy of pre-modern existence. Finally, gossiping can be said to hold an important place – instead of thinking – in 'post-modern' intellectual life as well. For some similar

comments, see Bauman (1989b). Perhaps the most important common feature of daily life seems to be the same in traditional villages, under bolshevik-type party-states and in the post-modern 'global village', though the modalities are quite different. It is dullness.

7 THE SPECIFICITIES OF THE INSTRUCTOR'S WORK

1 By the way, one of our most surprising experiences was the almost complete absence of cynicism among our respondents and interviewees. We experienced fear and the courage to speak; defence, reproach and complaints; faith and the loss of faith; hopelessness and hope; but did not meet anyone with outward cynicism. And, on second thoughts, this should not be surprising. The cynicism of the power-holders is based on a wavering faith in their own truth and morality and at the same time a belief in the stability of their power. The end of this stability eliminated the possibility of cynicism.

2 We took this question from Kirkpatrick *et al.* (1974).

3 Some lines written by Max Weber about military classes are particularly relevant here. See Weber (1968).

8 A GOVERNMENTAL TECHNOLOGY RESURRECTED BY THE PARTY: THE EARLY MODERN 'POLICE'

1 Our guess is that the closer the apparatus became to the population at large in its daily life, the less effective and useful it was for the leadership. At that point, it was discarded, as at least some leaders had confidence in their personal public appeal and popularity. Even the blame laid on the apparatus 'as such' could have been conceived as a way to increase this popularity. They did not foresee, apart from international events, that by ending the strict nomenclatura system and destroying the apparatus the whole system would collapse almost immediately.

2 See the quotation at the head of this chapter. The source is Pasquino (1978: 47).

3 Aristotle, *Politics*, ed. and trsl. by Ernest Barker (London, Oxford University Press, 1958). See also Barker's Introduction on the Greek meanings of the terms, pp. lxv–lxxi.

4 For example, in the words of the famous rhetorician, Isocrates: 'The soul of a *polis* is nothing else than its *politeia*, having as much power over it as does the mind over the body.' (Isocrates (1928–45): v. 2., p. 113).

5 Chevallier (1967). See Le Clère (1980).

6 See the discussion in Chapter 1.

7 See Duchesne (1767: 1–2); and see also Pasquino (1978).

8 On Machiavelli's concept of 'fortuna', see Pitkin (1984), especially Chapter 6.

9 See Pasquier (1607). On Pasquier, see Huppert (1970).

10 See Turquet (1611); and Mothe Le Vayer (1662: v.1.).

11 For the concept of 'voluntary compulsion', see Unger (1974: 31). On the 'mystical' attributes of party membership, see also Glazov (1988).

12 In the words of De La Mare, whenever anything troublesome happens, 'the

first thing that should come into one's mind and the first remedy to be used should be a recourse to a *commissaire* of police'. Moreover, this should include not only floods, murders, or accidents, but 'even the differences that arise in families among the closest persons, or between neighbours or people of the same occupation; these should be brought before them [i.e. the commissaires], and they should be the first judges for instructions [investigations]; and, most often, the pacifiers.' (De La Mare, 1705–1738: v.1, p. 205). In this sense, it is particularly intriguing that the country where this maxim was realised the most thoroughly is the United States (about the extremely wide range of welfare-type daily police activity there, see also Wilson 1968; this was the country considered to be the true home of civil society by both Hegel and Say.

13 This duality is a recurrent feature in the works of Foucault.

14 See Say (1828–9). By the way, this light was lit under very special circumstances in the case of Adam Smith. His Glasgow lectures contain all the basic ideas of the first book of the later *Wealth of Nations*, in the section on 'Police' in his *Lectures on Jurisprudence* (Smith 1978). And the career of Say himself was not very different from his master's. His first published work, *Olbie*, belonged to the genre of utopias about well-policed cities, so popular in the period around the French Revolution. See Say (1848).

15 As an illustration of this point, let's present here in a nutshell the history of the d'Argenson family in seventeenth- and eighteenth-century France. René de Voyer, seigneur d'Argenson (1596–1651), received his military education in the Netherlands, at the most advanced school of its kind at that time, to become a *maître des requêtes* in Paris, and later an intendant of justice, finances and police of Colbert in Berry and Burgundy. He finished as ambassador to Venice. All that is listed above had a particularly strong impact in general on the development of police technology, as, besides the obvious connections in the French administration, there is a direct link between the Dutch methods of social disciplining and the administrative methods used in the Brandenburg-Prussian *Polizeistaat* (see Oestreich 1982: ch. 6); the methods of administration employed in the Burgundian state served as models for German mercantilism and the science of 'police' (see Knemeyer 1980); and the Venetian methods for the collection of diplomatic information were taken over by all later domestic intelligence services. His son, Marc-René de Voyer, comte d'Argenson (1623–1700), was also a *maître des requêtes* and ambassador to Venice. With this background, it should not be surprising that the son of the latter, Marc-René de Voyer, marquis de Palmy, comte d'Argenson (1652–1721), became the second, and perhaps the most famous, *lieutenant de police* of Paris. He was such a famous personality of the age that both Saint-Simon and Fontenelle paid special tribute to him (see Saint-Simon, R. (1961): esp. v. 5., pp. 909–13; and Fontenelle (1766): v.6., pp. 122–36). His son, René-Louis de Voyer de Palmy, marquis d'Argenson (1694–1757), followed in his footsteps, and also became a *lieutenant de police* of Paris for a couple of years, but his career led in a different direction. He became disappointed with the direct methods applied by his father, and pressed for reforms inside the administration. According to Silberner, he was the first person to utter the statement 'laissez faire' (Silberner 1939: 176), and the inventor of the statement 'laissez faire, laissez passer'. Gournay, who was also an intendant, belonged to his circle of friends (see Schelle, 1897: 122).

Obviously, all this cannot prove or disprove anything, but may serve as an indication of how frameworks of thought, mentalities and models of behaviour have constructed a specific series, where the successive steps were built both positively and negatively on the previous ones, pointing out in this case that the cradle of the very idea of 'laissez faire' was rocked by disillusioned police administrators. On the history of the d'Argenson family, see also *La Grande Encyclopédie* (Paris, Lamirault, 1887–1902), v.3., pp. 833–8; and Buisson (1958).

16 See Justi (1769). Tribe, incidentally, calls attention to the fact that Soviet planners in the early 1920s quite explicitly went back to this mercantilist tradition (1988: 4). On Justi see also Pasquino (1978), and Foucault (1981).

17 On Sonnenfels, see Small (1909), Tribe (1988), Axtmann (1990).

18 See the writings of Thomas More, Erasmus and Vives.

19 About this, see Hirschman (1977) and Keohane (1980).

20 A particularly interesting example here is Montchrétien (1615). On the one hand, it is the first book bearing the title *Political Economy* (although the term itself was used earlier, by Turquet); on the other, it is one of the last work in the genre of the 'mirror of princes'. And while Machiavelli subverted this genre by neglecting the whole humanistic discourse about the traditional virtues of the king, Montchrétien 'subverted' Machiavelli by re-positing the king as the individual servant of each and every inhabitant, in the framework of economic welfare and the growth of the forces of the state.

21 See the works of social historians like Eric Hobsbawm, George Rudé, Nathalie Davis, E.P. Thompson or Charles Tilly.

22 On d'Argenson, see Keohane (1980), Schelle (1897) and Silberner (1939).

23 This is well documented in Keane (1988b).

24 See especially the pieces by Rosanvallon; and Hinrichs, Offe and Wiesenthal.

25 Following Pocock (1975), one could almost talk about a 'liberal moment'.

26 First, both regions were confronted with the need for reorganisation after long, bitter wars. The importance of the Second World War in making communism possible in Eastern Europe is usually neglected, though contemporary observers did make similar points. In the case of Hungary, one can refer to the testimonies of Sándor Márai and György Faludy, perhaps the most influential figures of the literary emigration. See also Gross (1989). This issue of anti-fascism, considered with some justification as a mere ideology in the last twenty years, also played an important role at that level. Second, the relative backwardness of the region in terms of earlier attempts to increase the strength of the state made a civilising process aiming to start everything all over again conceivable.

27 On this question, see Bruszt (1988) and Hankiss (1990).

9 CONCLUSION: THE SUCCESS OF A FAILURE?

1 The ambivalences of the party's claim that it keeps the whole society together are well reflected in the following interview:

Q: To what extent is the party [apparatus] a vital institution?
A: To the extent that, if for some reason the party were suddenly eliminated from the life of society, it would collapse immediately.

Q: Society?

A: Yes, the society. If you like, we can say that the party is the caricature of this society, or this society is the caricature of the party. One is defined by the other. So, this is a party-centred structure. If the party were eliminated, this social formation would collapse.

Q: In your opinion, if the district PC said for once that 'for a month, I will not intervene in public administration', would public administration be able to function independently?

A: Yes, it would be. It would be rather perplexed, but it would.

Q: This seems to contradict your previous statement. You said that if the party ceased to exist, society would collapse.

A: But you assumed one month in your [last] question.

Q: O.K., the time horizon was ill defined. So, in the long run, without the party – '

A: It could function, but then this system would not be the same. This would not be called The Hungarian People's Republic, but The Hungarian Republic [this change of name was actually made on 23 October 1989 – A. Sz. and A.H.]. Thus, the formation would collapse. Not society. It would find a different form of government, without any difficulties. Probably in a bourgeois way, but perhaps in a socialist one. But that this formation would collapse without the party [apparatus] is certain. I do not want to judge whether this is good or bad. This party [apparatus] is like the pole in a tent. It keeps the whole thing together. [. . .] The point is not that the party is a leading force, but that it keeps the building together.

(G.D.)

It is especially interesting that these remarks were made by a political instructor, in the spring of 1988. (We inserted the word 'apparatus' above, because the context of the interview makes it obvious that, in the conversation, the word 'party' referred to the concrete reality of the apparatus, and not just to the 'party' in general terms.)

2 Interestingly enough, this statement can be supported by a recent Hungarian publication, the memoirs of a former high-ranking police officer, who – not without a certain demagogy – claims that the key to the party-state was without doubt contained in the organisational rules of the communist party. See Hudy (1990: 61).

3 The ambivalent relationship between the apparatus and the members can be illustrated by the following interview details:

Q: Does the party need members at all?

A: Of course it does!

Q: Or just an apparatus?

A: I see now, that is a good question. My feeling is that this apparatus would not even notice if the members disappeared. It could work by itself without any difficulties.

(G.D.)

4 This common persistance in spite of the differences is a general topic in Fosdick's classic work, originally published in 1915. In his Introduction to the 1969 reprint, D.E. J. McNamara remarked that this book testifies that 'the

more things have changed in the police field, the more they have remained the same' (Fosdick 1969: i).

5 Current events in the Baltics (Winter 1990–1) provide an illustration for this statement. There are attempts to redefine, wherever a legal loophole can be found, buildings and institutions that were formerly considered to be 'state property' as 'party property'. It is an attempt to formalise the previous informal methods of control, once the flexible system has broken down. It also shows that, no matter who will win in this game, the result will be profoundly different from the former system: democracy or authoritarian dictatorship, independence or being part of the Soviet empire. All discussions about 'communism' are over; not at the level of ideology, but of daily government.

6 Sakwa (1990) is criticising the use of the term 'party-state' along similar lines.

7 Though we cannot give a conclusive account, one of our interviews shed some interesting light on the practice of large housing complexes, extremely widespread in Hungary and in the region in general, one of the ugliest, most perplexing features of the landscape of these countries. It is common knowledge that, in Hungary, one out of every six persons lives in such blocks of flats, though about 50 per cent of the population lives in rural areas. All this happened, it was often said, because of the centrally planned economy; because there were only a few, large building companies. But, perhaps, these were only consequences. The underlying reason may have been that the development plan of an area was in the hands of the district PC. Given this factor, it could have only been rational that the party committee used uniform plans for the different housing units, and that it preferred to deal with only one large company, and not bother itself with – from its perspective – pointless discussions and differences with smaller companies.

8 For a recent assessment of the literature on terror and Stalinism, see Sakwa (1989a: ch. 3).

9 To mention just a few, one can refer to the plays of Mrozek, Örkény or Ievgeni Shvarts; the films of the Georgian school (let's just recall the *Repentance* of Abuladze), or the Czechoslovakian 'new wave' of the 1960s (Forman, Menzel, Passer, Chytilova); or the novels of Kundera, Hrabal, Rozewicz or Bulgakov.

10 Some related aspects of Saint-Simon's work are discussed in Szakolczai (1987, 1990).

11 An elaboration of this concept by Nietzsche can be found in Foucault (1977a).

12 This is not to deny either the seriousness of the whole problematic, or the integrity of those persons who sincerely adhered to this view. On the one hand, communism was connected to some major ideas of modern Western political thought (about this, see Sakwa 1987b, 1989b; and the epigraphs of Rigby 1969, quoting Plato and St Paul). On the other, it motivated individuals who attempted to help people and alleviate suffering. The problem is with the concrete answers given, the methods used. It is interesting that, near the end of their lives, many major figures of communism may have realised the tragic absurdity of the whole undertaking.

13 As an illustration of the peculiar game between faith and fear, degenerating into cynicism and frustration, we can refer to the complete lack of humour, constrained gravity and ponderousness masked as a sense of responsibility toward the 'people' that characterised so many aspects of these systems.

Communism dreaded laughter, and restricted it to certain well-defined, limited occasions. It feared that, at any point, a laugh could go to the heart of the system. Probably nobody there had read Saint-Simon, but the system instinctively feared the situation described by Cicero that Saint-Simon liked so much to quote: Roman religion died when two augurs could not meet in public places without bursting into laughter (see Saint-Simon, C-.H. 1966: v. 5, pt. 2, p. 167). A genuine, healthy grin was not something that was seen in the last forty years on the faces of communist politicians – even if sometimes they afforded a slight fatherly smile. The ability to laugh, by the way, can be a good test for assessing the impact of the recent system on each and every individual. The expression 'laugh and I can tell you who you are' could be a good indication of how 'contaminated' a person was in the past. This again was a factor not restricted to the party.

14 See the article by Csanádi (1990b) on the work done by the apparatus in one of the districts of Budapest to eliminate the old structure and prevent hard-liners – the organisers of the 'new' Hungarian Socialist Workers' Party – from taking over the old networks, and convincing former party members that they should join the new socialist party. All at a time when they knew that it would be the final act of their official careers.

15 See, for example, the contrasting statements of Haraszti (1990), a former dissident and a leading member of the Free Democrats, and Jeszenszky (1990), the foreign secretary and a member of the ruling Democratic Forum.

16 This is analysed by Hankiss (1990) and Staniszkis (1990b).

17 In his only public interview on his childhood, Foucault was talking about his experiences of 'everyday fascism' at the period of the Ethiopian war (Foucault 1983c). Reinhart Koselleck's famous book (1988) was an attempt to analyse what made fascism intellectually possible.

18 This is analysed especially in the third essay of *On Genealogy of Morals*, but references can be found throughout his writings.

19 The well-known Hungarian poet, Gyula Illyés, in his 'One sentence on tyranny' written in 1950 had already noted that in this system the positions of prisoners and guards cannot be clearly separated.

20 Perhaps not surprisingly, as this 'devilish' character may have been a simple reflexion of an early Christian attitude according to which the forces of life were controlled by the devil, if 'we' did not pay close enough attention. It is well known how this strict asceticism and hostility to life were characteristic of the bolshevik mentality. Ságvári's (1989) book presents especially interesting details about how the joyous, happy activities of young communists after 1945 were frozen by the hostile, suspicious world-view of the Moscovite leaders. This is not an opposition between faith, enthusiasm and a sense of mission on the one hand, and bureaucratic rigidity on the other. The Moscovites were also motivated by faith in their mission, but it was connected not to the happiness of life, but to the necessity of discipline, asceticism and punishment.

21 An excellent account of the lasting impact of the fact of the decision, and the consequences of particular choices, can be found in Glazov (1988).

22 For the impact on subjectivity, see also Hill and Frank (1981: 23), Simecka (1984, esp. pp. 36–43) and Glazov (1988).

23 See, for example, the discussion in Haraszti (1987).

24 See the discussion on the different uses of 'no man's land' in Chapter 8.

25 This by no means implies that other social strata were not affected or impaired. On the question concerning workers under communist systems, see Haraszti (1977), Sabel and Stark (1982), Burawoy (1985).

26 See, for example, the frightening accounts by Genchev (1990) and Kozovoi (1990). A December 1990 news item on the Soviet Union that reported that German food aid was being distributed with the help of the KGB was also revealing in this respect.

27 To give an example, in June 1988, the police still used force against demonstrators commemorating the thirtieth anniversary of the execution of Imre Nagy. In September 1988, at the time of our survey, there were also some demonstrations. During an interview, we could see the reports, with full details, on the desk of a district secretary. Yet, this time, nothing happened. This should qualify the allegations that the secret police still worked in Hungary in January 1990 (see, for example, Haraszti, 1990). It may be that there were agents who still wrote reports. But nobody cared about them. There was no intention and no mechanism to use this information in the government of society.

Bibliography

Althusius, J. (1610) *The Politics of Johannes Althusius*, ed. F. S. Carney, 1965 edn, London: Eyre and Spottiswoode.

Arato, A. (1981) 'Civil Society against the State: Poland 1980–81', *Telos*, 47: 23–47.

Arendt, H. (1958) *Origins of Totalitarianism*, 2nd edn, New York: Harcourt.

Ariès, P. (1975) *Centuries of Childhood*, Penguin: Harmondsworth.

Aristotle (1958) *The Politics*, ed. and trsl. Ernest Barker, London: Oxford University Press.

Ash, T.G. (1989) *The Uses of Adversity: Essays on the Fate of Central Europe*, Cambridge: Granta Books.

Avtorkhanov, A. (1966) *The Communist Party Apparatus*, Chicago: Henry Regnery.

Axtmann, R. (1990) "Police" and the formation of the modern state. Legal and ideological assumptions on state capacity in the Austrian lands of the Habsburg Empire, 1500–1800' mimeo.

Banac, I. (1990) 'Continuing EEPS', *Eastern European Politics and Societies* 4, 1: 1–3.

Barber, B.R. (1969) 'Conceptual Foundations of Totalitarianism', in C.J. Friedrich, M. Curtis and B.R. Barber (eds) *Totalitarianism in Perspective: Three Views*, New York: Praeger.

Barsi, T. (1985) *A pártélet kisszótára* (A Dictionary of Party Life), Budapest: Kossuth.

Bauman, Z. (1974) 'Officialdom and Class', in F. Parkin (ed.) *The Social Analysis of Class Structure*, London: Tavistock.

—— (1989a) 'Intellectuals in East-Central Europe: Continuity and Change', in G. Schöpflin and N. Wood (eds) *In Search of Central Europe*, Cambridge: Polity.

—— (1989b) 'The sociology of postmodernity', *Thesis Eleven*, 1.

Bayley, D.H. (1975) 'The Police and Political Development in Europe', in C. Tilly (ed.) *The Formation of National States in Western Europe*, Princeton University Press.

Beik, W. (1985) *Absolutism and Society in Seventeenth-Century France* Cambridge: Cambridge University Press.

Bell, D. (1973) *The Coming of Post-Industrial Society*, New York: Basic.

Belohradsky, V. (1989) 'A legalitás térhódítása avagy az Osztrák Birodalom mint metafora' (The spread of legality or the Austrian Empire as a metaphor), *Századvég*, special issue.

Benda, V., Simecka, M., Jirous, I.M., Dienstbier, J., Havel, V., Hejdánek, L. and Simsa, J. (1988) 'Parallel Polis, or An Independent Society in Central and Eastern Europe: An Inquiry', *Social Research* 55, 1–2: 211–46.

Benson, L. (1990) 'Partynomialism, bureaucratism, and economic reform in the Soviet power-system', *Theory and Society* 19, 1: 87–105.

Bialer, S. (ed.) (1989) *Politics, Society and Nationality under Gorbachev's Russia*, London: Western Press.

Bibó, I. (1986) *Válogatott tanulmányok* (Selected works), Budapest: Magvetö.

Bihari, M. (1987) 'Reform és demokrácia' (Reform and Democracy), *Medvetánc*, 2: 165–225.

Bjørn-Andersen, N. (1982) *Information Society for Richer, for Poorer*, selected papers from a conference, Amsterdam: North-Holland.

Black, A. (1984) *Guilds and Civil Society in European Political Thought from the 12th Century to the Present*, London: Methuen.

Bozóky, A. (1990) 'Post-Communist Transition: Political Tendencies in Hungary', *Eastern European Politics and Societies* 4, 2: 211–30.

Braudel, F. (1977) *Afterthoughts on Material Civilisation and Capitalism*, Baltimore: The John Hopkins University Press.

Brown, A. and Gray, J. (eds) (1977) *Political Culture and Political Change in Communist States*, London: Macmillan.

Bruszt, L. (1988) "Without Us but For Us?" Political Orientation in Hungary in the Period of Late Paternalism', *Social Research* 55, 1–2.

—— (1990) '1989: The Negotiated Revolution in Hungary', *Social Research* 57, 2: 365–87.

Bugajski, J. and Pollack, M. (1987) *East European Fault Lines*, Boulder, CO: Westview.

Buisson, H. (1958) *La Police: son histoire*, Paris.

Bunce, Valerie (1990) 'The Struggle for Liberal Democracy in Eastern Europe', *World Policy Journal* 7, 3: 395–430.

Burawoy, M. (1985) *The Politics of Production*, London: Verso.

Burchell, G., Gordon, C. and Miller, P. (eds) (1991) *The Foucault Effect*, Brighton: Harvester.

Canguilhem, G. (1978) *The Normal and the Pathological*, Boston: Riedel.

Chapman, B. (1970) *Police State*, London: Macmillan.

Chevallier, P. (1967) *Les Philosophes et le lieutenant de Police, J. Ch. Pierre Le Noir* (1775–85), Troyes.

Church, W.F. (1972) *Richelieu and Reason of State*, Princeton University Press.

Coleman, C. and Starkey, D. (eds) (1986) *Revolution Reassessed: Revisions in the History of Tudor Government*, Oxford: Clarendon.

Crucé, E. (1623) *The New Cyneas*, ed. Thomas W. Balch, 1909, Philadelphia: Allen, Lane & Scott,

Csanádi, M. (1987) 'A döntési mechanizmus szerkezetéröl' (On the structure of the decision-making process), *Társadalomkutatás*, 4.

—— (1990a) 'Beyond the Image: the Case of Hungary', in *Social Research* 57, 2: 321–46.

—— (1990b) 'Egy hanyatlás krónikája: esettanulmány a pártállam felbomlásáról Budapest egy kerületében' (The chronicle of a decline: a case study of the disintegration of the party state in a district of Budapest), *Mozgó Világ* 16, 8: 52–60.

Curry, J.L. (ed.) (1983) *Dissent in Eastern Europe*, New York: Praeger.

Curtis, M. (1969) 'Retreat from Totalitarianism', in C.J. Friedrich, M. Curtis and B.R. Barber (eds) *Totalitarianism in Perspective: Three Views*, New York: Praeger.

Davis, N.Z. (1975) *Society and Culture in Early Modern France*, Stanford University Press.

De La Mare, N. (1705–38) *Traité de la Police*, Paris.

Deleuze, G. (1962) *Nietzsche et la philosophie*, Paris: PUF.

—— (1988) *Foucault*, London: The Athlone Press.

Djilas, M. (1957) *The New Class*, New York: Holt.

Donzelot, J. (1979) *Policing the Families*, New York: Pantheon Books.

Dreyfus, H.L. and Rabinow, P. (1983) *Michel Foucault: Beyond Structuralism and Hermeneutics*, Chicago: The University Press.

Duchesne (1767) *Code de la Police*, Paris.

Dyson, K.F. (1980) *The State Tradition in Western Europe*, New York: Oxford University Press.

Elias, N. (1978) *The Civilizing Process, Vol. One: The History of Manners*, Oxford: Blackwell.

—— (1982) *The Civilizing Process, Vol. Two: State Formation and Civilisation*, Oxford: Blackwell.

—— (1983) *The Court Society*, Oxford: Blackwell.

Eliot, J. (1632) *Monarchie of Man*, A.B. Grosart (ed.), 1879 edn, London.

Eribon, D. (1989) *Michel Foucault*, Paris: Flammarion.

Esterházy, P. (1981) *Függö* (Indirect), Budapest: Magvetö.

—— (1989) 'Az elefántcsonttoronyból' (From the Ivory Tower), *Hitel* 1, 3.

Fainsod, M. (1953) *How Russia is Ruled*, Cambridge, Mass.: Harvard University Press.

—— (1958) *Smolensk under Soviet Rule*, 2nd edn 1989, Boston: Unwin.

Fazekas, K. and Köllö, J. (1990) *Munkaeröpiac tökepiac nélkül* (Labour market without capital market), Budapest: KJK.

Fehér, F., Heller, A. and Márkus, G. (1983) *Dictatorship Over Needs*, Oxford: Blackwell.

Fidelius, P. (pseudonym for K. Palek) (1987) *L'Esprit post-totalitaire*, Paris: Bernard Grasset.

Finlay, M. (1987a) *Powermatics: A Discursive Critique of New Communications Technology*, London: Routledge.

—— (1987b) 'Technology as Practice', *The Canadian Journal of Political and Social Theory*, 11: 1–2.

Fleming, R.W. (1983) Foreword to J.L. Salvaggio (ed.) *Telecommunications: Issues and Choices for Society*, New York: Longman.

Fontaine, L. (1990) 'Affaire d'état, affaires de familles: Politique anti-protestante, stratégies privée, et vie communautaire dans une vallée alpine au XVIie siècle', mimeo.

Fontenelle, B. (1766) *Oeuvres*, Paris.

Fosdick, Raymond B. (1969) *European Police Systems*, Montclair, New Jersey: Patterson Smith. [1915]

Foucault, M. (1961) *Folie et déraison: Histoire de la folie à l'âge classique*, Paris: Plon.

—— (1963) *Raymond Roussel*, Paris: Gallimard.

—— (1965) *Madness and Civilization*, New York: Mentor Books. [1961]

—— (1967) 'Nietzsche, Freud, Marx', in *Nietzsche*, Paris: Cahiers de Royaumont.

—— (1973) *The Order of Things*, New York: Vintage Books. [1966]

—— (1975) *The Birth of the Clinic*, New York: Vintage Books. [1963]

—— (1976a) *The Archeology of Knowledge*, New York: Harper Colophon Books. [1969]

—— (1976b) *The Discourse on Language*, Afterword to Foucault (1976a), New York: Harper Colophon Books. [1970]

—— (1977a) 'Nietzsche, Genealogy, History', in D.F. Bouchard (ed.) *Language, Counter-Memory, Practice: Selected Essays and Interviews*, Oxford: Blackwell.

—— (1977b) 'Power and Sex: An Interview with Michel Foucault', *Telos*, 32, 152–61.

—— (1977c) 'What is an author?', in D.F. Bouchard (ed.) *Language, Counter-Memory, Practice: Selected Essays and Interviews*, Oxford: Blackwell.

—— (1978) 'Résumé du cours', *Annuaire de Collège de France* 78, 445–9.

—— (1979a) *Discipline and Punish*, New York: Vintage Books. [1975]

—— (1979b) 'Governmentality', *I & C* [*Ideology and Consciousness*], 6: 5–21.

—— (1979c) 'Résumé du cours', *Annuaire de Collège de France* 79, 367–72.

—— (1980a) *The History of Sexuality, Vol. One: The Will to Knowledge*, New York: Vintage Books. [1976]

—— (1980b) 'Two Lectures', in C. Gordon (ed.) *Power/Knowledge: Selected Interviews and Other Writings by Michel Foucault, 1972–1977*, Brighton: Harvester Press.

—— (1980c) 'Questions of Method', *I & C* [*Ideology and Consciousness*], 8: 5–20.

—— (1980d) 'Conversation With Michel Foucault', *Three Penny Review* 1, 1: 4–5.

—— (1981) 'Omnes et Singulatim: Towards a Criticism of Political Reason', in S.M. McMurrin (ed.) *The Tanner Lectures on Human Values*, Salt Lake City: The University of Utah Press.

—— (1983a) 'The Subject and Power', Afterword to H.L. Dreyfus and P. Rabinow, *Michel Foucault: Beyond Structuralism and Hermeneutics*, Chicago: The University Press.

—— (1983b) 'Structuralism and Post-Structuralism: An Interview with Michel Foucault', *Telos*, 55: 195–211.

—— (1983c) 'An interview by Stephen Riggins', *Ethos* 1, 2: 4–9.

—— (1984a) 'What is Enlightenment', in P. Rabinow (ed.) *The Foucault Reader*, New York: Pantheon Books.

—— (1984b) 'Space, knowledge, and power', in P. Rabinow (ed.) *The Foucault Reader*, New York: Pantheon Books.

—— (1984c) 'Preface to *The History of Sexuality*, Volume Two', in P. Rabinow (ed.) *The Foucault Reader*, New York: Pantheon Books.

—— (1984d) 'On the Genealogy of Ethics: An Overview of Work in Progress', in P. Rabinow (ed.) *The Foucault Reader*, New York: Pantheon Books.

—— (1984e) 'Polemics, Politics, and Problematizations: An Interview', in P. Rabinow (ed.) *The Foucault Reader*, New York: Pantheon Books.

—— (1984f) 'L'éthique du souci de soi comme pratique de liberté', *Concordia*, 6: 99–116.

—— (1986a) *The History of Sexuality, Vol. Two: The Use of Pleasures*, New York: Vintage Books. [1984]

—— (1986b) 'Kant on Enlightenment and Revolution', *Economy and Society* 15, 1: 88–96.

—— (1987) *The History of Sexuality, Vol. Three: The Care of Self*, New York: Vintage Books. [1984]

—— (1988a) 'On Problematization', *History of the Present*, 4: 16–17.

—— (1988b) '(Auto)biography of Michel Foucault', *History of the Present*, 4: 13–15.

—— (1988c) 'The Concern for Truth', in L.D. Kritzman (ed.) *Michel Foucault: Politics, Philosophy, Culture*, London: Routledge.

—— (1988d) 'The Return of Morality', in L.D. Kritzman (ed.) *Michel Foucault: Politics, Philosophy, Culture*, London: Routledge.

Foucault, M., Barret Kriegel, B., Thalamy, A., Beguin, F. and Fortier, B. (1976) *Les machines à guérir*, Paris: l'Institut de l'Environment.

Foucault, M. and Farge, A. (1982) *Le désordre des familles: Lettres de cachet des Archives de la Bastille*, Paris: Gallimard.

Fox, A. and Guy, J. (1986) *Reassessing the Henrician Age: Humanism, Politics and Reformation 1500–1550*, Oxford: Blackwell.

Fried, R.C. (1963) *The Italian Prefects. A Study in Administrative Politics*, New Haven: Yale University Press.

Friedrich, C. J. and Brzezinski, Z. (1956) *Totalitarian Dictatorship and Autocracy*, Cambridge, Mass.: Harvard University Press.

Gandal, K. and Kotkin, S. (1985) 'Governing Work and Social Life in the U.S.A. and the U.S.S.R.', *History of the Present*, 1.

Genchev, S. (1990) 'Bricks in a Pyramid: an interview', *East European Reporter* 4, 2: 23–4.

Gershuny, J. and Miles, I. (1983) *The New Service Economy*, London: Pinter.

Getty, J.A. (1985) *Origins of the Great Purges: the Soviet Communist Party Reconsidered, 1933–38*, Cambridge University Press.

Giddens, A. (1984) *The Constitution of Society*, Cambridge: Polity.

—— (1985) *The Nation-State and Violence*, Cambridge: Polity.

Gill, G. (1987) 'The Single Party as an Agent of Development: Lessons from the Soviet Experience', *World Politics* 39, 4: 566–78.

—— (1988) *The Rules of the Communist Party of the Soviet Union*, London: Macmillan.

Glazov, Y. (1988) *To Be or Not to Be in the Party*, Dordrecht: Kluwer.

Gombár, C. (1987) 'Velleitásaink' (Our velleities), *Századvég*, 4–5: 5–26.

Gordon, C. (1980) 'Afterword', in C. Gordon (ed.) *Power/Knowledge: Selected Interviews and Other Writings by Michel Foucault, 1972–1977*, Brighton: Harvester Press.

—— (1986) 'Question, ethos, event: Foucault on Kant and Enlightenment', *Economy and Society* 15, 1: 71–87.

—— (1990) "Histoire de la folie": an unknown book by Michel Foucault', *History of the Human Sciences* 3, 1: 3–26.

—— (1991) 'Governmental rationality: an introduction', in G. Burchell, C. Gordon and P. Miller (eds) *The Foucault Effect*, Brighton: Harvester Press.

Gouldner, A. (1979) *The Future of Intellectuals and the Rise of the New Class*, London: Macmillan.

Gramsci, A. (1975) *Note sui Machiavelli sulla politica e sullo Stato moderno* Torino: Editori Riuniti.

Grande Encyclopédie, La (1866–1902), sous la direction de A. Berthelot and C. Dreyfus, Paris: H. Lamirault et Cie.

Gregory, P.R. (1989) 'Soviet Bureaucratic Behaviour: Khozyaistvenniki and apparatchiki', *Soviet Studies* 41, 4: 511–25.

Gross, J.T. (1989) 'Social Consequences of War: Preliminaries to the Study of Imposition of Communist Regimes in East Central Europe', *Eastern European Politics and Societies* 3, 2: 198–214.

Gruder, Vivian R. (1968) *The Royal Provincial Intendants. A Governing Elite in Eighteenth-Century France*, Ithaca, N.Y.: Cornell University Press.

Guenée, B. (1987) *L'Occident aux XIVe et XVe siècles: Les Etats*, 3rd edn, Paris: PUF.

Halmos, P. (1978) *The Faith of the Counsellors*, 2nd edn, London: Constable.

Hankiss, E. (1986) *Diagnózisok 2* (Diagnoses), Budapest: Magvető.

—— (1990) *East European Alternatives* Oxford: Clarendon Press.

Hankiss, E., Manchin, R., Füstös, L., Szakolczai, A. (1983) *Kényszerpályán?* (Forced into a Siding), Institute of Sociology.

Hann, C.M. (1990) 'Second Economy and Civil Society', *The Journal of Communist Studies* 6, 2: 21–44.

Harasymiv, B. (1984) *Political Elite Recruitment in the Soviet Union*, London, Macmillan.

Haraszti, M. (1977) *A Worker in a Workers' State*, Penguin: Harmondsworth.

—— (1987) *The Velvet Prison*, New York: Basic Books.

—— (1990) 'A Choice between Resolution and Emotion: an interview', *East European Reporter* 4, 2: 76–7.

Harding, S. and Phillips, D. with Fogarty, M. (1986) *Contrasting Values in Western Europe: Unity, Diversity and Change*, London: Macmillan.

Hassner, P. (1984) 'Le Totalitarisme vu de l'ouest', in G. Hermet, P. Hassner and J. Rupnik (eds) *Totalitarismes*, Paris: Economica.

Havel, V. (1985) *The Power of the Powerless: Citizens against the State in Central-Eastern Europe*, ed. by J. Keane, London: Hutchinson.

Hill, R.J. and Frank, P. (1981) *The Soviet Communist Party*, London: Allen & Unwin.

Hintze, O. (1975) *The Historical Essays of Otto Hintze*, ed. by F. Gilbert, New York: Oxford University Press.

Hirschman, A.O. (1977) *The Passions and the Interests. Political Arguments for Capitalism before Its Triumph*, Princeton University Press.

Hirszowicz, M. (1980) *The Bureaucratic Leviathan: A Study in the Sociology of Communism*, New York University Press.

Hobsbawm, E.J. (1959) *Primitive Rebels*, New York: Norton.

Horváth, A. (1988a) 'Elit és hatalom' (Elite and power), mimeo.

—— (1988b) 'The Peculiar Power of the Party: Preliminary results of an empirical research done at a local party committee', mimeo.

Horváth, A. and Szakolczai, A. (1989) *Senkiföldjén: A politikai instruktorok tevékenységéről az állampártban* (In No Man's Land: the activity of political instructors in the state-party), Budapest: Akadémiai.

—— (1990) 'The Dual Power of the State-Party and Its Grounds', *Social Research* 57, 2: 275–301.

Hough, J.F. (1969) *Soviet Prefects: The Local Party Organs in Industrial Decision-Making*, Cambridge, Mass.: Harvard University Press.

Hsia, R.P. (1989) *Social Discipline in the Reformation: Central Europe 1550–1750*, London: Routledge.

Hudy, Zoltán (1990) *Pártrendőrség* (Party Police), Budapest: Interart.

Humboldt, W. von (1969) *The Limits of State Action*, Cambridge University Press.
Huppert, G. (1970) *The Idea of Perfect History*, University of Illinois Press.
Inglehart, R. (1977) *The Silent Revolution*, Princeton University Press.
Isocrates (1928–45) 'Areopagiticus', in *The Complete Works of Isocrates*, London: William Heinemann.
Janos, A.C. (1982) *The Politics of Backwardness*, Princeton University Press.
Jeszenszky, G. (1990) 'A Very Important Chapter in our History: an interview', *East European Reporter* 4, 2: 71–3.
Jowitt, K. (1990a) 'Comments', in *Eastern European Politics and Societies* 4, 2: 193–7.
—— (1990b) 'Gorbachev: Bolshevik or Menshevik?', in S. White, A. Pravda and Z. Gitelman (eds) *Developments in Soviet Politics*, London: Macmillan.
Justi, J. von (1769) *Elémens généraux de police*, Paris.
Kaiser, D.H. (ed.) (1987) *The Workers' Revolution in Russia: The View from Below*, Cambridge: Cambridge University Press.
Kassof, A. (1964) 'The Administered Society: Totalitarianism Without Terror', *World Politics* 16, 4: 558–75.
Katz, R.L. (1988) *The Information Society*, New York: Praeger.
Keane, J. (1984) *Public Life and Late Capitalism*, Cambridge University Press.
—— (1988a) *Democracy and Civil Society*, London: Verso.
—— (ed.) (1988b) *Civil Society and the State*, London: Verso.
Kenedi, J. (1982) *Do It Yourself: Hungary's Hidden Economy*, New York: Pluto Press.
Keohane, N.O. (1980) *Philosophy and the State in France*, Princeton University Press.
King, J.E. (1972) *Science and Rationalism in the Government of Louis XIV*, 1661–1683, New York: Octagon Books.
Kirkpatrick, J. (with the assistance of W.E. Miller) (1974) *The New Presidential Elite: Men and Women in National Politics*, New York.
Knemeyer, F.-L. (1980), 'Polizei', *Economy and Society* 9, 2: 172–96.
Kolosi, T. and Szabó, B. (1973) 'Kerületi döntés és munkamegosztás' (Decision-making and division of labour in the district), *Szociológia*, 3.
Konrád, G. (1984) *Antipolitics*, London: Quartet Books.
Konrád, G. and Szelényi, I. (1979) *The Intellectuals on the Road to Class Power*, New York: Harcourt.
Körösényi, A. (1990) 'Hungary', *Electoral Studies* 9, 4: 337–45. (Special issue: Elections in Eastern Europe.)
Koselleck, R. (1988) *Critique and Crisis: Enlightenment and the Pathogenesis of Modern Society*, Oxford, Berg.
Kovács, J.M. (1990) 'Reform Economists: The Classification Gap', *Daedalus* 119, 1: 215–48.
Kozovoi, V. (1990) 'Retour en URSS: un interview', *Le Monde*, 17 November.
Lampert, N. (1989) 'The "Anonimka" under Perestroika: a note', *Soviet Studies* 41, 1: 129–43.
Lane, David (1988) *Elites and Political Power in the USSR*, Aldershot: Edward Elgar.
Laval, A. de (1613) *Desseins de professions nobles et publiques*, 2nd edn, Paris.
Le Clère, M. (1980) *Bibliographie critique de la police*, Paris: Yzer.
Lengyel, L. (1989) *Végkifejlet* (Endgame), Budapest: KJK.

—— (1990a) 'Tavaszra várva' (Waiting for Spring), *2000* 2, 9: 3–6.

—— (1990b) 'Megjött a tél' (Winter came), *2000* 2, 12: 3–9.

Lévy, Y. (1966) 'Police and Policy', *Government and Opposition* 1, 4: 485–510.

Lipski, J.J. (1985) *KOR: A History of the Workers' Defense Committee in Poland 1976–1981*, Berkeley: University of California Press.

Lukes, S. (1974) *Power: A Radical View*, London: Macmillan.

—— (ed.) (1986) *Power*, New York: University Press.

Lyon, D. (1988) *The Information Society*, Cambridge: Polity.

MacDonell, D. (1986) *Theories of Discourse: An Introduction*, Oxford: Basil Blackwell.

Makhaïski, J.W. (1979) *Le socialisme des intellectuels*, ed. A. Skirda, Paris: Seuil.

Manchin, R. (1988) 'Individual Economic Strategies and Social Consciousness', *Social Research* 55, 1–2: 77–95.

Mann, M. (1986) *The Sources of Social Power, Vol. One: a history of power from the beginning to A.D. 1760*, Cambridge University Press.

Martin, J. (1978) *The Wired Society*, Englewood Cliffs, N.J.: Prentice-Hall.

Martin, W. J. (1988) *The Information Society*, London: Aslib.

Masuda, Y. (1981) *The Information Society as Post-Industrial Society*, Washington, D.C.: World Future Society.

Megill, A. (1987) 'The Reception of Foucault by Historians', *Journal of the History of Ideas* 48, 1: 117–41.

Meinecke, F. (1957) *Machiavellism: The Doctrine of Raison d'Etat and its Place in Modern History*, New York: Oxford University Press.

Meuret, Denis (1988) A political genealogy of political economy, *Economy and Society* 17, 2: 225–50.

Meyer, P. (1983) *The Child and the State: The Intervention of State in Family Life*, Cambridge University Press.

Michels, R. (1915) *Political Parties*, New York: The Free Press.

Michnik, A. (1985) *Letters from Prison and Other Essays*, Berkeley: University of California Press.

Miller, P. (1990) 'On the Interrelations between Accounting and the State', in *Accounting, Organisation and Society* 15, 4: 315–38.

Miller, P. and Rose, N. (1990) 'Governing economic life', *Economy and Society* 19, 1: 1–31.

Montchrétien, A. de (1615) *Traicté de l'œconomie politique*, ed. T. Funck-Brentano, 1889, Paris: Plon.

Moore, B. Jr. (1954) *Terror and Progress USSR: Some Sources of Change and Stability in the Soviet Dictatorship*, Cambridge, Mass.: Harvard University Press.

—— (1967) *Social Origins of Dictatorship and Democracy: Lord and Peasant in the Making of the Modern World*, Boston: Beacon Press.

Mosco, V. and Wasko, J. (ed.) (1988) *The Political Economy of Information*, The University of Wisconsin Press.

Mothe Le Vayer, F. de la (1662) *Oeuvres*, Paris.

Mumford, L. (1961) *The City in History*, New York: Harcourt.

—— (1967) *The Myth of the Machine, Vol. One: Technics and Human Development*, New York: Harcourt.

—— (1970) *The Myth of the Machine, Vol. Two: The Pentagon of Power*, New York: Harcourt.

Munoz Darde, Veronica (1990) 'The tradition of the Enlightenment and critical morality', mimeo.

Myers, J.L. (1927) *The Political Ideas of the Greeks*, New York: The Abingdon Press.

Neumann, S. (1965) *Permanent Revolution: Totalitarianism in the Age of International Civil War*, 2nd edn, New York: Praeger.

Nietzsche, Friedrich (1954) *The Viking Portable Nietzsche*, ed.W. Kaufmann, New York: Viking Press.

—— (1966) *Beyond Good and Evil*, New York: Vintage.

—— (1969) *On the Genealogy of Morals*, New York: Vintage.

Nove, A. (1982) 'Classes in Eastern Europe', in A. Giddens and D. Held (eds) (1982) *Classes, Power and Conflict*, London: Macmillan.

Oestreich, G. (1982) *Neostoicism and the Early Modern State*, Cambridge: Cambridge University Press.

Ottlik, G. (1959) *Iskola a határon* (School at the Border), Budapest: Magvető.

Ostrogorski, Mosei (1902) *Democracy and the Organisation of Political Parties*, two vols, London: Macmillan.

Parker, D. (1989) 'Sovereignty, Absolutism and the Function of the Law in Seventeenth-Century France, *Past and Present*, 122: 36–75.

Pasquier, E. (1607) *Recherches de la France*, Paris.

Pasquino, P. (1978) 'Theatrum politicum: the genealogy of capital–police and the state of prosperity', *I & C [Ideology and Consciousness]*, 4: 41–54.

Pelczynski, Z.A. (1984) 'The significance of Hegel's separation of the state and civil society', in Z.A. Pelczynski (ed.) *The State and Civil Society*, Cambridge: Cambridge University Press.

Pitkin, H.F. (1984) *Fortune is a Woman*, Berkeley: University of California Press.

Plato (1952) *The Dialogues of Plato*, London: Encyclopaedia Britannica, Inc.

Pocock, J.G. A. (1975) *The Machiavellian Moment*, Princeton University Press.

Polányi, K. (1944) *The Great Transformation*, New York: Rinehart.

Porat, M. (1977) *The Information Economy*, Washington D.C.: U.S. Department of Commerce.

Poster, M. (1984) *Foucault, Marxism, History*, Cambridge: Polity.

Raeff, M. (1983) *The Well-Ordered Police State*, New Haven: Yale University Press.

Rahr, A. (1990) 'The CPSU in the 1980s: Changes in the party apparatus', paper given at the IVth World Congress for Soviet and East European Studies, Harrogate, England, July.

Rajchman, J. (1985) *The Freedom of Philosophy*, New York: Columbia University Press.

Rakovski, M. (pseudonym for G. Bence and J. Kis) (1978) *Towards an Eastern European Marxism*, London: Allison & Busby.

Rigby, T.H. (1969) *Communist Party Membership in the USSR, 1917–67*, Princeton, N. J.: Princeton University Press.

—— (1990) *Political Elites in the USSR*, Aldershot: Edward Elgar.

Rigby, T.H. and Harasymiw, B. (1983) *Leadership Selection and Patron–Client Relations in the USSR and Yugoslavia*, London: Allen & Unwin.

Rose, E.D. (1983) 'Moral and Ethical Dilemmas Inherent in an Information Society', in J .L. Salvaggio (ed.) *Telecommunications: Issues and Choices for Society*, New York: Longman.

Rose, N. and Miller, P. (1989) 'Rethinking the State: governing economic, social and personal life', mimeo.

Rudé, G. (1964) *The Crowd in History*, New York: Wiley.

Rupnik, J. (1988) 'Totalitarianism revisited', in J. Keane (ed.) *Civil Society and the State*, London: Verso.

—— (1989) *The Other Europe*, Revised edn, London: Weidenfeld & Nicolson.

Rutland, P. (1990) 'Perestroika on the periphery: insights from the regional press in Russia and Ukraine', paper given at the IVth World Congress for Soviet and East European Studies, Harrogate, England, July.

Sabel, C.F. and Stark, D. (1982) 'Planning, Politics, and Shop-Floor Power: Hidden Forms of Bargaining in Soviet-Imposed State-Socialist Societies', *Politics and Society* 11, 4: 439–75.

Ságvári, A. (1989) *Mert nem hallgathatok* (Because I cannot remain silent), Budapest: Magyar Hirlap Könyvek.

Saint-Simon, C-.H. (1966) *Oeuvres complètes*, Paris: Anthropos.

Saint-Simon, R. (1961) *Mémoires*, ed. G. Truc, Paris: Gallimard.

Sakwa, R. (1987a) *Soviet Communists in Power: A Study of Moscow during the Civil War 1918–21*, London: Macmillan.

—— (1987b) 'The Commune State in Moscow in 1918', *Slavic Review* 46, 3–4: 429–49.

—— (1989a) *Soviet Politics*, London: Routledge.

—— (1989b) 'Commune Democracy and Gorbachev's Reforms', *Political Studies* 37, 2: 224–43.

—— (1990) *Gorbachev and his Reforms, 1985–1990*, Oxford: P. Allan.

Salvaggio, J.L. (ed.) (1983) *Telecommunications: Issues and Choices for Society*, New York: Longman.

Say, J.-B. (1828–9) *Cours complet de l'économie politique pratique*, Paris: Guillamin.

—— (1848) *Oeuvres choisies*, Paris: Guillamin.

Schapiro, L. (1971) *The Communist Party of the Soviet Union*, 2nd edn, New York: Vintage.

Schapiro, L. (ed.) (1972) *Political Opposition in One-Party States*, London: Macmillan.

Schelle, G. (1897) *Vincent de Gournay*, Paris: Guillamin.

Schiller, H.I. (1981) *Who Knows: Information in the Age of the Fortune 500*, Norwood, N.J.: Ablex.

—— (1983) 'Information for What Kind of Society?', in J.L. Salvaggio (ed.) *Telecommunications: Issues and Choices for Society*, New York: Longman.

Schöpflin, G. and Wood, N. (eds) *In Search of Central Europe*, Cambridge: Polity.

Schumpeter, J. (1954) *The History of Economic Analysis*, New York: Oxford University Press.

Schütz, A. and Luckmann, T. (1974) *The Structures of the Life-World*, London: Heinemann.

Seyssel, C. de (1515) *La Monarchie de France*, ed. J. Poujol, Paris: PUF.

Siklova, J. (1990) 'The "Gray Zone" and the Future of Dissent in Czechoslovakia', *Social Research* 57, 2: 347–63.

Silberner, E. (1939) *La Guerre dans la pensée économique du XVIe au XVIIIe siècle*, Paris: Sirey.

Simecka, M. (1984) *The Restoration of Order*, London: Verso.

Skilling, H.G. (1989) *Samizdat and Independent Society in Central and Eastern Europe*, London: Macmillan.
Skilling, H.G. and Griffiths, F. (eds) (1971) *Interest Groups in Soviet Politics*, Princeton University Press.
Skocpol, T. (1979) *States and Social Revolutions*, Cambridge: Cambridge University Press.
Small, A.W. (1909) *The Cameralists: The Pioneers of German Social Polity*, University of Chicago Press.
Smith, A. (1978) *Lectures on Jurisprudence*, eds R.L. Meek, D.P. Raphael and P.G. Stein, Oxford: Clarendon Press.
Solomon, S. (ed.) (1983) *Pluralism in the USSR*, London: Macmillan.
Spiegel, H.W. (1983) *The Growth of Economic Thought*, Revised edn, Durham, N.C.: Duke University Press.
Staniszkis, J. (1989a) 'The Dynamics of a Breakthrough in the Socialist System: an outline of problems', *Soviet Studies* 41, 4: 560–73.
—— (1989b) 'The Obsolescence of Solidarity', *Telos*, 80: 37–50.
—— (1990a) 'Patterns of Change in Eastern Europe', *Eastern European Politics and Societies* 4, 1: 77–97.
—— (1990b) "Political capitalism" in Eastern Europe', mimeo.
—— (1990c) 'Dilemmas for democracy in Eastern Europe', mimeo.
Starkey, D. (1977) 'Representation through Intimacy', in I. Lewis (ed.) *Symbols and Sentiments*, London: Academic Press.
—— (1985) *The Reign of Henry VIII: Personalities and Politics*, London: G. Philip.
Starkey, D., Morgan, D.A.L., Murphy, J., Wright, P., Cuddy, N. and Sharpe, K. (eds) (1987) *The English Court: from the Wars of the Roses to the Civil War*, London: Longman.
Stewart, P.D. (1968) *Political Power in the Soviet Union*, Indianapolis: Bobbs-Merrill.
Sweeney, G.P. (ed.) (1982) *Information and the Transformation of Society*, Papers from a Conference, Amsterdam: North-Holland.
Szakolczai, A. (1987) 'Concerning the Grounds of Modern Economic Society and Political Economy: an analysis of the writings of Say, Saint-Simon and Sismondi, using the works of Michel Foucault', unpublished dissertation, University of Texas at Austin.
—— (1990) *A fejlödés megkérdöjelezése* (Questioning development), Budapest: Akadémiai.
Szalai, E. (1990) 'Utelágazás' (The parting of roads), *Valóság* 33, 8: 44–54.
Századvég (1989) *Kell-e nekünk Közép-Európa?* (Do we need Central Europe?), a special issue.
Szelényi, I. (1983) *Urban Inequalities under State Socialism*, Oxford: Oxford University Press.
—— (1986–87) 'The Prospects and Limits of the East European New Class Project: An Auto-Critical Reflection on The Intellectuals on the Road to Class Power', *Politics and Society*, 2.
Thompson, E.P. (1963) *The Making of the English Working Class*, New York: Vintage.
Tilly, C. (1964) *The Vendée*, Princeton University Press.
—— (ed.) (1975) *The Formation of National States in Western Europe*, Princeton University Press.

Tismaneanu, V. (1989) 'The Tragicomedy of Romanian Communism', *Eastern European Politics and Societies* 3, 1: 329–76.

Tocqueville, A. (1955) *The Old Régime and the French Revolution*, New York: Anchor Books.

Tökés, R.L. (ed.) (1979) *Opposition in Eastern Europe*, London: Macmillan.

Tribe, K. (1988) *Governing Economy: The Reformation of German Economic Discourse 1750–1840*, Cambridge University Press.

Turquet, L. (1611) *La monarchie aristodemocratique*, Paris.

Unger, A.L. (1974) *The Totalitarian Party*, Cambridge University Press.

Urbán, L. (1989) 'Hungary in Transition: The Emergence of Opposition Parties', *Telos*, 79: 108–18.

Vajda, M. (1988) 'East-Central European Perspectives', in J. Keane (ed.) *Civil Society and the State*, London: Verso.

Veyne, P. (1978) 'Foucault révolutionne l'histoire', in *Comment on écrit l'histoire*, 2nd edn , Paris: Seuil.

Voslensky, M. (1984) *Nomenklatura: Anatomy of the Soviet Ruling Class*, London: The Bodley Head.

Wallerstein, I. (1974) *The Modern World-System I*, New York: Academic Press.

—— (1980) *The Modern World-System II*, New York: Academic Press.

—— (1989) *The Modern World-System III*, New York: Academic Press.

Walzer, M. (1967) 'Puritanism as a Revolutionary Ideology', in S.N. Eisenstadt (ed.) *The Protestant Ethic and Modernization. A Comparative View*, New York: Basic Books.

Weber, Max (1968) *Economy and Society*, New York: Bedminster Press.

Webster, F. and Robins, K. (1986) *Information technology: a Luddite analysis*, Norwood, N.J.: Ablex.

Wicklein, J. (1981) *Electronic Nightmares: The New Communication and Freedom*, New York.

Willerton, J.P. (1979) 'Clientelism in the Soviet Union: an Initial Examination', *Studies in Comparative Communism* 12, 2–3: 159–83.

Wilson, J.Q. (1968) *Varieties of Police Behavior*, Cambridge, Mass.: Harvard University Press.

Z. (pseudonym for M. Malia) (1990) 'To the Stalin Mausoleum', *Daedalus* 119, 1: 295–344.

Zinoviev, A. (1981) *Le communisme comme réalité*, Paris: Julliard.

Index

254   *Index*